The Facebook® Guide for
People Over 50

The Facebook® Guide for
People Over 50

by Paul McFedries

WILEY
Wiley Publishing, Inc.

The Facebook® Guide for People Over 50
Published by
Wiley Publishing, Inc.
10475 Crosspoint Blvd.
Indianapolis, IN 46256
www.wiley.com

ISBN: 978-0-470-87517-9

Manufactured in the United States of America

10 9 8 7 6 5 4 3 2 1

For general information on our other products and services or to obtain technical support, please contact our Customer Care Department within the U.S. at (877) 762-2974, outside the U.S. at (317) 572-3993 or fax (317) 572-4002.

Wiley also publishes its books in a variety of electronic formats. Some content that appears in print may not be available in electronic books.

Library of Congress Control Number: 2010939963

WILEY

About the Author

Paul McFedries is a technical writer who has been authoring computer books since 1991 and has more than 70 books to his credit. Paul's books have sold more than three million copies worldwide. These books include the Wiley titles *Twitter Tips, Tricks, and Tweets,* 2nd Edition, *MySpace Visual Quick Tips, Internet Simplified, iPad Portable Genius,* and *iPhone 4 Portable Genius.* Paul is also the proprietor of Word Spy (www.wordspy.com), a website that tracks new words and phrases as they enter the language. You can visit Paul on the web at www. mcfedries.com or on Facebook at www.facebook.com/paulmcfedries.

Credits

Senior Acquisitions Editor
Aaron Black

Project Editor
Chris Wolfgang

Senior Copy Editor
Kim Heusel

Editorial Director
Robyn Siesky

Vice President and Executive Group
Publisher
Richard Swadley

Vice President and Executive
Publisher
Barry Pruett

Business Manager
Amy Knies

Senior Marketing Manager
Sandy Smith

Project Coordinator
Kristie Rees

Graphics and Production Specialists
Jennifer Henry
Andrea Hornberger

Quality Control Technician
Rebecca Denoncour

Proofreading
Linda Seifert

Indexing
Steve Rath

Acknowledgments

As you'll soon see, this isn't so much a How-To book as a What-To book that aims to show you what's available on Facebook, no matter what you're interested in or concerned about. To that end, I spent inordinate amounts of time poking around the seemingly infinite nooks and crannies of Facebook, a task that was often ridiculously fun. Adding to the fun were the great people at Wiley that I got to work with. They included Acquisitions Editor Aaron Black, who was kind enough to ask me to write the book; Project Editor Chris Wolfgang, who has an endless supply of common sense and excellent suggestions; Copy Editor Kim Heusel, who made sure my i's were dotted and my t's were crossed, and not the other way around; and Technical Editor Jonny Thaw, who made sure my instructions didn't zig when they were supposed to zag. Very special thanks go out to the lovely and talented Karen Hammond, who helped unearth tons of the Facebook treasures found in this book. Many heartfelt thanks to all of you for outstanding work on this project.

C contents

Contents

Contents

introduction

When Facebook announced in May 2010 that it had reached 500 million users, the news appeared in all the usual places — technology blogs, major news media outlets, and Web sites dedicated to all things Facebook. However, you also saw a story on the announcement if you were a member of AARP, the nonprofit organization that focuses on people aged 50 and older. That seems slightly odd at first blush. Why would an organization devoted to older adults care about a site that seems to be dominated by teenagers and young adults? For the answer to that conundrum you could turn to AARP itself, which had recently published the results of a study that looked at, among other things, the use of social networking among people aged 50 and up. The main result was that of people aged 50+ who used the Internet, 31 percent used Facebook (out of a total of 37 percent who used social networking sites).

The reality is that Facebook is *not* a site just for the very young. People of all ages use Facebook, but the majority of Facebook users are over 35, and the fastest growing segment on Facebook are people aged 50 and over. Why is Facebook so popular with those of us in the 50+ set? Probably because the things you can do on Facebook are more or less the same as the things you already do in your life: Chat with friends; view photos of your kids or grandkids; talk politics or gossip; play a game of Scrabble or fill in a crossword; learn more about your favorite hobby.

And that's where *The Facebook Guide for People Over 50* comes in. Yes, this book shows you *how* to use Facebook with introductory guides to setting up your profile, learning the Facebook lingo, working with photos, and more. However, this is really a book about *what* you can do with Facebook. This book is mostly a comprehensive resource to the best that Facebook has to offer in a wide variety of topics: politics, history, charities, shopping, personal finance, fitness, health, medical conditions, aging, arts, media, hobbies, food, travel, and so much more.

Facebook is designed to help you improve and enhance your social life by keeping up with your family and friends, reconnecting with old friends and distant family members, and making new friends with similar interests and tastes. With *The Facebook Guide for People Over 50* at your side, you'll see that Facebook can also help you improve and enhance all the other aspects of your life.

A Note about the Links

I should point out here that although there are tons of Facebook resources sprinkled throughout this book, very few of those resources were created by Facebook itself. Rather, the vast majority of the links you see here were created by Facebook users who were passionate enough about a particular topic to share that passion with the Facebook community. I think you'll enjoy most of these resources, or at least find them useful, but just remember that the content on them was generated by the people who created and now maintain each resource, as well as the users who visit each resource.

For clickable links of all the resources discussed in this book, head to *The Facebook Guide* series' very own Facebook page: www.facebook.com/FBGseries.

| **Wall** | Info | Photos | Notes |

Getting Started

In this chapter, you get your feet wet by learning just what kinds of things you can do on Facebook and how to set up your own account. You also get a tour of your new Facebook home, and you learn how to build the profile that other people will see, including your pictures, your activities and interests, your schools and jobs, and your contact info. You also learn about the major Facebook concepts and features — including friends, the News Feed, photo sharing, and applications — that you'll be working with throughout your Facebook career.

Taking the Facebook Plunge

Are you ready to make the big leap and get yourself a Facebook account? If so, great! I tell you all about it a bit later in this chapter. However, if you're more of a look-before-you-leap person, then perhaps you have a few concerns you'd like addressed before going any farther. Perhaps you think Facebook is a kids-only thing? Perhaps you're not sure if there's anything on Facebook that would appeal to you? The next couple of sections tackle these legitimate concerns, and then I take you through the process of setting up an account on Facebook.

Isn't Facebook just for kids?

You might be forgiven for thinking that Facebook is only for kids because the service was literally created in a college dorm. Founder Mark Zuckerberg, along with his Harvard classmates Dustin Moskovitz, Chris Hughes, and Eduardo Saverin, created Facebook (it was originally called *Thefacebook*) in February 2004, and for the first year and a half or so it was available only to college students. Facebook opened its doors to high school students in the fall of 2005, and it wasn't until a year later that anyone (technically, anyone 13 years of age or older) could set up a Facebook account.

With university and high school students having been given such a head start, you might assume they dominate Facebook. Surprisingly, they don't. According to Facebook data, as of September 2010, 70 percent of Facebook's users were outside of college age.

Quote, Unquote: Facebook and Family

"I joined Facebook to be able to view pics of one of my nephews because my sister-in-law would only post on here. I have since got all the rest of my family linked up on here, and we are all able to share photos of the new babies back and forth so fast! In the past two years we have had like four or five babies born in our family, and there were photos posted on Facebook within 15 minutes of each child being born!" — H. B., Tampa, Florida

Okay, but certainly people 50 and up must comprise a mere fraction of the Facebook population. Again, you'd be surprised. By some measures, the 50+ demographic was as large as the total number of teenagers on Facebook. In fact, it may not be long before the 50+ cohort surpasses the teen group in total numbers. According to Facebook, as of September, 2010, the 65+ demographic was the fastest-growing group on Facebook, followed by the 55-to-64 demographic.

In short, yes, there are lots of kids on Facebook, but it's certainly not dominated by youngsters. Quite the opposite is true.

What can people 50 and older do on Facebook?

Worldwide Facebook demographic numbers are hard to come by (because the company breaks down its data by country), but I can tell you that as I write this Facebook has more than 500 million users around the world. That means one out of every 14 people on Earth use Facebook! Assuming age demographics break down more or less uniformly across all countries (a bold assumption, to be sure, but a simplifying one), there are approximately 76 million users who are 50 or older on Facebook. If we all gathered together, those of us in Facebook's 50+ population would form the 17th largest country in the world!

That physical gathering will never happen, of course, but it doesn't have to because we can all gather online at Facebook.com with just a few clicks of a mouse. And surely it goes without saying that 76 million people wouldn't do just that if there wasn't something interesting or instructive or fulfilling or fun for them to do on Facebook. Most of this book is focused on specific things you can do on Facebook, but they all fall into one of the following six categories:

- **Keep in touch.** Facebook enables you to stay in touch with people you might otherwise see or hear from only infrequently. Whether you're talking about far-flung family members or friends, colleagues, or college roommates, those people can use Facebook to send you messages, photos, videos, and more so you can keep up with what's going on, whether they live across town, across the country, or halfway around the world.

- **Share your life.** The significant events of your life are almost always more significant when you share them with people you know. Other folks may not be able to attend your birthday bash or your retirement party, but they can still share in the news when you share it with them on Facebook. In fact, you can use Facebook to share just about anything you want, whether it's significant or not: the book you just read or the movie you just saw; a recent family photo or video; a link to a particularly interesting Web site; some thoughts or opinions that you just need to get off your chest. You can share as much or as little as you feel comfortable with.

- **Make connections.** As you learn in Chapter 2, it's relatively easy to locate people you know on Facebook: family, friends, coworkers, neighbors, and so on. But one of the major benefits of Facebook (and one of its biggest surprises, for most people) is that you can also connect with people you don't already know. Facebook offers a number of different features and resources that enable you to connect with people who share your interests.

- **Learn new things.** Most people think of Facebook as a social service, but it's home to an amazing amount of information as well. Whether you're into fitness or fishing, cooking or crosswords, politics or personal finance, there's a wealth of data to be found. Much of this data is on Facebook itself and has been shared by professionals, experts, and passionate amateurs, but Facebook is also a great place to find out about other Web sites that contain useful information. If you're just learning a new topic or you want to take your knowledge of a subject to a higher level, Facebook is a great place to start.

- **Make a difference.** At a glance, Facebook might appear to be a place that encourages and rewards self-interest, egotism, and a focus on the trivial. And yes, it's certainly true that these superficial qualities exist in abundance (as they would with any group that includes half a billion people). But Facebook rises above all that by making it easy for people to organize around and raise awareness of causes, movements, and activism, and to facilitate helping others, volunteering, and charity work. If you're looking to make a difference in the world, the best places to start are often the Facebook resources that are available for whatever interests you.

Quote, Unquote: Reunions

"Facebook has helped me have a very close relationship to my cousin who I had not seen in over 30 years! She lives in Mississippi and I live in Indiana. After finally seeing each other for a couple of hours in 2009, we started chatting on Facebook. I have found the most wonderful person in my family to share stories with, to laugh with, to cry with." — S. F., Indianapolis, Indiana

| **Quote, Unquote: Facebook and Friends** |

"My husband was diagnosed on June 16, 2010, with terminal cancer and given 6–9 months with chemo. My Facebook friends joined together and set up a Cancer Fund at a bank local to us. Pretty soon donations began coming in and cards of encouragement were sent to us both. Most of these people we have never met, yet they did this for us. Facebook Friends are the best." —D. H., Benson, North Carolina

Have fun. Although you certainly can (and should) use Facebook for work, activism, politics, and other serious pursuits, the dominant vibe on Facebook is a strong sense of fun. Whether it's a too-cute-for-words picture of a grandchild, a link to a funny cartoon or YouTube video, or a good joke shared among friends, Facebook interactions are often quite fun. And Facebook also offers a diverse and thriving community of games and the people who play them, so whether you're into cross-words or Scrabble or poker, there's a Facebook game (or three) for you.

Setting up your account

Unlike most Web sites where all or most of the content is open to anyone who surfs on by, most of the content on Facebook is only available to people who have an account, and you can't do anything on Facebook (such as make friends and post photos) unless you sign up.

Fortunately, getting a Facebook account isn't a long, involved process. To get started, follow these steps:

1. **Navigate your Web browser to www.facebook.com.**
2. **Use the Sign Up form to type your first and last names, your e-mail address, and a password.**
3. **You also have to select your sex and specify your date of birth (to ensure you're at least 13 years old).**
4. **Submit the form, and Facebook sends a confirmation message to your e-mail address.**
5. **To confirm your new account, click the link that appears in the message and then type the confirmation code that appears in the message.**

Then Facebook takes you through a four- (or possibly three-) step process designed to get your Facebook experience off to a rousing start. You actually don't have to perform any of these steps right now (I show you how to perform all of them later in the book). If you feel like getting started immediately though, here's a summary of each step:

- **Add Friends.** If Facebook believes there are people already on the service that you may know, it displays a list of those people to enable you to add them as friends right away.

- **Find Friends.** In this step you allow Facebook to log on to your e-mail account and search your contacts list to see if any of them are already on Facebook. Note that this only works if you have an online e-mail account, such as a Gmail or a Hotmail account.

- **Profile Information.** In this step, Facebook prompts you to type the names of your high school, college or university, and current employer. This info is added to your Facebook profile, and you can later use it to find friends who went to the same schools or who work at the same place.

- **Profile Picture.** You use this step to add a picture to your Facebook profile. You can either upload a photo from your computer, or you can take a picture with your computer's webcam (if it has one).

Facebook automatically logs you in to your new account, and you can log out at any time by clicking Account and then Log Out. To log in again, go to www.facebook.com, type your e-mail address and password, and then click Login.

Rather than logging in to Facebook every time you visit the site, you can tell Facebook to keep you logged in. The next time you go to www.facebook.com to log in, select the Keep me logged in check box.

Understanding How Facebook Works

Even if you're an experienced Web surfer, you've probably never come across a service quite like Facebook. The site itself is unique on the Web; the Home page you see when you log in to Facebook is focused on one person (you); and, perhaps Facebook's most unique attribute, you see its features scattered on other sites all over the Web. The next few sections demystify these and other Facebook head-scratchers.

Understanding the site

If you surf to www.ebay.com, www.microsoft.com, or www.nytimes.com (the main sites for, respectively, the eBay online auction site, Microsoft Corporation, and *The New York Times* newspaper), you see the usual Web page suspects: text, images, links, and so on. You see what every other surfer is seeing at the same time because these sites present the same content to everyone who visits.

However, if you surf to www.facebook.com and you're already logged in to your account from a previous visit, you don't see a standard page that every other surfer sees. Instead, you see your Home page, which I describe in more detail in the next section. In other words, Facebook.com isn't about Facebook itself; it's about you and helping you connect to, share with, and find people, products, businesses, causes, and so on.

 NOTE If you want to start using Facebook, you should be aware that like people, the site strives relentlessly to improve itself. Don't be surprised if one day you log in to the site to find your pages completely changed. If this happens, don't panic; you'll quickly adapt to the improvements.

Taking a tour of your Home page

When you log in to Facebook (or, if you're already logged in, any time you surf to www.facebook.com), you see your Home page. If you just created your account and you haven't yet added any friends, you see the Welcome to Facebook version of the page, which is similar to the one shown in Figure 1.1. You use this version of the Home page to find friends on Facebook, edit your profile, and other setup tasks.

The Home page looks quite busy, but it helps if you understand the various sections. There are five main areas of the page:

- **Navigation area.** You use this area to navigate the main features of your Facebook account, such as the News Feed, your Photos, and your Friends, all of which are covered later in this chapter.

- **Content area.** When you click an item in the Navigation area, that item's content appears here.

Facebook links

Message bar   Content area   Toolbar

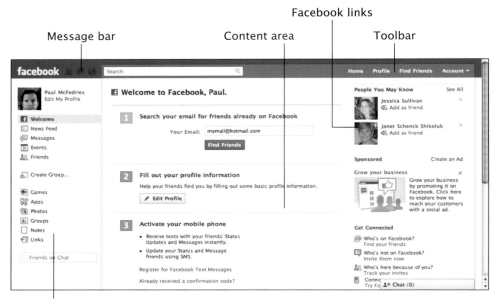

Navigation area

1.1 If you haven't added any Facebook friends as yet, you see the Welcome to Facebook version of the Home page.

- **Message bar.** This area consists of three icons to the right of the Facebook logo. The icons are, from left to right: Friend Requests, Messages, and Notifications, each of which represents a type of message that is sent to you. When you have one or more messages pending, you see the number of messages beside the icon, as shown in Figure 1.2. Click the icon to see the message or messages.

1.2 The message bar icons display the number of friend requests, direct messages (as shown here), or notifications you have waiting.

- **Toolbar.** This strip across the top of the Home page includes the Search box, which you can use to find any type of content on Facebook.

- **Facebook links.** The right side of the Home page displays your upcoming events, friend recommendations, Facebook ads, and other links generated by Facebook.

Interacting with Facebook on other Web sites

One of the unique features of Facebook is that its interface extends well beyond Facebook.com. Facebook has created a number of features that it calls *social plugins*, which enable you to interact with other sites via your Facebook account. There are a number of social plugins that site developers can use, but the two you see most often are the Like button and the Facebook login:

- **Like button.** This button (see Figure 1.3), enables you to indicate that you like content on other sites. This information appears on your Facebook profile, and you also see whether any of your Facebook friends have liked the same content.

1.3 You can use the Like button on another site to indicate to your Facebook friends that you like or recommend the site content.

- **Facebook login.** This feature (see Figure 1.4) enables you to log in to a site using your Facebook e-mail and password rather than creating new login credentials at the site. In most cases, this also makes it easy for you to post information from the site directly to your Facebook profile.

1.4 You can use the Facebook login feature to log in to the site using your Facebook credentials.

Building Your Profile

Your profile is the information that you add to your Facebook account for other people to see and to allow you to connect to people with similar interests. It can include the city where you live, your political views, and your contact info. If you're worried about posting this and similar data online, good for you. Everyone should be wary about sharing too much information online, and your Facebook profile data should be no exception. Fortunately, you can exercise control over your profile in two ways:

- Almost all the profile data is voluntary, so if you're not comfortable divulging something like your religious views or your cell phone number, you don't have to.

- Facebook's privacy settings give you control over who can see specific parts of your profile. For example, you can configure unique privacy settings for your birthday, your religious and political views, your phone numbers, and so on. In each case, you can allow everyone to view the data, just your Facebook friends, only yourself, and more.

Filling in at least *some* of your profile is a good idea because sharing information with your friends is at the heart of the Facebook experience. As you'll see, it's also the easiest way to get in touch with old classmates and coworkers and to find people who share your interests.

Facebook divides your profile data into the following categories, which vary depending on the likes and interests you've added:

- **Profile Picture.** This is the picture that appears in your profile page and anywhere in Facebook that displays lists of users or friends. Most people display a simple head shot, but you can use anything you want (or no image at all).

- **Education and Work.** You use this section to specify your high school, college or university (or more than one, if needed), and your current and past employers.

- **Arts and Entertainment.** This section is where you share the things that you enjoy. You can specify one or more activities and interests;

your favorite musical groups, singers, or genres; the books, authors, or reading genres you prefer; your favorites movies, actors, directors, or film genres; your preferred TV shows, actors, and genres; and your favorite games on Facebook.

Basic Information. This section includes boxes for your current city, your hometown, your sex, and birth date. If you want to use Facebook to help find romance, you can also select what sex you're interested. This section also includes boxes where you can add your languages and a short bio.

Including your birth date is a fun part of Facebook because it means your friends get information when your birthday comes around. If you don't want others to see the year you were born, be sure to choose the Show Only Month & Day in My Profile setting.

Contact Information. This section includes your e-mail address, instant messaging screen name, phone numbers, physical address, and Web site address (if you have one).

Viewing your Facebook profile

To take a peek at your Facebook profile, either click the Profile link in the tool-bar, or click your name in the upper-left corner of your Home page. Figure 1.5 shows the profile page for a new user, which as you can see displays only the basic info you added during the account setup.

Editing your Facebook profile

To make changes to your profile, either click the Edit Profile link that appears in the upper-right corner of your profile, or click any of the Edit links (which in some sections appear as just pencil icons without the word "Edit"). Figure 1.6 shows an example of the Edit Profile page that appears (in this case, for the Arts and Entertainment section). You use the links on the left to navigate the sections, and you use the controls that appear with each section to type your data. As you make your edits, be sure to click Save Changes to save your work.

1.5 Your Facebook profile is a barebones affair when you just start out.

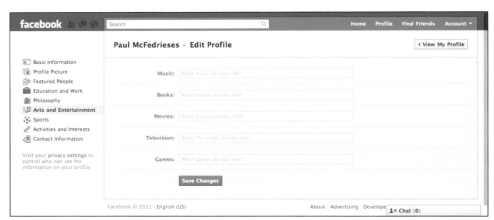

1.6 Click a section on the left to displays its controls, and then use those controls to fill in your Facebook profile.

Understanding Facebook's Features

When you just start out with Facebook, the site can seem a bit intimidating with all this talk about friends, profiles, wall sections, likes, messages, notifications, pages, networks, and on and on. Facebook is actually home to more than 20 features, and although it's unlikely you'll use all 20 in your Facebook career, it's very likely that, taken as a group, the people you interact with on Facebook will use all of them. Therefore, it pays to learn at least a little about each of Facebook's available features, which will help you get more out of the ones you can't avoid, decide which optional ones you might want to check out, and understand what's happening when someone you know makes use of a feature you don't use yourself.

The rest of this chapter takes you through a list of these features and a few other fundamental Facebook concepts. Think of what follows as your general reference guide to all things Facebook.

NOTE As mentioned, Facebook is a moving target that is constantly adding new features and tweaking existing ones. So this list represents a snapshot of Facebook as it was configured when this book when to press, but it's a certainty that *something* will have changed by the time you read this. For up-to-the-minute information about changes to Facebook, you can visit the site's main page (www.facebook.com/facebook) and The Facebook Blog (blog.facebook.com); that's where new features are announced and explained. You can also check out Facebook's Help Center (www.facebook.com/help) for answers to common questions.

Understanding friends

Social networking refers to using a Web site to connect with people you know or who share similar personal or professional interests. Facebook is, therefore, a social networking site, and although the word *social* has many meanings on Facebook, the most important by far is embodied in the concept of the *friend*. Put simply, a Facebook friend is a person with whom you've agreed to share information.

The "agreed" part here is crucial, because both people must give their blessing before Facebook considers them to be friends. What happens is that one person sends a *friend request* to another, and the recipient then either accepts or declines the request. (See Chapter 2 for the details on all this.) If the person accepts the request, both parties are added to each other's *friends list*, and the sharing begins right away.

Quote, Unquote: Facebook and Friends

"Last year I had an operation which left me unable to speak for quite a while. I couldn't go out, nor could people visit me. Facebook kept me in touch with friends, their children, real life 'out there' and it all made my life a lot less isolated." —G. V., Trowbridge, England

What gets shared? If a person is your Facebook friend, that person can see your profile and is also automatically alerted if you change your profile, update your status, like something, upload a photo, and so on. These features are covered in more detail later in the chapter. Similarly, you can view the other person's profile, and on your News Feed you see the other person's Facebook activity.

However, as I mentioned earlier, you can use your privacy settings to control all this. In particular, you can prevent a particular person from seeing aspects of your profile and your Facebook activities.

Viewing your News Feed

When you connect with someone on Facebook as a friend, it usually means you want to stay abreast of what that person is up to, not just on Facebook, but also in regular life (depending, of course, on how much that person is willing to share). Once you're friends with someone, you can go to that person's Facebook profile page and poke around to see what's new: profile changes, status updates, uploaded photos or videos, and so on.

That's fine if you have just a few friends, but the average Facebook user has more than 130 friends. If the idea of accessing dozens of Facebook profiles every day just to keep up with what your friends are doing makes you exhausted, you're not alone. That's why Facebook completely automated the process. Rather than you going out to all your friends' Facebook pages to see what's new, Facebook automatically gathers what's new with your friends and displays it in your News Feed on your Home page.

To see what I mean, click Home. (If you're already viewing some other part of your Home page, you can also click the News Feed link in the Navigation area.)

Facebook displays the News Feed page, which shows you what's happening with your friends, as seen in Figure 1.7.

1.7 Click the News Feed link to open the News Feed page, which tells you what's new with your friends.

The News Feed actually comes with two views, and you switch between them by clicking the links that appear in the top-right corner of the News Feed:

- **Top News.** This is the default view, and it represents only those friend activities that Facebook has calculated are relevant to you. That sounds a tad Orwellian, but all it really means is that based on your previous activity on Facebook (particularly content you've added and friend activity that you've liked or commented on), the site makes calculated guesses on what is meaningful to you. In the same way that a newspaper editor decides the important news of the day, your News Feed acts as your Facebook friend newswire, with Facebook (and, indirectly, you) as the editor.

- **Most Recent.** This view shows you all of your friends' recent activities, sorted chronologically, with the most recent at the top. If you don't want to miss anything your friends have posted or done on Facebook, then this is the view for you.

In keeping with the news metaphor, Facebook calls each item that appears on the News Feed a *story*, so that's the terminology I use here as well.

Updating your status

The simplest way to share information with your Facebook friends is to post a status update. This is a simple message that you use to share what you're doing, where you're going, how you're feeling, or whatever happens to be on your mind. In fact, the text box you use to type your status update (it's called the Publisher) contains the text "What's on your mind?"

Status updates might seem trivial, but they can be amazingly useful. As an extreme example, CNN first learned about the 2010 Haitian earthquake when a producer saw status updates from family members who were in Haiti at the time!

To see this text box, you have two choices:

- **Click Home.** The Publisher appears with the text "What's on your mind?" near the top of the News Feed.
- **Click Profile.** The Publisher appears just below the Wall tab (see Figure 1.8).

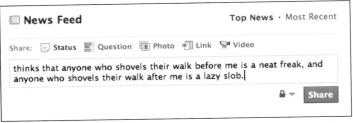

1.8 Type your status update and then click Share

From here, you click the Status link; then type your status message and then click Share. Note that it's traditional (although by no means mandatory) to write your status update under the assumption that your name will appear at the beginning of the text when other people view it. Figure 1.9 shows what my Facebook friends see when the status update comes through on each person's News Feed.

Paul McFedries
thinks that anyone who shovels their walk before me is a neat freak, and anyone who shovels their walk after me is a lazy slob.

2 seconds ago · Like · Comment

1.9 Your status update as it appears on each friend's News Feed.

The text-only status update is the easiest and most basic way to let your friends know what's happening in your life, but Facebook also lets you attach four kinds of items to a post: a link to a Web page, one or more photos, a video, or a question. More about all these later in this chapter.

Liking stories

At first glance, you might think your News Feed is simply something you read and then move on with your life. You can certainly do that if you choose, but Facebook emphasizes social interaction, where each person is no longer a passive consumer of the News Feed stories but is an active participant in the feed. Facebook gives you three main ways to interact with News Feed stories:

- Like
- Comment
- Share

I talk about liking stories here, and the next two sections cover commenting and sharing.

The easiest way to interact with the News Feed is to say if you liked a particular story. Most News Feed items come with a Like link (for example, refer to Figure 1.9), and all you have to do is click that link.

When you do that, two things happen:

- The Like link turns into an Unlike link, which you can click if you change your mind.
- A notice that you liked that particular item goes out to your friends.

Commenting on stories

A second way to interact with your News Feed is to write a comment about a story. You can comment on status updates, as well as posted links, photos, videos, events, notes, questions, and more. How you go about this depends on whether anyone has commented on the story before you:

- If you're the first person to comment, click the Comment link (see the upper of the two items shown in Figure 1.10), type your comment in the box that appears, and then click Comment.

- If other people have added comments already, you see the "Write a comment" box below the existing comments (see the lower of the two items shown in Figure 1.10). Click inside that box, type your comment, and then click Comment.

1.10 To comment on a story, ether click the Comment link (if you're the first commenter), or click inside the "Write a comment" box (if other people have beaten you to it).

When you add a comment to a story, three things happen:

- The comment appears below the story, both on your News Feed and in the News Feeds of anyone else who is friends with the same person.
- A notice that you commented on that story goes out to your friends.
- Facebook "remembers" that you commented on this story, and it uses that data to help choose stories for the Top News view of your News Feed.

Sharing stories

The third way to interact with your News Feed is to share a story by adding it to your profile. For example, if one of your friends posts a particularly noteworthy link or photo, you can share that story. When you share a story, Facebook adds it to the Wall tab on your profile page, and anyone who visits your profile page will see it. You can share links, photos, videos, events, and notes, but not status updates.

To share a story, click the Share link, type a message to go along with the story when it appears on your profile, and then click Share.

Posting links

A simple status update is the easiest way to tell your friends what's on your mind, what you've been doing lately, and how you're feeling. However, some of the most interesting people on Facebook go beyond simple status updates by telling their friends about fascinating, useful, or amusing Web pages that they've found in their online travels. Facebook's Publisher lets you attach a link to a status update, and once the update is posted your friends can simply click the link to check out the page.

Before posting the link, first use your Web browser to navigate to the page, then copy the Web page address. Facebook then gives you two ways to attach a link to an update:

- Go to the Publisher at the top of your home page or Profile page, click Link, paste the address into the Link box that appears, and then click Attach. A text box will appear where you can also add your own thought or comment about the link.
- Click Status and then paste the address.

Facebook then populates the Link box with the Web page title, address, and opening text, as well as a thumbnail image from the page. Feel free to use the Publisher to add your own text that introduces or comments on the Web page. For example, in Figure 1.11, I introduce a Web page article and add a quotation from the article.

1.11 When you attach a link to an update, Facebook displays the Link box with information about the Web page.

When you post a link, two things happen:

- Facebook adds it to the Wall tab of your profile.
- The link goes out to your friends and appears in each person's News Feed.

Sharing photos

Facebook is full of surprises, but one of the biggest is that, by far, it is the most popular place on the Web for sharing photos. You might have heard of sites such as Flickr (www.flickr.com) and Picasa Web Albums (picasaweb.google.com) that specialize in storing photos online and sharing them with other people. These are excellent sites, but Facebook stores and shares way more photos, despite not having nearly as many bells and whistles as the dedicated sites. In fact, each day Facebook users upload 200 million photos.

Facebook's secret to photo success is the same one that lies behind all of its successes: the social component. When you attach a photo to a status update, upload a photo, or create a new album of photos, your friends know about it, and then can like or comment on your photos. Even better, you can also *tag* any friends that happen to appear in your photos. Tagging just means that you identify a person in a photo as one of your Facebook friends.

Photos are such a popular topic on Facebook that I devote an entire chapter to them (see Chapter 4). However, for now I just let you know that you have two main ways to work with photos on Facebook:

- **Attach a photo to an update.** In this case, you click the Photo link in the Publisher at the top of your Home page or Profile page and then upload an existing photo, take a new photo, or create an album.

- **Use the Photos application.** Click Profile and then click Photos from the applications in the Navigation area of your home page. From here, you can view your photos, create a photo album, and edit your existing albums.

Sharing videos

With inexpensive digital video cameras available everywhere, and with many cellphones now including built-in video capabilities, digital videos are more popular than ever. If you have a video you shot yourself, you can share it with your friends by attaching it to an update.

To do this, you click inside the Publisher and then click the Video link. Facebook adds a Video box, which you can then use to either upload an existing video or shoot a new video using the webcam attached to your computer.

Posting notes

A status update is useful for relatively short messages, perhaps up to a few dozen words or so. However, what if you have something to say or share and it's several hundred words, or even several thousand? In that case, forget the status update and opt instead for a *note*. A Facebook note is a message that can be as long as you need (or as long as you think your friends can stand!). If you're familiar with blogging, then notes are the Facebook equivalent.

To forge a new note, follow these steps:

1. **Click the Notes link in the navigation area of your profile page.**

2. **Click Write a Note.** Facebook displays the Write a Note page.

3. **Use the Title text box to type a title for your note.**

4. **Use the Body text box to write your text, as shown in Figure 1.12.** You can use the buttons that appear above the body text box to format your note text.

5. **When you're done, click Preview to take a sneak peek at your note to make sure everything looks okay.**

6. **If everything meets your approval, click Publish to share it with your friends.**

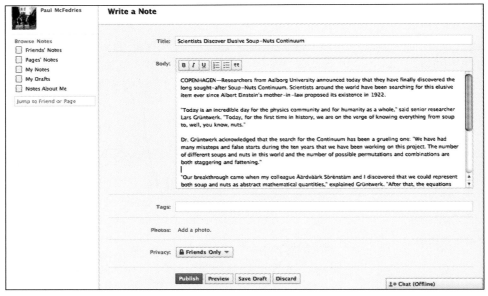

1.12 Add the Notes tab to your profile, click Write a New Note, and then use the Write a Note page to compose your note.

Getting the hang of Wall sections

You've no doubt seen those community corkboards that appear in many super-markets and other public locations; people and organizations post ads, notices, flyers, and other messages on them. And you've also no doubt seen guest books at weddings and other functions that enable you to write a short note and sign your name. Finally, you may have also seen in your office or in another workplace a whiteboard where team members or other employees are encouraged to jot down ideas and other brainstorming bits.

What the corkboard, guest book, and whiteboard have in common is that each is a (relatively) public medium where people can write messages and offer information, and that in essence is what a Facebook *Wall* is all about. Your Wall is a section of your Facebook profile where your friends can add stories. Any other friend who drops by your profile can also see those stories, and can like, comment on, or share those stories.

When a friend visits your profile and clicks the Wall tab, she sees the Publisher at the top, and she can use it to post a story to your Wall section. This can be a simple text update, or it can include a link, photo, or video she wants to share with you. (And, of course, you can visit any of your friends' profiles and add stories to their Wall sections using the same technique.)

As a final note, Wall sections are everywhere on Facebook. When you learn about Pages, Groups, and Events a bit later in this chapter, you'll see that all these Facebook features come with a Wall section of their own, and in most cases you can post stories on them.

 It's possible to prevent people from writing on a Wall section. If you want to do this for your own Wall section, click on Privacy Settings under your Account menu, select Customize, and then deselect the Friends may post to my Wall check box that appears within the Things others share section.

Exchanging messages

Writing on a person's Wall section is an easy way to communicate with a friend, but it's not exactly private. In fact, in most cases not only can your other friends see your Wall posts, but so can *their* friends. (Fortunately, you can change this, as you learn later in this chapter.)

If you have something to say to a friend and you don't want other friends (or friends of friends) listening in, you can send that person a *message*, which is text (possibly augmented with a link, photo, or video) that is sent directly to the friend. Think of it as Facebook's version of sending someone an e-mail message.

NOTE I'm talking about friends here, but you can actually send a message to *anyone* on Facebook, unless that person only allows friends to send messages.

You have two ways to get started:

- Navigate to a person's Profile page and then click the Message button, which appears in the upper-right corner of the friend's profile.

- In the Navigation area, click the Messages icon (pointed out earlier in Figure 1.1) and then click New Message. In the New Message dialog box, click inside the To box and type the friend's name.

Fill in the Subject line and the Message box (see Figure 1.13), optionally attach a link, photo, or video, and then click Send.

1.13 Use the New Message dialog box to compose and then send your message.

When you receive a message, the Messages icon displays a red badge telling you the number of waiting messages. Click the Messages icon to see the message (as shown in Figure 1.14), and then click the message to see the full text. In the message window that appears, you can send a reply or delete the message.

1.14 Click the Messages icon to see your incoming messages.

Understanding notifications

As you've seen so far, there's a lot to do on Facebook: Ask a person to be your friend; post status updates and other stories; see your friends' stories in your News Feed; like, comment on, or share your friends' stories; communicate by writing on Wall sections or sending messages. The list seems endless, but it doesn't begin to cover the constant hive of activity that goes on elsewhere on Facebook: A person accepts your friend request; your friends like, comment on, or share your stories; your friends post stories to your Wall section; someone tags you in a photo.

What's the common denominator in all these extra activities? That's right: *you*. There's just one problem, though. If all these activities that are related to you happen elsewhere on Facebook, how do you keep tabs on them? How do you know when someone accepts your friend request or comments on one of your stories? The answer is a Facebook feature called *notifications*, which are simple messages that Facebook sends you whenever someone else does something on Facebook that relates to you.

When you receive a notification, the Message bar's Notifications icon (pointed out earlier in Figure 1.1) displays a red badge telling you the number of waiting notifications. Click the Notifications icon to see the notifications, as shown in Figure 1.15.

1.15 Click the Notifications icon to see the notifications you've received from Facebook.

TIP

Facebook also sends notifications to your e-mail address. If you get tired of seeing these extra messages, you can turn some or all of them off. Click Account, click Account Settings, and then click the Notifications tab. For each type of notification you want to avoid, deselect the Email check box.

Understanding Pages

So far you've seen that each person who sets up a Facebook account gets a profile page that includes the person's Wall section, profile info (location, likes and interests, contact data, and so on), photos, notes, and more. However, although your social self may be mostly focused on other people, it's not exclusively so. In your daily life, you also interact with businesses and organizations, watch TV shows and movies, read books, listen to music, and pursue favorite interests and hobbies.

In the pre-Facebook way of doing things, relationships with these nonpersonal entities were almost entirely one-way: You'd consume, watch, read, listen to, pursue, or otherwise interact with the entity, but that entity would rarely (if ever) interact with you. So lumping these entities in with your social self might seem like a bit of a stretch.

However, Facebook changes everything by making relationships with nonpersonal entities two-way instead of just one-way. It does that by enabling companies, organizations, products, TV shows, movies, actors, books, authors, bands, Web sites, governments, and even cities to each build a presence on Facebook called a *Page*. A Page is a special, nonpersonal Facebook profile designed to help businesses communicate with customers, organizations to communicate with users, and public figures or entities to communicate with fans.

A Page includes many of the same features as a personal profile, including a Wall section and an Info tab, but it also includes extra features such as tabs that offer content specific to the Page owner. For example, a Page for a band might have a Tour Dates tab, or a Page for a book might offer an Excerpt tab.

Where things get social is that most Pages offer interactive features. For example, it's common to see a Page with a Discussion Board tab where people can discuss multiple topics related to the Page subject. Even better, each Page comes with a Like button, as shown in Figure 1.16.

Clicking Like sets you up as a *fan* of the Page, which is the Page equivalent of a friend. This means that any stories posted to the Page appear in your News Feed, and in many cases you'll also be able to post to the Page's Wall section.

It's important to note that even if you've never clicked a Like button on any Page, you're probably already a fan of several Pages. That's because Facebook automatically sets you up as a fan of one or more Pages based on the info in your profile. For example, if you specified your current city in your profile, Facebook automatically sets you up as a fan of that city's Page.

Similarly, if you added one or more TV shows, movies, or books to your profile, you're automatically made a fan of those Pages. For your schools, interests, and activities, chances are Facebook has set you up as a fan of the associated *Community Page*, which is a collection of shared knowledge on the topic.

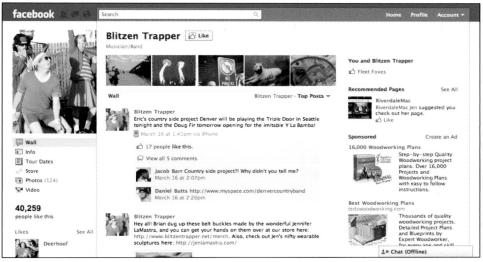

1.16 Each Page comes with a Like button that you can click to become a fan of the page.

Figuring out Groups

When you're exploring Facebook, you'll come across two kinds of resources called *Groups*. The old style of Group was a collection of people who share a common interest. It might be a hobby, a passion, a cause, a protest, or just something fun or silly. The Group profile includes a Wall section, an Info tab, and usually multiple extra tabs for things like having discussions with other Group members, posting photos and videos, scheduling upcoming events, and more.

You'll still see these old Groups around Facebook, but they've been supplanted by a new type of Group that is a subset of your friends. Why would you need such a thing? Mostly because your full list of friends probably includes a wide range of people: close family, distant family, pals, acquaintances, current colleagues, former colleagues, college classmates, high school classmates, teammates, and so on.

Quote, Unquote: Facebook and Groups

"I started a Group on Facebook called 'Mothers raising a child with Aspergers.' It's a way we mothers who are in the same position dealing with our daily struggles can support each other and give advice and tips to one another to help with certain issues we may be struggling with. I now don't feel as alone knowing there are so many other mums who live my life each and every day." — T. B., Queensland, Australia

If you want to share a status update or link, in most cases it's probably fine to share it with all your friends, but what if you just want to share it with *some* of your friends? For example, a work-related link might be of interest to your current work colleagues, but not to anyone else in your friend list. Similarly, some minutiae concerning an upcoming family wedding or birthday is certainly suitable for family, but might glaze the eyes of anyone else.

To avoid these situations, you can create a Group that consists of just a subset of your friends (family, workmates, or whatever). You can then use the Group to communicate just with the Group members, including sharing status updates, links, photos, videos, events, and more. Facebook's new Group feature even includes group chat. To create a Group, click Home and then click Create a Group in the navigation area. To access a Group of which you are a member, click the Group's name in the Navigation area of your Home page.

NOTE Be aware that others can add you to a Group without your permission. To remove yourself from a Group, open the Group's page and click the Leave Group link on the right side of the screen.

Learning about events

After you've been on Facebook for a while, it might seem like all your socializing is happening online, but chances are you still have a social life offline. Facebook recognizes that and can even make offline socializing easier. Facebook includes a feature called Events that makes it a snap for people to create a profile page (see Figure 1.17) for and invite people to some offline event, such as a wedding, celebration, rally, or simple get-together.

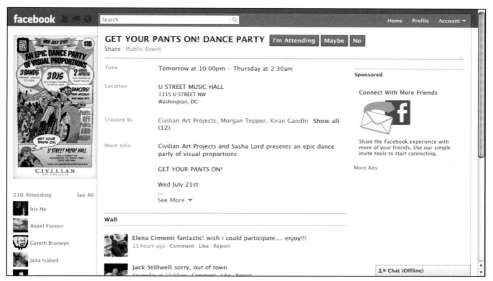

1.17 A typical Facebook event page, which contains information about the event, a list of who's attending, and a Wall section.

To add your name to an event guest list, you have three ways to go:

- **Browse your friends' events.** Probably the easiest way to look for events is to check out the ones your friends have accepted. Click Home to load your Home page, click Events, and then click Friends' Events. If you see an event that looks interesting, click it and, if it's an open event, click I'm Attending.

- **Respond to an event invitation.** If one of your friends invites you to an event, you can accept that invitation. Click Home to open your Home page and then click Events. (You may also be able to click Home and then click See All in the Events section in the upper-right corner.) For the event you want to work with, click Respond, click Attending, and then click RSVP.

- **Search for an event.** Use the Facebook Search feature to search for a topic that interests you, then click Events in the search results. If you locate an event you want to attend, click it and, if it's an open event, click I'm Attending.

NOTE You can also create your own events. You'll learn how in Chapter 3.

Finding answers about Questions

Facebook Questions is a feature that enables you to pose questions to the Facebook community. When you ask a question, it appears in your friends' News Feeds. Your question is also visible to the greater Facebook community, meaning you might just receive an answer from a certified expert. To ask a question, simply click the Questions link that appears in the Publisher at the top of your home page and your profile page, type your question, and click Share.

Checking in with Places

Facebook lets you share many things with your friends: status updates, links, photos, videos, and much more. These are all "What's on your mind?" items that, taken together, give your friends an excellent sense of who you are and what you are all about. But what about giving your friends a sense of *where* you are? Sure, you can just post a status update that says where you are, or a photo of your current location, but Facebook's Places feature makes sharing your location much easier.

Places works using the Facebook mobile application, which is available for the iPhone and other types of smartphones. The Facebook app determines your whereabouts and then displays a list of locations in your area — stores, schools, libraries, and so on. You select the location, write a short message, tag a Facebook friend who's with you (if any), and then post the location to your profile. This is called *checking in*, and you can do it for existing locations or for new locations that you set up yourself.

To check in with Places — in this example, on an iPhone — follow these steps:

1. **Open the Facebook application on your iPhone.**
2. **Tap the Places icon on the main screen.** The Places screen appears.
3. **Tap Check In.** Your phone pinpoints your location and creates a list of stores, restaurants, schools, libraries, churches, and other public places nearby.
4. **Tap your location.** A screen appears where you can indicate what you're doing at the location and tag any friends who are with you.

5. **Tap Check In.** Places reminds you that when you check in, friends nearby will be able to see your location.

6. **Tap I Agree.**

Getting to know applications

As you've seen so far, Facebook is loaded with features that ought to keep you busy. Just in case they don't (or even if they do), there's another aspect of the site that lets you extend Facebook with even *more* features. These are called *applications*, and they're small programs that run within the Facebook site. There are thousands of applications to choose from, everything from serious business programs to silly trifles that don't do much of anything.

To locate applications, Facebook gives you three options:

- **Check out your friends' applications.** To see which apps your friends are using, click Home to load your Home page, and then click Applications. The Applications page has a Friends' Applications section that lists two or three applications for each friend. If you see an application you might like, click it.

- **Browse the Applications Directory.** This is a Facebook feature that lists applications by category (such as Business, Entertainment, and Games). Click Home to open your Home page, click Applications, and then click Applications Directory. Click a category, browse through the results, and then click on any application that you think you might like to use.

- **Search for an application.** Use the Facebook Search feature to search for a keyword that interests you, then click Applications in the search results. If you locate an application that looks interesting, click it.

When you get to the application's page, you can click the Info tab to learn more about it, and click the Reviews tab to see what other people think of it. If you want to install the application, click the Go to Application button. You then see the Request for Permission page, as shown in Figure 1.18. Most applications require access to your Facebook profile so that they can display your profile picture and name, and show you things like which of your friends are using the application. Click Allow to give the application permission to access your profile.

1.18 When you install a Facebook application, you usually need to give the application permission to access your profile.

After you add an application to your profile, you can return to it at any time by clicking Home to open your Home page, clicking Applications in the Navigation area, and then clicking the application in the list of applications that Facebook displays. If you have an application that you use frequently, you can add the application as a bookmark to get faster service:

This means that the application appears in the Navigation area (although you may need to click the More link to see it). To set up an application as a bookmark, click Account, then click Application Settings. Click the Edit Settings link beside the application, click the Bookmark tab, and then click the Bookmark *Application* check box (where *Application* is the name of the program).

Playing games

You might think that games are just for kids, but Facebook offers thousands of games that are fun for all ages. Whether you're into Scrabble, crosswords, poker, or Sudoku, Facebook has a game (more likely a few games) that will help you become less productive!

Games are just applications, so everything that I talked about in the previous section applies here. However, Facebook does come with some specific techniques for finding games:

- **Check out your friends' games.** Click Home to open your Home page, and then click Games. The Games page has a Friends' Games section that lists two or three games for each friend. If you see a game that looks fun, click it.

- **Browse the Games Directory.** This is a list of the games that are available on Facebook. Click Home to open your Home page, click Games, and then click Games Directory. Browse through the games, and then click on any game that looks appealing.

- **Search for a game.** Use the Facebook Search feature to search for a keyword that interests you, and be sure to include the word *game* in the search text. Click Applications in the search results. If you locate a game that looks interesting, click it.

Searching Facebook

One of the key principles of this book is that Facebook is loaded with interesting, useful, and entertaining content, so no matter what you're into, Facebook's resources — people, stories, links, photos, videos, notes, Wall sections, Pages, Groups, Events, applications, and games — are a great place to start.

However, the key is *finding* those resources that are pertinent to your needs and interests. Your friends can help, as always, but connecting to the resources that are best suited to you will almost always require the use of the Facebook Search feature.

To run a Facebook search, click inside the Search box in the Facebook toolbar, then type a word or two that best characterize what you're interested in. If you want to search on a phrase, include the words in quotation marks. As you can see in Figure 1.19, Facebook usually displays a few results that it thinks best matches your search text.

If you see what you want, you can click it in the top results. To view additional matches, click the See More Results link at the bottom of the results menu. This displays a results page (see Figure 1.20) that enables you to break down the results by Facebook feature: People, Pages, Groups, Applications, Events, Posts by Friends, and Posts by Everyone.

1.19 When you type in the Search box, Facebook displays the top results right away.

Controlling your privacy

Depending on the type of content, Facebook offers up to four privacy settings:

- **Friends Only.** With this setting, only people you're friends with can see the content.

- **Friends of Friends.** With this setting, people you're friends with can see the content, and so can their friends.

- **Everyone.** This setting shows the content to anyone, even those who don't have a Facebook account.

- **Customize.** This setting enables you to create a custom privacy setting. For example, you can make the content visible to only certain people, or you can hide the content from specific users.

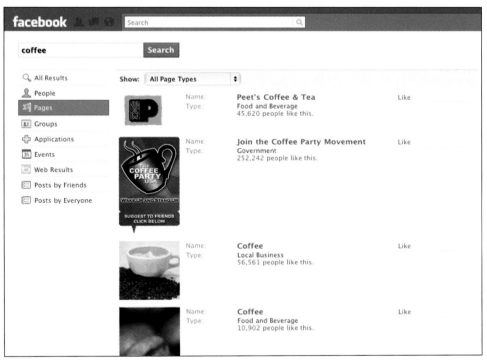

1.20 Click See More Results to display a page like the one shown here, where you can break down the results by the type of feature you want.

To view your current Facebook privacy options, click Account and then click Privacy Settings. The Choose Your Privacy Settings page is divided into two main sections:

- **Connecting on Facebook.** This section includes privacy settings that govern your basic profile data. By default, Facebook shares this data using a mixture of Everyone and Friends Only settings. To change this, click View Settings, then use the lists in the Connecting on Facebook page (see Figure 1.21) to choose a privacy setting for each type of information.

- **Sharing on Facebook.** This section (see Figure 1.22) determines how you share your other Facebook data. The default Recommended setting shares some data with Everyone, some with Friends of Friends, and some with just Friends. You can use the preset Everyone, Friends of Friends, or Friends Only settings to modify all the settings with a single mouse click. If you want more fine-grained control, click Customize Settings and then use the lists to choose a privacy setting for each type of content.

Choose Your Privacy Settings ▸ **Connecting on Facebook**

| ◂ Back to Privacy | | Preview My Profile |

Your name, profile picture, gender and networks are visible to everyone (learn more). We also recommend setting the other basic settings below open to everyone so friends can find and connect with you.

🔍 **Search for you on Facebook** — This lets friends and family find you in Facebook search results. Set this to Everyone or you could miss friend requests. — 🔒 Everyone ▾
  ✓ Everyone
  Friends of Friends
  Friends Only

👥 **Send you friend requests** — This lets you receive friend requests. Set this to Everyone to avoid missing out on chances to connect with people you know.

💬 **Send you messages** — This helps you make sure you know people before adding them as friends. — 🔒 Friends Only ▾

👥 **See your friend list** — This lets you connect with people based on friends you have in common. Your friend list is always available to applications and your connections to friends may be visible elsewhere. — 🔒 Friends Only ▾

📷 **See your education and work** — This helps you connect with classmates and colleagues, and discover new professional opportunities. — 🔒 Friends Only ▾

1.21 Use the lists in the Basic Directory information page to determine who can see your basic profile data.

For example, suppose you want to control who can post stories on your Wall section and who can see those stories. Click Customize Settings and then scroll down to the Things Others Share section, which offers two Wall-related privacy settings:

- **Friends can post on my Wall.** Deselect this check box if you don't want anyone else adding stories to your Wall.

- **Can see Wall posts by friends** If you're allowing friends to post to your Wall, use this list to select who can see those posts: Everyone, Friends of Friends, Friends Only, or Customize.

Choose Your Privacy Settings

Connecting on Facebook
Control basic information your friends will use to find you on Facebook. View Settings

Sharing on Facebook
These settings control who can see what you share.

	Everyone	Friends of Friends	Friends Only
Your status, photos, and posts	●		
Bio and favorite quotations	●		
Family and relationships	●		
Photos and videos you're tagged in		●	
Religious and political views		●	
Birthday		●	
Permission to comment on your posts			●
Places you check in to [?]			●
Contact information			●

Everyone

Friends of Friends

Friends Only

Recommended ✔

☑ Share a tagged post with friends of the friend I tag

✎ Customize settings   ✔ This is your current setting.

1.22 The default Recommended setting offers a good mixture of privacy and sharing, but you can click Customize Settings to set up your own privacy scheme.

2 chapter

Wall | **Info** | **Photos** | **Notes**

Making Friends

Facebook would be just another lonely outpost on the frontiers of the Web if all anyone ever did was post status updates and stories. Facebook is, instead, a vibrant, noisy place because it goes beyond mere broadcasting and embraces its social side by letting you make friends with fellow Facebookers. This means that you see that person's status updates, stories, profile changes, and activities such as likes and comments. They all appear in your News Feed, so you can easily keep track of what that person shares with his Facebook friends. By friending (yes, it's a verb) your pals, family, and colleagues, and by liking, commenting on, and sharing stories, and exchanging messages with your friends, you begin to get the full Facebook experience.

Finding Friends

Sociologists often use the term *social capital* to refer to the value generated by a person's social relationships. The more an individual relationship or a collection of relationships — that is, a social network — fosters benefits such as good will, civility, empathy, fellowship, support, and mutual assistance, the more social capital that relationship or network generates. As you might expect, studies have consistently shown that the greater your social capital, the greater your overall well-being and the higher your self-esteem. Social capital is, in short, a good thing.

Facebook is a social network, of course, so it raises an obvious question: Does having a Facebook account raise your social capital? To answer that question, in early 2010 Facebook's data researchers decided to try to measure social capital among Facebook users. They recruited 1,200 people to take surveys that measure social capital, and they examined each user's Facebook data and activities over the previous two months: total number of friends, News Feed clicks, likes, and comments, Wall posts, and so on. The results clearly showed that the more friends you have on Facebook — and, crucially, the more you interact with those friends — the greater your social capital.

So all the more reason to go out and find yourself a few (or, better, a few dozen) Facebook friends. The next few sections take you through the various techniques that Facebook offers for tracking down friends.

Searching Facebook for people you know

Perhaps the most straightforward way to track down a friend on Facebook is to simply search for that person by name. Click inside the Search box at the top of any Facebook Page, type the person's name, and then do one of the following:

- If Facebook displays a results menu of matches for things like actors, authors, and public figures, click the See More Results for *Name* link (where *Name* is the name you typed).
- If you don't see the results menu, just press Enter or Return.

When the results page appears, click the People category to see just the Facebook folks who match your search.

As you can see in Figure 2.1, Facebook also enables you to refine your search by applying one or more filters to the results. You can type a location (a city, town, state, or province), a school, or a company name. Click Refine Search when you're done.

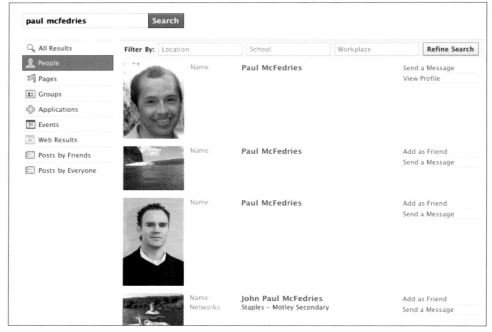

paul mcfedries		**Search**			

| | **Filter By:** | Location | School | Workplace | **Refine Search** |

Q All Results

👤 People

📄 Pages

👥 Groups

➕ Applications

📅 Events

💬 Web Results

📋 Posts by Friends

📋 Posts by Everyone

| Name: | **Paul McFedries** | Send a Message |
| | | View Profile |

| Name: | **Paul McFedries** | Add as Friend |
| | | Send a Message |

| Name: | **Paul McFedries** | Add as Friend |
| | | Send a Message |

| Name: | **John Paul McFedries** | Add as Friend |
| Networks: | Staples – Motley Secondary | Send a Message |

2.1 To refine your search, click People and then use the Filter text boxes to narrow your search by location, school, or company.

TIP

If you happen to know the person's e-mail address, you can save yourself a lot of time by searching on that address instead of the person's name (particularly if the person has a common name). Because e-mail addresses are unique on Facebook, any match that comes up is guaranteed to be the person you're looking for.

If you're not sure whether a search result is the person you seek, click the person's name to go to his or her profile page. Most people share only a limited amount of data with nonfriends, but you should at least see the person's current city and hometown.

Quote, Unquote: Facebook Friends

"Facebook reconnected me to childhood friends. It did change my life, because I no longer feel that old times are lost. My life is more complete with Facebook." — I. R., Budapest, Hungary

If you find the person you're looking for, follow these steps:

1. **Click Add as Friend.** Facebook displays a dialog box like the one shown in Figure 2.2, asking you to confirm that you want to send the friend request.

2. **If you want to personalize your request, click the Add a personal message link.**

3. **Type your message.**

4. **When you're done, click Send Request.**

2.2 Facebook asks you to confirm that you want to send a friend request.

NOTE Most people don't bother personalizing their friend requests, and few people will feel slighted if you don't. However, there are some situations where adding a personal message comes in handy. For example, if it has been a while, you might want to include a short note reminding the person how you know him or her. Similarly, if you're still not sure whether you have the right person, you could include a note asking the person to confirm.

Finding friends using your address book

You already have a collection of friends: the list of people in your e-mail address book. These friends, family members, colleagues, clients, and acquaintances are, by definition, people with whom you've had at least some contact, and with over half a billion people on Facebook there's a good chance that a large percentage of those contacts also have Facebook accounts.

So one very easy way to generate a large number of friend requests is to check if the people in your address book or contacts list have Facebook accounts. Facebook gives you two ways to do this: using a Web-based e-mail account and using a contact file generated from your computer's address book. The next two sections provide the details.

Finding friends through an online e-mail account

If you use a Web-based e-mail account from a service such as Gmail, Windows Live, Hotmail, or Yahoo! Mail, you can give Facebook's friend finder feature permission to access your online address book and look for those contacts who have Facebook accounts (based on the e-mail address you have stored for each person).

To give this a try, follow these steps:

1. **Click Home to load your Facebook Home page.**

2. **Click Friends in the Navigation area to open the Friends page.**
   For some Facebook accounts, you can also open the Friends page by clicking Find Friends in the toolbar.

3. **In the Find People You Email section, type your online e-mail address.** From here, there are two ways you can go:

   • If Facebook doesn't recognize the domain name (such as gmail.com, live.com, or yahoo.com), it will continue to display the Password text box. You'll need to type your e-mail account password, and then click Find Friends.

   • If Facebook does recognize the domain name, it will hide the password box, so go ahead and click Find Friends. Facebook connects with the online e-mail service, which then prompts you to log on to your account.

NOTE The thought of giving out your e-mail password is probably more than a little alarming. Not to worry, though: Facebook does not store your password. Instead, it uses it once only to connect to your e-mail account, then it forgets the password.

In most cases, your e-mail provider asks if you want to allow Facebook to access the information in your account.

4. **Click Allow to let Facebook access your contacts.** Facebook connects with your account, downloads your address book, and then displays a list of the contacts who have Facebook accounts, as shown in Figure 2.3.

5. **Select the check box beside each person you want to request to be your friend.** Alternatively, select the Select All Friends check box to select everyone.

6. **Click Add as Friends to ship out the requests.** Facebook then presents you with a list of your contacts who are not on Facebook, and asks if you want to invite them to join.

NOTE If, instead of Facebook successfully accessing your contacts, you see an error message such as Unsupported Email Address, it means that Facebook can't connect with your e-mail service. In this case, you may still be able to use a contact file, as described in the next section.

2.3 Facebook connects to your e-mail service and then displays a list of your contacts who are on Facebook.

7. **If you're sure this won't be seen as intrusive by your friends, select the check box beside each person you want to invite.**

8. **Click Invite to Join.**

NOTE If you use instant messaging, you may have a long list of buddies, some of whom might be on Facebook. To find out, display the Friends page, scroll down to the Find People You IM section, click the instant messaging service you use, type your credentials, and then click Find Friends.

Using a contact file to find friends

Facebook's automatic friend finder makes it easy to see which of your contacts are already on Facebook, but it's not for everyone. For example, you might not use an online e-mail service, Facebook might not recognize your service, or you might not be comfortable entering your e-mail account password.

Whatever the reason, friend finder offers an alternate route to seeing which of your friends are on Facebook. You can export your address book to a contact file and then import that file into friend finder. Facebook scours the file to look for existing Facebook accounts.

For this to work, you must export your address book to a file in one of three formats:

- comma-separated values (.csv)
- vCard (.vcf)
- Lightweight Directory Access Protocol (LDAP) Data Interchange Format (.ldif).

Here are the instructions to follow to get started in various programs and Web sites:

- **Microsoft Outlook.** Click File, click Import and Export, select Export to a file, click Next, select Comma separated values (Windows), click Next, click the Contacts folder, and then click Next.

- **Windows Live Contacts.** In Windows, run Windows Live Mail, click Contacts, click the Menus icon (or press Alt+M to display the menu bar and then click File), click Export, and then click Comma Separated Values (.CSV).

- **Outlook Express.** Click File, click Export, click Address Book, select Text File (Comma Separated Values), and then click Export.

- **Mac OS X Address Book.** Click File, click Export, and then click Export Group vCard.

- **Gmail.** Log in to your Gmail account, click Contacts, click Export, select Everyone, select Outlook CSV, and then click Export.

- **Windows Live Mail.** Log in to your Windows Live account, click Mail, click Contacts, click Manage, click Export, type the verification text, and then click Export.

- **MobileMe.** Log in to your MobileMe account, click Switch Apps (the cloud icon), and then click Contacts. Click Actions (the gear icon), click Select All, click Actions again, and then click Export vCard.

- **Yahoo! Mail.** Log in to your Yahoo! Mail account, click Contacts, click Tools, click Export, and then click the Microsoft Outlook Export Now button.

In each case, you're then prompted to type a filename and choose a location for the file. Remember where you store the file, because you'll need that information when you import the file into Facebook.

Once your contact file is safely stowed on your computer, return to Facebook and open the Friends page. Click the Upload Contact File link, click Choose File, click your contacts file, click Choose, and then click Find Friends. You can then send friend requests to people already on Facebook (as described in the previous section) or e-mail Facebook invitations.

TIP

After you send out a bunch of friend requests, you might forget which people you've sent requests to, or you might want to know who has yet to respond to a friend request. Unfortunately, Facebook doesn't have any direct way to get a list of what it calls "pending friend requests." The next best thing is to click Account, click Edit Friends, and then click Friends. In the friend list that appears, you see Friend Request Pending beside each person who has yet to handle your request.

Finding your old high-school pals

One of the aspects of Facebook that many people really enjoy is getting back in touch with old friends, particularly from one's high school days. It has all the benefits of a high-school reunion, but without the awkwardness of face-to-face meetings.

To make finding your old high-school friends easy, you should first add your high school to your profile, if you haven't done so already:

1. **Click Profile to open your Profile page.**
2. **Click Edit Profile.**
3. **Click Education and Work.**
4. **In the High School field, type the name of your school.** Facebook displays matching schools as you type, so if you see your school before you complete the name, click it in the list.
5. **Use the Class Year list to choose the year you graduated.**
6. **Click Save Changes.** Facebook adds the school to your profile.

Quote, Unquote: Facebook Friends

"The pleasures of Facebook have been multitude. A memorably sweet reunion for fellow refugees from my tiny, now shuttered high school would never have happened had we not found each other on FB." — Mary Elizabeth Williams, Salon.com

To search for people from your high school, follow these steps:

1. **Open the Friends page.**

2. **Click Other Tools.**

3. **Click the Find Classmates from *School* link, where *School* is the name of your high school and the year you graduated.** Facebook displays a list of the people with Facebook accounts who have added the same school and graduating year to their profiles.

4. **For each high school buddy you see, click the Add as Friend link to send a request.**

Finding your university friends

Facebook also makes it easy to locate people you went to college or university with. Again, to make this easier, you should add your college or university to your profile:

1. **Click Profile to open your Profile page.**

2. **Click Edit My Profile.**

3. **Click Education and Work.**

4. **In the College/University text box, type the name of your school.** Facebook displays matching schools as you type, so if you see your school before you complete the name, click it in the list.

5. **Use the Class Year list to choose the year you graduated.** If you're looking for friends from a different class, choose the year that those friends graduated, instead.

6. **Use the Concentrations text boxes to type your majors.**

7. **Select either College or Graduate Studies.**

8. **Click Save Changes.** Facebook adds the school to your profile.

To search for people from your college or university, open the Friends page, click Other Tools, and then click the Find classmates from *School* link, where *School* is the name of your college or university and the year you graduated. Facebook displays a list of the people with Facebook accounts who have added the same school and graduating year to their profiles. For each college or university friend you see, click the Add as Friend link to send a request.

> College and university searches tend to produce long lists of results, so it might take a while to scroll through all the people. Use the sections on the left (such as Hometown and Current City) to filter the results using either the check boxes or by typing items in the text boxes.

Finding your work colleagues

Many people find Facebook to be an invaluable place to communicate and collaborate with work colleagues, particularly those who work in a different location. If you want to find out who in your company has a Facebook account, the best way to start is to add your current job to your Facebook profile:

1. **Click Profile to surf to the Profile page.**

2. **Click Edit My Profile.**

3. **Click Education and Work.**

4. **In the Employer text box, type the name of your current employer.** If Facebook displays your employer as you type, click your employer in the list.

5. **Use the Position text box to type your current job title.**

6. **Use the City/Town text box to type the location of your work.**

7. **Use the Description text box to briefly describe your job.**

8. **Select the I currently work here check box.**

9. **Use the Month and Year lists to specify when you started at the company.**

10. **Click Save Changes.** Facebook adds the job to your profile.

To search Facebook for people from your company, open the Friends page, click Other Tools, and then click the Find former coworkers from *Company* link, where *Company* is the name of your employer. Facebook displays a list of the people with Facebook accounts who have added the same company to their profiles. For each coworker you want to friend, click the Add as Friend link to send a request.

> If you work for a large company, your search will likely generate a distressingly long list of results. In that case, you can use the sections on the left (such as Hometown and Current City) to filter the results.

Quote, Unquote: Facebook Friends

"I've become reacquainted with so many friends and colleagues from my past. It's just been incredible. I can see their families, see how they are doing, catch up, and simply just read up on their posts. It's been totally great!" — B. G., Philadelphia, Pennsylvania

Handling Friend Requests

The more Facebook activities you engage in — friending people, liking and commenting on stories, writing on Wall sections, and so on — and the more people who sign up for Facebook accounts, the more likely it is that friend requests will come your way. On the surface, a friend request seems like such a simple thing because you can only do one of three things: confirm the request and become that person's friend; decline the request; or do nothing, putting off your decision to a later date if you can't make up your mind right now.

It all seems simple enough, but the calculus involved in deciding whether to accept a friend request can be quite complex. Sure, it's not a problem with people you're close to or find interesting, but it can get uncomfortable when a request comes in from someone you barely know, someone you know but have no real connection to, someone you had a falling out with long ago, or someone you don't find all that interesting.

If you decline or ignore a request, the person who made the request will receive no notification of your action. Even so, most Facebook folk generally know who they've sent friend requests to, and when you decline or ignore a request from someone, that's kind of a snub. Because of that, ignoring a friend request is actually not an easy thing to do, and many people end up just accepting the request rather than snubbing someone. However, building a too-large list of friends (the maximum is 5,000!) can lead to problems:

- The more friends you have, the more stories you see in your News Feed, particularly in the Most Recent view. This isn't a problem with just a few friends, but as your friend list grows you could end up wading through hundreds of stories each day.

TIP Facebook gives you the option of hiding News Feed stories that come from a particular friend, which is an easy way to keep your News Feed relevant. This is covered later in this chapter.

- In the default Facebook privacy settings, if Person A writes on Person B's Wall section, the friends of Person B can see that Wall post. So if you're Person A, you need to realize that all of Person's B's friends can see your writings on Person B's Wall section. If Person B happens to be friends with someone you dislike or are in some way uncomfortable with, you might not want that user to see your posts, so that might argue against accepting Person B's friend request. (The alternative would be to accept Person B's friend request and then only send Person B private messages.)

- The more you stray outside your circle of true friends, family members, close work colleagues, and people you genuinely like, the more likely it is that at least some of your "friends" will send you boring or inane status updates, uninteresting stories, irrelevant requests to join Groups and like Pages, and so on.

None of this means that you have to restrict your Facebook friends to only those closest to you (although many on Facebook do exactly that), but it does mean that you should think in advance about the type of experience you want on Facebook. If the idea of seeing myriad status updates, profile changes, stories, comments, Wall posts, Group and Event invitations, and Page suggestions from a diverse range of people sounds appealing, then go right ahead and confirm your friend requests with abandon.

To handle a friend request, you have two ways to get started:

- Click the Friend Requests icon in the Message bar, as shown in Figure 2.4.

- Click Home to load your Home page, then click Friends in the Navigation area.

2.4 Click the Friend Requests icon to see a list of the friend requests that people have sent you.

You have three ways to handle the friend request:

- If you want this person as your friend, click Confirm.
- If you want to decide later, click Not Now to have Facebook hide the request. To display the request later on, click the Friend Requests icon in the Message bar, click See All Friend Requests, and then click See X Hidden Requests (where X is the number of requests you put off until later).
- If you don't want this person as your friend, click Not Now, use the technique from the previous bullet to display the hidden request, and then click Delete Request. Note that you can also indicate that you don't know the person; this prevents him or her from sending you additional friend requests in the future.

As you add friends (and as you add more details to your profile, particularly school and work data), Facebook begins looking around for people you might know on the site. For example, if several of the people you're friends with are all friends with a particular person, Facebook will likely assume you might also want to be friends with that person. To check out these friend suggestions, open your Friends page and scroll down to the Suggestions section. These recommendations may also appear in the Suggestions box on the right side of your home page.

Working with Friends

Sending your own friend requests and confirming (or ignoring) the friend requests that come your way is only the beginning of the friend-related activities that Facebook offers. Once you have your Facebook friend list going, you'll see incoming status updates, profile updates, stories, and other friend-generated content come your way, and you'll be able to read, like, comment on, and share that content. However, Facebook also offers a number of useful techniques for working with and managing your list of friends, and you learn the most useful of these techniques in the rest of this chapter.

Viewing your friends' updates

Before getting to the behind-the-scenes techniques for working with friends, let's take a look at a couple of little-known front-of-the-scenes techniques for working with friend updates. You learned in Chapter 1 that friends can post all kinds of stories, from links to photos to videos to Event invitations. However, for many people on Facebook, the most important friend posts are the updates:

the status updates that give you insight into each friend's actions, moods, concerns, and thoughts, and profile updates that alert you to changes in relationships, employers, interests, and activities.

One way to view updates is to visit your friends' profile pages. Another approach is to view the News Feed on your Home page, where you can see status updates and other stories from several friends at once. As great as the News Feed is, however, it sometimes shows more information than you want to see — your coworker's latest acquisition in FarmVille and other similar stories. If you only want to view status updates or profile updates, you can filter your feed. Here's how:

- **Status updates.** Click Home to open your Facebook Home page, choose Most Recent from the options at upper-right. Click on the down arrow, and then click Status Updates. Facebook displays the Status Updates page, which shows only the recent status updates posted by your friends.

- **Profile updates.** Click Home to see your Home page, click Friends in the Navigation area, then click Recently Updated. Facebook displays the Friends page, which shows only the recent profile changes made by your friends.

Viewing your friends

Every now and then you might want to see a list of your Facebook friends, either to remind yourself who you're friends with or to visit a specific friend's Facebook Profile page. To view your friends, click Profile to open your Profile page. In the left column of the Profile page, you see a Friends list like the one shown in Figure 2.5. This box displays a random sampling of ten people from your list of friends. (That is, if you reload the page, you see a different set of ten friends.) To see all your friends, click the Friends link. Facebook displays the Friends page, which lists all your friends in

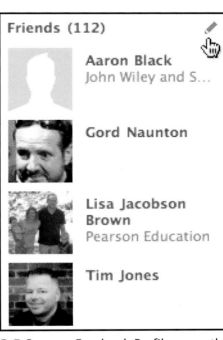

Friends (112)

Aaron Black
John Wiley and S...

Gord Naunton

Lisa Jacobson Brown
Pearson Education

Tim Jones

2.5 On your Facebook Profile page, the Friends box randomly displays ten of your friends.

alphabetical order by first name. To see a subset of your friends, click the Search button, click the type of search (such as Search by Name or Search by Hometown, as shown in Figure 2.6) and then type your search text.

2.6 You can click Search, choose a search type, and then type some text to filter your friends.

TIP To customize the people that appear in the Friends box, click the Edit box (the pencil icon), then use the Featured Friends area to specify an existing friend list or group, or create a new list of friends.

Quote, Unquote: Facebook Friends

"These days, when you meet someone new, you get to know them better through a social networking site like Facebook. I met some of my very best friends through Facebook, and to this day, adding or requesting someone on Facebook could be a sure way to develop friendships that could last a very long time." — S. A., Chicago, Illinois

---

Quote, Unquote: Facebook Friends

"Using Facebook has allowed me to reconnect with family and friends all over the country! I can see pics and I share my pics. My BFF of 30 years and I had lost touch over the years and because of Facebook we are now in touch every day!" — G. W., Duncansville, Pennsylvania

Creating and using lists

Facebook treats your collection of friends as a single unit. This means, for example, that when you post a status update or story, it's displayed on the News Feed of each of your friends. Similarly, when you configure a privacy setting (as described in Chapter 1) and you choose the Friends option, Facebook applies that privacy option to all your friends.

However, it's unlikely that your friends are that monolithic. Your thoughts on or photos from last weekend's family barbeque are appropriate for your family members and perhaps your close friends, but it's unlikely your work colleagues or clients will be all that interested. Similarly, an inside joke from work might be appreciated by your colleagues, but it's likely to mystify anyone from outside the company.

To work around these sorts of problems, one solution would be to create a Group (see Chapter 1) that includes a subset of your friends. Another is to create lists for different collections of friends. Once you create a list, you can then use the list to tailor your Facebook activity. Here are some examples:

- **Send a status update or story to just the people in a list.** For example, if you have several Facebook friends who are interested in wine, you can create a list called, for example, Wine Lovers, and then post any wine-related updates or stories just to that list.

- **Restrict a photo album to just the friends in a list.** For example, if you have a photo album that you only want your family to see, you can create a list with a name such as Family Members and then configure the album so that only the people in that list can view it.

- **Configure your profile data privacy so that only the people in a list can see that data.** If you want your contact data to be visible only to a select set of friends, you can create a list of those friends and configure your profile contact information privacy settings so that only the friends in the list can view your contact data (phone numbers, address, and so on).

● **Invite the people in a list to an Event.** For example, if you're planning a company gathering, rather than picking your colleagues one by one when selecting the guests, you can create a list called, say, Work Colleagues, and use that list to choose the attendees.

Creating a list

To create a friend list, click Account, and then click Edit Friends to open the Edit Friends page. In the Lists section on the left side of the page, click Friends to display your complete friend list. Click Create New List to open the Create New List dialog box. Type a name for the list, and then click each friend you want to include in the list, as shown in Figure 2.7. (If you select someone by accident, click that person again to deselect him.) When you're done, click Create List. Facebook builds the list and then adds it to the Lists category of the Edit Friends page.

2.7 Click Create New List and then use this dialog box to name your list and select the friends you want to include in the list.

To add more people to a list later on, Facebook gives you a couple of ways to go. First, click Account and then click Edit Friends to display the Edit Friends page. One method is to click Friends, locate the friend you want to add, click that person's Add to List button, and then click your list. Alternatively, click your list in the Lists section, and then click Edit List.

 NOTE Facebook's Groups feature is evolving to perform many of the same functions as lists. You may find Groups to be a better and easier way to communicate with a small set of friends.

Posting a story to a list

Once you have at least one friend list on the go, you can compose a status update or story and tell Facebook to send it only to the people in the list. Here's how:

1. **Compose your status update or other story.**

2. **Click the Privacy icon to the left of the Share button.**

3. **Click Customize.**

4. **In the Custom Privacy dialog box, use the Make this visible to list to choose Specific People.**

5. **Type the list name in the text box, as shown in Figure 2.8.**

6. **Click Save Setting.**

7. **Click Share to post your update or story to the list.**

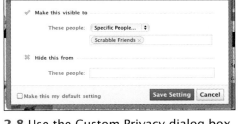

2.8 Use the Custom Privacy dialog box to specify the friend list you want to use for the status update or story.

Applying a list to a privacy setting

I mentioned in Chapter 1 that by default Facebook gives you four possible options for most privacy settings:

- Everyone
- Friends of Friends
- Friends Only
- Only Me

For many settings, however, there's a fifth option called Specific People, which you can use to apply the setting to specific friends or, more conveniently, to a list of friends.

To set up a specific list of friends, follow these steps:

1. **Display the options associated with the privacy setting you want to configure.**

2. **Click Customize.** Note, however, that some privacy settings don't offer a Customize option.

3. **In the Custom Privacy dialog box, use the Make this visible to list to choose Specific People.**

4. **Type the list name in the text box.**

Hiding a friend's updates

It's an unfortunate fact of Facebook life that not everyone is always interesting or entertaining or fun. That, I realize, is a statement that applies to life in general, not just to Facebook. However, just as we forgive our offline friends for being occasionally dull or self-centered, it's often necessary to forgive our Facebook friends when their status updates or stories fail to scintillate.

Sometimes, however, you end up with a friend who isn't merely occasionally uninteresting or trivial or self-involved, but is always so. Your eyes glaze over just thinking about the possibility of a story from that person in your News Feed. Unfortunately, one of the other unfortunate facts of Facebook life is that the more trivial or self-absorbed a person is, the more often she seems to post stories.

Rather than cluttering your News Feed with these kinds of stories, you can tell Facebook to hide all updates from that person. This includes not only stories, but also status updates, profile changes, likes, comments, and so on.

To hide someone from your News Feed, follow these steps:

1. **Click Home to display your News Feed.**

2. **Hover your mouse over an update from the person you want to hide.** As shown in Figure 2.9, Facebook displays an X on the right side of the update.

Akela Einzelganger I had a grilled cheese sandwich for lunch, washed down with a soda, and topped off with a candy bar. Yum yum. 4 minutes ago · Comment · Like

What are you planning?

Remove sored   Create an Ad

2.9 Move your mouse over a person's update, then click the X to remove all that person's updates from your News Feed.

3. **Click the X.**

4. **When Facebook asks you to confirm, click Hide all by *User,* where *User* is the name of the friend.**

Removing a friend

It's one thing if one of your Facebook friends is consistently boring or trivial, because the easy remedy is to hide that person's updates, as described in the previous section. However, you might find yourself in the uncomfortable position of having a friend who's often rude, nasty, crude, or hostile, either to the world in general or to you in particular. Life's too short to put up with that! You should seriously consider unfriending that person. Facebook gives you two ways to do this:

- Display the person's Profile page and then click the Unfriend link that appears near the bottom of the left column.

- Click Account and then click Edit Friends to open the Edit Friends page. In the Lists section, click Friends to display your complete list of friends. Locate the person you want to remove, then click the Remove Connection (X) icon beside that person. When Facebook asks you to confirm, click Remove from Friends.

Note that no matter which method you use, the ex-friend does not receive any notification that you've unfriended him or her. Instead, you just quietly disappear from that person's friend list.

TIP If you want to ensure that this person never contacts you again on Facebook, or if you're dealing with someone who isn't your friend but is sending you unpleasant messages, you can block the offending user. Display the person's Facebook profile and then click the Report/Block this Person link, which appears near the bottom of the left column.

3 chapter

Wall	Info	Photos	Notes

Connecting with Family

When people are asked what they like most about Facebook, the most common answer by far is that it helps them to connect with family. Whether it's a cousin who lives across the country, a distant relative they barely know, or someone from a forgotten limb of the family tree, Facebook helps people connect the disparate parts of their families. Facebook also helps parents and their children, grandparents and their grandchildren, siblings, aunts, uncles, nieces, and nephews get closer by sharing messages, photos, videos, and more. Finally, Facebook is a great place for family-related information, including info on parenting, grandparenting, genealogy, pets, and more.

Friending Your Kids and Grandkids

One of the first questions that all parents ask when they sign up for Facebook is, "Should I friend my kids?" And if you're a bit further along in life's journey, a second question pops up immediately after: "Should I friend my grandkids?"

For most parenting and social media experts, the answers are actually simple and straightforward:

- If you're the parent of a young child (say, 13 or 14 years old; remember that the minimum Facebook age is 13), then yes, you should friend your child to ensure that he or she isn't oversharing or making other Facebook mistakes.

- For all other children, whether you're a parent or grandparent, ask. That is, sit your child or grandchild down and have a talk about whether he or she would be comfortable having you as a friend.

If you do friend your child or grandchild, here are a few tips for getting the most out of the experience:

- If you're dealing with a teenaged child, you're well within your rights to ask that child to uphold certain rules online: No swearing, no inappropriate photos, no posting of future party locations.

- Do not try to friend any of your child's friends. That's just embarrassing.

- For younger children or grandchildren, resist the temptation to constantly like or comment on the child's stories, or to write on his or her Wall section. Most youngsters don't want frequent reminders that mom, dad, grandma, or grandpa is listening in.

- Forgive as much as you can. None of us is perfect on Facebook, and so it's almost certain that your kid or grandkid will post status updates, stories, and other content that you think is inappropriate, inane, or offensive. If you comment on or send a message about every little Facebook faux pas, you'll get unfriended in a hurry. Save your indignation for the worst of the offenses, and be sure to send your response using a private channel, such as sending a message (if a face-to-face talk isn't possible right away).

- Remember that your child or grandchild can also see your status updates, stories, and Facebook activities. This means that you should be on your best behavior on Facebook, particularly when you're dealing with younger children or grandchildren and you're still in role model mode.

Adding Family Members to Your Profile

One of the benefits of friending your family members is that you can then add them to your profile to show them off to the rest of your friends. (For non-spousal relationships, Facebook also allows you to add family members who don't have a Facebook account.) You can add your relationship status and your significant other (if any), and you can add other family members, such as your parents and children.

Adding your current relationship

To add your current relationship status and, if you're in a relationship, the name of your significant other, follow these steps:

1. **Click Profile to open your Facebook Profile page.**
2. **Click Edit Profile.**
3. **Click Featured People.**
4. **Use the Relationship Status list to select your current status, such as Married, Widowed, or It's Complicated.**
5. **If you indicated you're in a relationship, use the text box to type the person's name, and you can also fill in the Anniversary fields, as shown in Figure 3.1.**

3.1 Specify your relationship status and then add the name of your significant other, if applicable.

6. **When you're done, click Save Changes.** If you indicated you're in a relationship, Facebook then sends a confirmation message to that person.

If you're in a relationship and you filled in your anniversary, Facebook is kind enough to remind you when the big day approaches by including a message in the Events box of your Home page, as shown in Figure 3.2.

3.2 If you told Facebook the date of your anniversary, it adds a reminder to your Home page's Events box a few days before.

Currently only you and your significant other see this message, although Facebook has indicated that your anniversary will eventually be shown to your other friends as well.

Adding other family members

You can also add other members of your family to your profile, although for now Facebook only supports six types of relationships: daughter, son, mother, father, sister, and brother.

To add a family member, follow these steps:

1. **Click Profile to see your Profile page.**

2. **Click Edit Profile.**

3. **Click Featured People.**

4. **Use the Family Member text box to type the person's name, and then use the Select Relation list to specify the relationship, as shown in Figure 3.3.**

   3.3 Use the Family Member area to type the name of the family member and your relation type.

5. **If you want to add more family members to your profile, click the Add another family member link and repeat the process.**

6. **When you finish, click Save Changes.** Facebook sends a confirmation message to each family member you added.

Quote, Unquote: Facebook and Family

"Through Facebook, I connected with family across the ocean, over in Norway. One day I searched for an old family name on Google, and thanks to Facebook's high ranking in search results, a distant cousin with that name was on the first page. It has been awesome to get to know them and continue to keep in touch with them on Facebook. I am planning a trip to visit them in the future." — M. M., Great Falls, Montana

Quote, Unquote: Facebook and Family

"My elderly family members are in love with Facebook now. It helps everyone keep in touch. Nowadays, we can contact our great aunts and uncles to say, 'Hey! Let's grab lunch!'" —R. P., Torrance, California; quoted in The Facebook Blog, June 21, 2010

Here are two other things to note when adding family members:

- If you add a son or daughter, you can also add your child's birth date, as shown in Figure 3.4.

- If you add a family member who is not on Facebook, you can have that person confirm the relationship via e-mail, as shown in Figure 3.4.

3.4 You can specify your son's or daughter's birth date, and you can add family members who aren't on Facebook.

Using Facebook to Organize a Family Gathering

The social web that Facebook helps you build and maintain operates not only on Facebook.com, but also on many other Web sites, as I describe in Chapter 1. But Facebook helps you be more social offline as well, thanks to its Events application, which enables you to use your profile to create and manage real-world gatherings. So the next time you want to get your family together — it could be for a birthday, a barbecue, an anniversary, a holiday, or just because — use the Events application to set up the details and send out the invitations, even to family members who aren't on Facebook!

To create an event, follow these steps:

1. **Click Home to open your Facebook Home page.**

2. **Click Events in the Navigation area.**

3. **Click Create an Event.**

4. **You then use the Create an Event page, shown in Figure 3.5, to specify the particulars of the event: when it happens, what it is, and where it occurs.** Here are two important things to note:

   ● Your guest list can consist of Facebook friends and family members who aren't on Facebook. To create the guest list, click Select Guests to open the Select Guests dialog box, then click each family member you want to invite in the list of friends. For family folks not on Facebook, type their e-mail addresses in the Invite by E-mail Address text box, separating each one with a comma.

   ● You probably don't want nonfamily ogling your event, so be sure to deselect the Anyone can view and RSVP check box, which turns your gathering into a private Event that's viewable only by invitees.

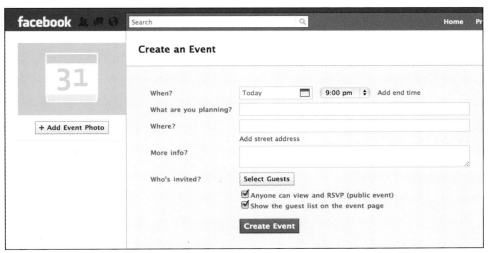

3.5 Use the Create an Event page to specify the details of your family gathering.

The resulting Event page (which you can view by clicking Home, Events, and then clicking the event) offers the guest list, information about the Event, and a Wall section that guests can write on, as shown in Figure 3.6. You can also send a message to all the guests by clicking the Message Guests link in the upper-right corner.

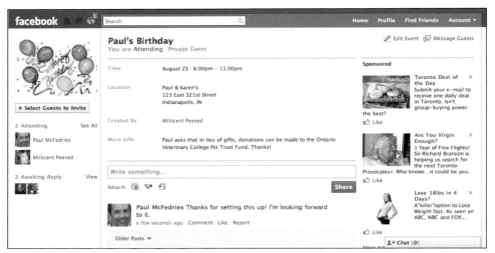

3.6 The Event page includes event information, the guest list, and a Wall section that guests can use to share stories about the event.

Working with Birthdays

Facebook is big on birthdays. The service not only has a few birthday-related features baked in, but it also hosts tons of useful birthday-themed applications. If you want to get in on the birthday fun (that is, if you want to have lots of friends use your Wall section to wish you well when your birthday rolls around), be sure to edit your profile to include your birth date:

1. **Click Profile.**
2. **Click Edit Profile.**
3. **Click Basic Information.**
4. **Fill in the Birthday month, day, and year.**

TIP

If you don't like the idea of sharing your birth year with your friends or (depending on your privacy settings) the rest of the world, you can hide it. When you edit your profile, use the list beside the Birthday controls to choose Show only month & day in my profile.

Viewing your friends' birthdays

Facebook keeps tabs on your friends' birthdays, and when one rolls around, Facebook lets you know by adding a birthday reminder in the Events box of your Home page, as shown in Figure 3.7. Click your friend's name to display his or her Wall section where you can then write a birthday greeting.

3.7 The Events box lets you know when any of your friends' birthdays rolls around.

It's certainly great that Facebook reminds you of a friend's birthday, but getting that reminder on the day of the birthday doesn't give you much time to rush out and get a card and present. If you need more time, you can see a complete list of upcoming birthdays by clicking Home, then Events, then Birthdays. Facebook opens the Birthdays page, as shown in Figure 3.8, which lists the upcoming friend birthdays in chronological order.

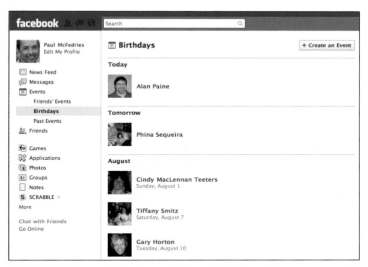

3.8 Click Home, Friends, and then Birthdays to see a complete list of your friends' birthdays.

Facebook birthday applications

Facebook's native birthday features are useful, but they're a tad simple, so many Facebook developers have jumped into the fray by offering applications that enable you to send birthday cards, track birthdays, and get birthday reminders. Here are a half-dozen applications to check out:

NOTE There are many Facebook addresses in this section. All of them are case sensitive, and some of them quite long. Rather than typing the addresses by hand, see the Facebook page for this series: www.facebook.com/FBGseries. Alternatively, you can type a page's name in Facebook's Search box to locate it. Please note that Facebook does not endorse the sites listed in this book.

- **Birthday Cards.** This application (see Figure 3.9) by RockYou! is the most popular Facebook birthday application by far. It not only enables you to send a predesigned card to a friend, you can also create your own cards, see a list of upcoming birthdays, view a birthday calendar, and much more.

  www.facebook.com/apps/application.php?id=14852940614

- **Birthday Greeting Cards.** This application by Socialsoft lets you create birthday cards to send to your friends. You also get a birthday calendar and you can set up birthday alerts.

  www.facebook.com/birthdaycard

- **Fun Cards — Birthday & More!** This application by SocialCash offers a large set of predefined cards that you can send to your friends. You can also create your own card or send a video card via YouTube.

  www.facebook.com/apps/application.php?id=6651249934

- **Birthday Calendar.** This application by BigDates Solutions shows your friends' birthdays on a calendar, and you can also create alerts to get birthday reminders.

  www.facebook.com/BirthdayCal

- **Hallmark Social Calendar.** This application by Newput offers a full-service social calendar for not only birthdays, but also your Facebook events, anniversaries, holidays, and more.

  www.facebook.com/SocialCalendar

- **Birthday Alert.** This simple but useful application by JibJab lets you configure alerts for upcoming birthdays.

  www.facebook.com/apps/application.php?id=4326036791

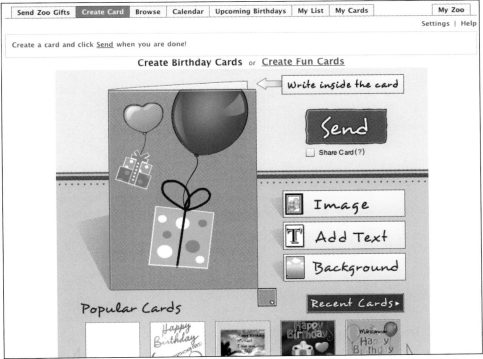

| Send Zoo Gifts | Create Card | Browse | Calendar | Upcoming Birthdays | My List | My Cards | | My Zoo |

Settings | Help

Create a card and click <u>Send</u> when you are done!

Create Birthday Cards or <u>Create Fun Cards</u>

Write inside the card

Send

☐ Share Card (?)

🖼 Image

T Add Text

Background

Popular Cards

Recent Cards▸

3.9 With the Birthday Cards application, you can create your own birthday cards from scratch and send them to your friends.

Planning a Wedding

A wedding may be the most social event we attend, because it brings together two people's closest family members and friends for one big celebration. The wedding happens offline, of course, but there's no reason you can't celebrate the big day both before and after using Facebook's social tools. For example, you could create an event for the wedding itself, use the bride or groom's Wall section to send wedding-related messages, follow the couple's wedding prep stories on your News Feed, and use the Photos app to post wedding photos and tag the participants who have Facebook accounts.

TIP

To keep members of your wedding party apprised of relevant wedding details, consider creating a special Facebook Group just for them.

There are also third-party applications that can help plan and get ready for the wedding:

- **Wedding Buzz.** This full-featured and very popular application (see Figure 3.10) lets you enter the wedding details, specify the wedding party and the guest list, set up wedding registries, create a guestbook, add photos, and much more.

  www.facebook.com/weddingbuzz

3.10 Use Wedding Buzz to set up your wedding, define the wedding party and guest list, add registries, and more.

- **Daisypath Wedding and Anniversary Ticker.** Use this app to keep a countdown to your wedding date. (The ticker also works for anniversaries or even upcoming vacations.)

  www.facebook.com/apps/application.php?id=16675062575

- **WeddingWire.** This application enables you to create your own personal blog within Facebook, as well as read about other weddings near you. As an added bonus, the application maintains a database of more than 100,000 local wedding vendors, along with real reviews from satisfied (or not) customers.

  www.facebook.com/apps/application.php?id=26507478183

> ### A Facebook Romance
>
> After an unexpected divorce, Jenece Whitted was discouraged by the prospect of finding love again. She decided in February 2009 to post a status update on Facebook voicing her frustration with the "game" of dating, and she was surprised when an old friend from elementary school, Adam, commented in agreement. The two began chatting on Facebook, Adam moved to Arizona at the end of May, and in September he found a unique way to pop the question. "I woke up in the morning and checked Facebook like I always do," said Jenece, who noticed a new picture on Adam's Wall section. "I clicked on it, thinking he had just drawn another comic." This was no ordinary picture, though; it was Adam's proposal. The two are planning a June 2010 wedding. — S.L., The Facebook Blog, February 12, 2010

If your interest in weddings is more abstract, I suggest you check into the Weddings Community Page, which although sparse with content as I write this, will one day soon be a major source of wedding information:

www.facebook.com/pages/Weddings/108189402545995

Learning about Parenting and Grandparenting

Facebook abounds in useful information on parenting and even grandparenting. Facebook's Community Pages are always good places to get started when researching any topic, and the topics of parenting and grandparenting are no exceptions. The following Pages should have lots of good content:

- **Parenting:** www.facebook.com/pages/Parenting/112349262114200
- **Grandparent:** www.facebook.com/pages/Grandparent/107817579240779
- **Children:** www.facebook.com/pages/Children/107910772575139
- **Mothers:** www.facebook.com/pages/Mother/107944305900606
- **Fathers:** www.facebook.com/pages/Father/103103389729220

Quote, Unquote: Facebook and Family

"I want to thank you. I found my daughter after 20 years. I am so grateful."
— J.G., San Diego, California

Here's a list of a few other parenting Pages on Facebook:

- **Parenting.com.** This Page is the Facebook home of the popular Parenting.com Web site.

  www.facebook.com/Parenting

- **Attachment Parenting.** This Page promotes the attachment parenting style.

  www.facebook.com/pages/Attachment-Parenting/20646286418

- **Natural Parenting Tips.** This Page promotes natural parenting.

  www.facebook.com/NaturalParentingTips

- **Proud Parenting.** This Page is an excellent parenting resource for gay and lesbian parents.

  www.facebook.com/pages/Proud-Parenting/6372775731

TIP Why not create a Facebook Group for all the members of your immediate and extended family?

Researching Genealogy

Facebook specializes in helping you connect with family members who are alive right now, but what about the other branches of your family tree? Your ancestors weren't around when Facebook was created, but you can use Facebook's genealogy resources to help you discover and learn about your family's past.

Two promising places to start are Facebook's Community Pages related to genealogy, which should soon have lots of useful and interesting content about the theory and practice of genealogy:

- **Genealogy:** www.facebook.com/pages/Genealogy/106154876082188

- **Genealogy Research:** www.facebook.com/pages/
  Genealogy-Research/369610238741

There are also tons of useful Facebook Pages dedicated to genealogy:

- **AfriGeneas.** This is the Facebook Page for the AfriGeneas Web site (afrigeneas.com), which specializes in African-American or Africa-related genealogy.

  www.facebook.com/afrigeneas

- **Ancestorville Genealogy.** This is the Facebook Page for the Ancestorville Web site (Ancestorville.com), which deals with genealogy, particularly genealogy antiques.

  www.facebook.com/Ancestorville

- **Genealogy.** This Page offers lots of Wall posts, photos, and discussions related to genealogy.

  www.facebook.com/pages/Genealogy/96653184251

- **Genealogy Center.** This is the Facebook Page for the famous Genealogy Center of the Allen County (IN) Public Library, which offers many useful resources for genealogy researchers.

  www.facebook.com/GenealogyCenter

- **Genealogy Tip of the Day.** This Page offers daily tips related to genealogical research.

  www.facebook.com/genealogytip

Quote, Unquote: Facebook and Family

"I have been my family's genealogist for a long time. After others in my family got me to connect with them on FB, I decided to put up a page ... hoping to connect with some of my paternal grandmother's family. Nothing happened for the longest time. One day, I checked the page and there was a message from an unknown cousin, Frans, from Holland!! Since then, we have 'met' more cousins!" — B. S., Hartford, Connecticut

Finally, be sure to check out Facebook's third-party applications for building family trees using your Facebook friends. Here's a good place to start:

- **We're Related.** This application, from FamilyLink.com, lets you build a family tree based on your Facebook friend list.

  www.facebook.com/myrelatives

Playing with Pets

Pets are part of the family, and although few pets have their own profiles on Facebook, they're still well represented by their owners' pet-related stories, photos, videos, and more. Facebook may not encourage pet profiles, but that doesn't mean your pet can't have friends on Facebook. Two very popular applications allow you to give your pet the next best thing to being on Facebook:

- **Catbook.** Yes, it's Facebook — for cats! You can create a profile for your cat, tag your cat in photos, request friendships with other cats, and more.

  www.facebook.com/Catbookapp

- **Dogbook.** This is the dog equivalent, and it too lets you set up your pooch with a profile. You can friend other dogs, tag your dog in photos and videos, and even add your dog's favorite parks.

  www.facebook.com/Dogbookapp

As you might imagine, there are lots of pet-themed Pages on Facebook, too. For starters, here are the Community Pages related to pets, cats, and dogs:

- **Pets:** www.facebook.com/pages/Pets/106252142744198
- **Cats:** www.facebook.com/pages/Cats/111851445501172
- **Dogs:** www.facebook.com/pages/Dogs/114197241930754

Here's a list of some of the more popular pet-related Pages on Facebook:

- **Lazy Pets by The Animal Rescue Site.** This is a great Page that features very cute photos of pets being, well, lazy.

  www.facebook.com/LazyPets

- **PetSmart.** This is the Facebook home of the national pet product retailer.

  www.facebook.com/PetSmart

Quote, Unquote: Facebook and Pets

"On Dec. 31, 2009, my three pugs got out of my house. The temps in my hometown were below zero. I am happy to report that all three are now home safely (1/5/2010) but without Facebook, they would most likely have frozen. I was able to get the message and photos of the dogs out to several hundred people in a matter of minutes who then spread the word. Before I knew it, nearly half the town was looking for my lost pugs." — H. W., Des Moines, Iowa

- **Cats.** This Page offers nearly 20,000 photos of cats!
  www.facebook.com/pages/cats/19252983523
- **Cat Lovers.** This Page features lots of photos of cats.
  www.facebook.com/catowners
- **Dogs.** This popular Page is home to many dog-related discussions.
  www.facebook.com/pages/Dogs/6223702909
- **Dogs.** This Page offers many dog-related Wall posts and photos.
  www.facebook.com/pages/Dogs/82955505846
- **Dog Lovers.** This Page features lots of photos of dogs.
  www.facebook.com/doglovers
- **Pet Loss Grief Support.** This is the Facebook Page for the Web site PetLoss.com, which helps pet owners deal with the passing of their beloved pets.
  www.facebook.com/pages/Pet-Loss-Grief-Support-Petlosscom/279101266589

Dealing with Death

Facebook is a celebration of life, particularly social life, but death is part of life, and as a site with more than half a billion users, Facebook is smart enough to know that it can't ignore death. So Facebook offers a form that enables you to report a deceased person's profile. You can either have Facebook remove the profile entirely, or you can convert it to a memorialized profile, which retains its Wall section so that people can write remembrances, but hides some profile information and ensures the person does not come up in a search or in friend suggestions.

The form (see Figure 3.11) is here:

www.facebook.com/help/contact.php?show_form=deceased

NOTE Use the Proof of Death field to enter the URL of the deceased's online obituary, if one exists. Otherwise, you can copy the obituary text into the field.

3.11 Use the Report a Deceased Person's profile form to either remove or memorialize a deceased person's profile.

Quote, Unquote: Facebook and Family

"My daughter died in a car crash two years ago. The day after she died, a school friend of hers set up a dedication page in her memory. It helped us in our grief and it was nice to be able to look at all the comments, memories, and photos that her friends posted. It showed us what a great person she was, and we saw what she was like with her friends." — L. B., Croydon, UK

If, instead, you're grieving the loss of someone close, Facebook can be useful here as well by offering Pages that specialize in helping people cope with grief:

- **Grief Loss & Recovery.** This is the Facebook Page for the Web site GriefLossRecovery.com, which helps people who are grieving the loss of a loved one.

  www.facebook.com/pages/griefflossrecovery

- **How to Survive Your Grief When Someone You Love Has Died.** This is the Facebook Page for the book of the same title.

  www.facebook.com/SurviveYourGrief

- **Hello Grief.** This Page is a support group for surviving the loss of a loved one, particularly a child.

  www.facebook.com/Hello-Grief/164559842054

And of course, when you are grieving, your circle of friends becomes ever more important. Facebook helps in this way, too, by offering one-click access to people who are only too eager to provide comfort.

4 chapter

Sharing Photos

When talking about Facebook and photos, it's tempting to talk about numbers: 99 percent of Facebook's users have uploaded at least one photo to their profile, and Facebook users upload more than 200 million photos every day. However, these impressive numbers don't tell the whole story. Facebook has become the Web's largest repository of photos (no other site is even close), because not only can you share your photos with your friends, but you can also point out your friends in your photos, a process known as tagging. Sharing photos is one of the favorite pastimes of all Facebook users, so this chapter shows you how it's done.

Adding a Photo to Your Wall Section

The simplest way to get a photo onto Facebook is to add it to your Wall section. Your friends will see a News Feed notice about the new photo, and any friend who visits your profile will see it in your Wall section where they can then like it or comment on it. You can add a photo to your Wall section directly or by sending the photo to a special e-mail address.

Adding a Wall photo

You add a photo to your Wall section by posting it as a story with the photo attached. Here's how it's done:

1. **Click Profile to open your Facebook Profile page.**

2. **Click the Wall tab.**

3. **In the Publisher, click the Photos link. Facebook displays several options for adding photos.**

4. **Click Upload a Photo.** Facebook prompts you to select a file.

5. **Click Browse.** If you're using a Mac, click Choose File instead.

6. **Click the photo you want to upload.**

7. **Click Open.** If you're using a Mac, click Choose instead.

8. **Use the text box to type a caption for your photo.**

9. **Click the Share options listed above the text box, and then click who you want to see the photo.** You can choose Everyone, Friends of Friends, or Friends Only. You can also click Customize to show the photo to or hide it from specific people.

10. **Click Share.** Facebook uploads the photo and adds it to your Wall section.

E-mailing a photo to your Wall section

If you're out roaming around, you might take a picture with your mobile phone and then decide you'd love to share it with your Facebook friends. Rather than waiting until you get home to copy the photo to your computer and then upload it to Facebook, you can send the photo to your Wall section immediately by e-mailing it to a special address.

To see your special email address (it's unique for each Facebook user), surf to www.facebook.com/mobile. The Upload via Email box shows your personal upload address, which always takes the following form:

word1NNNword2@m.facebook.com

Here, *word1* and *word2* are random words, and *NNN* is a random three-digit number.

To upload your photo, follow these steps:

1. **Use your mobile phone's software to create a new e-mail message with the photo attached.**
2. **Use the To field to type your unique Facebook upload address.**
3. **Use the Subject field to type a description of the photo (see Figure 4.1).** Facebook uses this text as the photo caption.
4. **Send the message.** When Facebook receives the message, it automatically posts the photo and the caption to your Wall section, as shown in Figure 4.2.

4.1 On your mobile phone, attach the photo to a message and send the message to your special Facebook upload address.

TIP If your photo shows up sideways, you can rotate it. Click Profile, click the Photos tab, click the Mobile Uploads album, and then click the photo you want to fix. Below the photo and above the Share link, you see two icons: Click the one on the left to rotate the photo counterclockwise; click the one on the right to rotate the photo clockwise.

4.2 When Facebook receives the message, it adds the photo to your Wall section with the message subject as the caption.

Quote, Unquote: Facebook and Photos

David Slade's fiancée Kelly was the first to find the lost little dog. Standing in the driveway on her way to shop for wedding dresses in January, Kelly was surprised when the disoriented animal cheerfully ran up to her. Kelly brought the pup, which she nicknamed "Mouse," inside from the incoming rainstorm to play with her and David's own dogs. ... Fortunately, David's neighborhood of Hillcrest, a small, older area within Little Rock, Ark., has an active Facebook Page with nearly 2,500 fans. David posted a photo of Mouse, along with the following short message to the Page's Wall section:

FOUND: white, little, really cute male dog. He's got a blue collar but no tags. We found him on Saturday, 1/23/2010 at around 12 PM on Lee and Monroe. If you have any ideas as to who his owner is, please get in touch.

Amazingly, within only a few hours, a woman named Lin Chan commented: "That's our TYSON! Thank you!" Lin had been alerted to David's

continued

continued

post by a phone call from a friend who had seen the post. "I quickly logged onto Facebook and was relieved and in disbelief when I saw Tyson's photo posted by David," Chan said. "My son, who is 4, actually cried when he saw the photo because he 'wanted Tyson home now'." —S. L., The Facebook Blog, March 5, 2010

Working with Photo Albums

Posting a photo to your Wall section is convenient and easy if you have just a single photo to show your friends. However, it's common to have multiple photos to share. It could be a collection of photos about a vacation, a party, your kids or grandkids, a new puppy, or even yourself. In such cases, rather than posting multiple photos to your Wall section, you can post everything at once using a photo album. This not only makes it easier to upload a bunch of photos, but it also makes it easier for your friends to view and navigate your photos.

The next few sections take you through creating, viewing, and working with Facebook photo albums.

Creating a photo album

Here are the steps to follow to create a photo album:

1. **On your Facebook home page, click the Photos link in the Navigation area.** The Photos page opens.

2. **Click the Upload Photos button.** The Create Album page opens.

3. **Fill in the album particulars, including the album name, location (if any), and description.**

4. **Use the Privacy list to choose who can view your album.** You can choose Everyone, Friends of Friends, or Friends Only. You can also click Customize to show the album to or hide it from specific people.

5. **Click Create Album.** Facebook creates the photo album and prompts you to upload some photos to it.

6. **Click Select Photos.** Facebook prompts you to select the photos you want to include in the album.

7. **In Windows, hold down Ctrl, click each photo you want to upload, and then click Open.** If you're using a Mac, instead, hold down ⌘, click each photo, and then click Select.

8. **Click Upload Photos.** Facebook transfers the photos from your computer to your photo album. If you want to let your friends know about the new album right away, skip to step 12.

9. **For each photo that you want to describe, type some text in the photo's Caption box (see Figure 4.3).**

10. **If a friend appears in a photo, click the friend's face and then click the friend in the list that appears.**

11. **To use a photo as the album cover, select the This is the album cover option below the photo.**

12. **Click Publish Now. Facebook adds the album to your profile and lets your friends know that you've published a new album.**

4.3 Use the Caption boxes to add captions to your photos.

NOTE To add more photos to the album later on, click the Photos link in the Navigation area on your Home page, click My Uploads, click the album to which you want to add more photos, and then click Add More. Follow steps 6 to 12 from this section to upload the new photos to the album.

Viewing a photo album

To take a look at your new album, click the Photos link in the navigation area of your Home page, click My Uploads, and then click the album. Facebook displays the album's photos, as shown in Figure 4.4.

To begin, click the first photo you want to view, and Facebook displays a full-size version of the photo. To navigate the album, use the following techniques:

- To move to the next photo, either click the photo or click Next.
- To move to the previous photo, click Previous.

When you finish, click Back to Album to return to the album, or click My Photos to return to your profile's Photos tab.

TIP You can control the order that your photos appear in the album. Click Profile, click the Photos tab, click the album, and then use your mouse to drag each photo into the position you prefer. When you're finished, click Save Changes.

Quote, Unquote: Facebook and Photos

"Last year I volunteered in an orphanage in Kenya. It was so hard to leave a 3-year-old boy with whom I became so close that I became his sponsor. Thanks to FB, I'm able to keep in touch with other volunteers and see pictures of him growing up and changing. I had tears of joy when I came across a picture on FB of him with the biggest smile on his face, showing off a photo of the two of us that I sent him in the mail." — J. R., London, Ontario

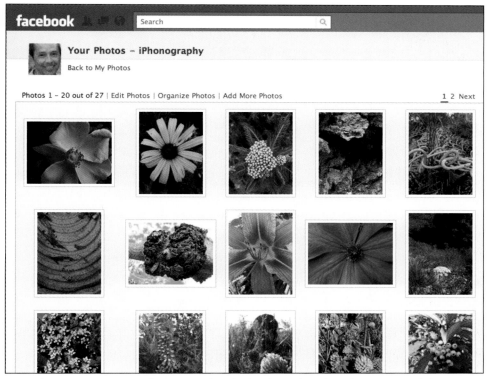

4.4 When you open an album, Facebook displays thumbnail versions of the album's photos.

Identifying Facebook friends in photos

If there's one thing that sets Facebook's Photos application apart from all the other photo-sharing services on the Web, it's that you can connect your photos to your friends. You do this by telling Facebook when a friend appears within a photo, a process known as tagging. (Some other photo-sharing services are starting to offer similar features, but none of them have a massive social network behind them, so this remains a key feature for Facebook photos.) When you tag a friend in one of your photos, three things happen:

- Facebook sends a notification to the friend to let him or her know about the tag.

- Facebook adds the photo to the friend's profile. That is, in that person's Photos tab, he or she now sees a Photos of Name section (where Name is the person's first name), which displays all the photos in which that friend has been tagged.

When others view the photo, below the photo they see the text "In this photo" and a link to the tagged friend's profile.

Here are the steps to follow to tag a friend in one of your photos:

1. **On your Facebook home page, click the Photos link in the Navigation area.** The Photos page opens.
2. **Click the My Uploads link.**
3. **Click the album that contains the photo you want to work with.**
4. **Click Tag This Photo.**
5. **Click on the face of the friend you want to tag.** Facebook displays a list of your friends, as shown in Figure 4.5.
6. **Click the friend.** Facebook tags the friend.
7. **Repeat steps 5 and 6 to tag any other friends in the photo.**
8. **Click Done Tagging.** Facebook saves your changes.

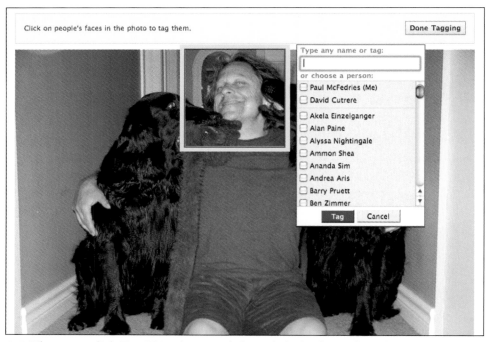

4.5 When you click Tag This Photo and then click the face of the friend in the photo, Facebook displays a list of your friends.

Quote, Unquote: Facebook and Photos

"I was separated from my family at age 4 and adopted at age 6. Through Facebook, I finally reached one of my brothers over 40 years later. Within one day and on my 50th birthday, I reunited with my seven siblings. On Facebook, we were able to tag pictures of each other and send them to my daughter, who has been introduced to all her new aunts/uncles and new cousins." — C. G., Valrico, Florida

Deleting a photo album

If you decide against sharing a particular album, you can delete it from your profile by following these steps:

1. **On your Facebook home page, click the Photos link in the Navigation area.** The Photos page opens.
2. **Click the My Uploads link.** Facebook displays your photos and albums.
3. **Click the Edit Album link under the album you want to remove.**
4. **Click the Delete tab.** Facebook asks you to confirm.
5. **Click Delete.** Facebook removes the album and all of its photos from your profile.

Working with Friends' Photos

Besides uploading and working with your own Facebook photos, you can also view your friends' photos. This is one of Facebook's best features, and one of the most popular pastimes among people who use the site, because it enables you to get a visual record of your friends' activities. Even if your kids, grand-kids, siblings, or old friends live far away, you can still see them now and then by viewing their photos of birthday parties, weddings, family gatherings, vacations, graduations, and all the other day-to-day activities that make a life. You can also perform actions such as liking, commenting on, sharing, and tagging these photos. The next few sections provide the details.

Quote, Unquote: Facebook and Photos

"Last year my sister-in-law, an NICU nurse, was in labor with my second nephew. My brother was at the hospital with her, but both sets of grandparents weren't there for the delivery. Through Facebook's photo sharing, all the grandparents, great-grandparents, uncles, aunts, and cousins were able to share the joy of the miracle of life within days. One Web site helped unite an entire family. — D. C., New York, New York

---

Viewing a friend's photos

Facebook gives you three main ways to get to your friends' photos:

- View new Wall photos and albums in your News Feed.
- Navigate to a friend's Profile page and then click the Photos tab.
- Click Home and then click Photos in the Navigation area to see a list of the recent photos and albums posted by your friends, as shown in Figure 4.6.

Whichever route you choose, click a photo to open it, or click the album name to see thumbnail versions of the album photos, and then click the photo you want to see. You navigate a friend's photo album the same way you navigate one of your own:

- To move to the next photo, either click the photo or click Next.
- To move to the previous photo, click Previous.

If a friend's photo really strikes your fancy, Facebook offers several ways to share your appreciation:

- You can like the photo by clicking the Like link.
- You can leave a comment for the photo by clicking inside the Comment box, typing your note, and then clicking Comment.
- You can post the photo to your profile by clicking Share to open the Post to Profile dialog box, and then clicking Share. The photo appears on your Wall section, with links back to the friend's photo album and profile.

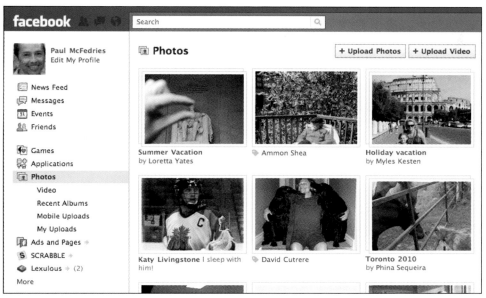

4.6 Click Home and then Photos to see the recent Wall photos and albums posted by your friends.

Identifying people in a friend's photo

As you're perusing a friend's album, you might stumble upon one of your other friends in a photo. If so, you can tag that person, even though you're not the owner of the photo.

Here are the steps to follow to tag a friend in one of your friends' photos:

1. **Use any of the techniques from the previous section to display the photo you want to work with.**
2. **Click Tag This Photo.**
3. **Click on the face of the friend you want to tag.** Facebook displays a list of your friends.
4. **Click the friend.** Facebook tags the friend.
5. **Repeat steps 3 and 4 to tag any other friends in the photo.**
6. **Click Done Tagging.** Facebook saves your changes.

Removing your tag from a friend's photo

If one of your friends tags you in a photo, Facebook sends you a notification to let you know, as shown in Figure 4.7. You can click the notification to jump directly to the photo. Facebook also adds the photo to the Photos tab on your Profile page in a section titled Photos of You (where You is your first name); you can also click that photo to open it.

NOTE Facebook also sends you an e-mail message when someone tags you in a photo. That message includes a link that you can click to display the photo directly.

Most of the time, getting tagged in photos is a good thing because it further connects you to your friends, and it helps you know when other people are posting photos that include you. However, every now and then you might not want people to know you're in a particular photo. For example, if a photo isn't all that flattering, you might not want other people to know that's you.

4.7 Facebook sends you a notification when someone tags you in a photo.

Fortunately, Facebook makes it easy to remove your tag from a photo. First, use any of the techniques from earlier in this chapter to display the photo you want to work with. As you can see in Figure 4.8, Facebook displays "In this photo" followed by your name (as well as the names of other people who have been tagged in the photo). Click the remove tag link, and Facebook immediately deletes the tag.

4.8 If you've been tagged in a photo, Facebook displays your name beside the "In this photo" text.

Quote, Unquote: Facebook and Photos

"All my family and extended family can keep in touch with our young son — our first child — and watch him grow as I post photos of him on Facebook. Now family and extended family far away can watch him grow up and stay connected to him and us! — S. R., Aurora, Ontario

Facebook's Photography Resources

Photos are one of the most popular ways of sharing and connecting with people on Facebook, so it will come as no surprise that Facebook is also home to a huge number of photography resources. These range from general photography information to tips and techniques for taking better photos.

General photography resources

If you're interested in photography as a technology, art form, or cultural touchstone, Facebook offers lots of general resources for you. You can start on the many Community Pages, which should soon have tons of useful and interesting information on photography and photographers:

NOTE There are many Facebook addresses in this section. All of them are case sensitive, and some of them quite long. Rather than typing the addresses by hand, see the Facebook page for this series: www.facebook.com/FBGseries. Alternatively, you can type a page's name in Facebook's Search box to locate it. Please note that Facebook does not endorse the sites listed in this book.

- **Photography:** www.facebook.com/pages/Photography/108170975877442

- **Photographer:** www.facebook.com/pages/Photographer/107600619269865

Here's a list of a few other general photography Pages on Facebook:

- **New York Institute of Photography.** This Page is the Facebook home of the New York Institute of Photography, which offers photography courses, podcasts, and other educational resources (see Figure 4.9).

  www.facebook.com/NYIPhoto

- **World Photography Organization.** This is the Facebook Page of the World Photography Organization, which runs the World Photography Awards and other photography-related activities.

  www.facebook.com/WorldPhotographyOrganisation

4.9 The New York Institute of Photography has a home on Facebook.

- **Los Angeles Time Photography, Video, and Multimedia.** This Page features slide shows and other multimedia from the Los Angeles Times.

  www.facebook.com/latimesmultimedia

- **Houston Center for Photography.** This Page is the Facebook home of the Houston Center for Photography, which is an advocacy group for photography as an art form.

  www.facebook.com/houstoncenterforphotography.

- **The Center for Alternative Photography.** This Facebook Page is devoted to teaching the original methods for processing photographs that were used in the 19th and early 20th century.

  www.facebook.com/CAPWorkshops

- **Get Photography Jobs.** This Page lists jobs for professional photographers.

  www.facebook.com/GetPhotographyJobs

> ## Quote, Unquote: Facebook and Photos
>
> "Impossible to count the number of amazing people and opportunities (both business and personal) that occurred to me or to my life just because Facebook exists! From being a photographer and assisting with Facebook to expose my photography to a greater audience to countless people I have met in person through the years who became my dear friends.
> — B. H., London, England

Viewing famous photographers

Thousands of professional photographers show their wares on Facebook, as any search on the word "photographer" immediately reveals. Fortunately, some of the world's best photographers have also set up shop on Facebook, and most are only too happy to share samples of their work (see Figure 4.10). Here's a sampling:

- **David Bailey.** www.facebook.com/pages/David-Bailey/35115191712
- **Tim Flach.** www.facebook.com/pages/Tim-Flach/47595439651
- **Tony Howell.** www.facebook.com/pages/Tony-Howell-Photography/129294303763964
- **David Lachapelle.** www.facebook.com/pages/David-Lachapelle/109689315736474
- **Annie Leibovitz.** www.facebook.com/AnnieLeibovitz
- **Duane Michals.** www.facebook.com/pages/Duane-Michals/36112884101
- **James Nachtwey.** www.facebook.com/jamesnachtwey
- **Mario Testino.** www.facebook.com/pages/Mario-Testino/77062935105
- **Spencer Tunick.** www.facebook.com/pages/Spencer-Tunick/45119274946
- **Tim Walker.** www.facebook.com/pages/Tim-Walker/10401714874
- **Dave Walsh.** www.facebook.com/davewalshphoto

- **William Wegman.** www.facebook.com/WilliamWegman
- **Grace Weston.** www.facebook.com/pages/Grace-Weston-Photography/ 49552975917

4.10 Photographer Grace Weston uses her Facebook page to show off many of her fantastic staged miniatures.

Taking and editing photos

If your goal is to take and edit better photos, Facebook has lots of useful Pages. You can begin at the main Community Pages, which offer a great deal of useful information:

- **Taking Photos.** www.facebook.com/pages/Taking-Photos/ 360520604066
- **Photo Editing.** www.facebook.com/pages/Photo-Editing/377717261596

Here are some Pages for photography magazines and other resources that offer lots of useful content for improving your craft:

- **Popular Photography.** This Page is maintained by *Popular Photography* magazine, which is the world's most popular photography publication. You'll find lots of links to articles on equipment, techniques, buying guides, and more.

  www.facebook.com/pages/Popular-Photography/324110192620

- **Professional Photographer.** This is the Facebook Page for the magazine *Professional Photographer*, which is published by Professional Photographers of America. It includes links to articles, cover photos, subscription information, and more.

  www.facebook.com/ppmagazine

- **Photography Monthly.** This Page is the Facebook home of the British magazine *Photography Monthly*. It offers tutorials, podcasts, and lots of other resources.

  www.facebook.com/photographymonthly

- **Better Photography.** This Facebook Page is the home of *Better Photography* magazine. It includes photos, a lively discussions board, frequent events for workshops, and more.

  www.facebook.com/betterphotography

- **Digital SLR Photography.** This is the Facebook home of the magazine *Digital SLR Photography*. It includes photos, links to articles, and more.

  www.facebook.com/DSLRMY

- **Spectrum Photography Tips.** This Page offers tips for photographers of all levels.

  www.facebook.com/spectrumphototips

- **I love photography but am not a pro photographer...YET.** This is a Page for photography amateurs to post photos and share tips and experiences.

  www.facebook.com/pages/I-love-photography-but-am-not-a-pro-photographer-YET/332016092020

Working with cameras

Photography is heavily focused on equipment, of course, and Facebook offers some good resources for cameras and other gear. First, there are three main Community Pages:

- **Camera.** www.facebook.com/pages/Camera/104010966300653
- **Cameras.** www.facebook.com/pages/Cameras/112165425476541
- **Digital Cameras.** www.facebook.com/pages/Digital-Cameras/ 115995478411167

Here's a list of a few Facebook pages related to cameras and other equipment:

- **Canon Cameras.** This is the official product page for Canon's line of camera equipment.

  www.facebook.com/pages/Canon-Cameras/6158898850

- **Leica Camera.** This product Page features notes, discussions, and information related to Leica camera equipment.

  www.facebook.com/LeicaCamera

- **Olympus Cameras.** This is the product Page for Olympus gear.

  www.facebook.com/pages/Olympus-Cameras/23847657116

chapter 5

Wall Info Photos Notes

Politics and Society

With more than half a billion people now on Facebook, it has grown well beyond its beginnings as a place for college kids to check each other out. In fact, Facebook is now so large, so widespread, and so diverse, that you can safely say that the interests, activities, and passions of Facebook users mirror those of society at large. So, for example, if you're into politics, there are Facebook resources — pages, groups, events, and more — that will interest you, no matter where you fall in the political spectrum. Facebook offers similarly impressive resources for government, history, and the environment. And if you're itching to make a difference in the world, Facebook can help there, too, by offering terrific resources for connecting with charities, finding volunteer work, and connecting with like-minded activists.

Politics on Facebook

In June 2008, *Reader's Digest* magazine published an article titled "The Facebook Election," which predicted that young people would heavily influence the 2008 U.S. presidential election campaign. That prediction proved true, as we now know, and one of the main tools in then-Senator Barack Obama's election campaign was his Facebook page. Whether it was spreading the candidate's message, organizing canvassers, recruiting volunteers, or getting out the vote on election day, the Obama campaign used Facebook and the millions of people who were fans of the Barack Obama page to galvanize their support and capture not only the Democratic Party nomination, but the presidential election itself.

President Obama's Facebook presence remains strong, with well over 20 million fans of his page (which you can find at www.facebook.com/barackobama). However, this doesn't mean that Facebook is exclusively liberal (or left-wing or progressive or whatever label you want to use). Facebook is home to political views across the spectrum. For example, Sarah Palin's Facebook page (www.facebook.com/sarahpalin) has more than 3 million fans as I write this. In fact, politics is one of the most popular topics on Facebook. The site is home to resources on political theory, current political news and views, political parties, and much more.

NOTE If you're into politics yourself, don't forget to add your favorite political party to your Facebook profile. Click Profile, click Edit Profile, choose the Philosophy section, and then use the Political Views text box to type the name of the party. Be sure to click Save Changes. As with items in your profile — particularly your activities and interests — Facebook creates a link to the Page associated with the political view you enter, if one is available.

For general information on politics and political science, start with the Facebook community pages, which offer lots of useful content:

NOTE There are many Facebook addresses in this section. All of them are case sensitive, and some of them quite long. Rather than typing the addresses by hand, see the Facebook Page for this series: www.facebook.com/FBGseries. Alternatively, you can type a page's name in Facebook's Search box to locate it. Please note that Facebook does not endorse the sites listed in this book.

- **Politics.** www.facebook.com/pages/Politics/112519432094249
- **Political Party.** www.facebook.com/pages/Political-party/104044382966320
- **Political Science.** www.facebook.com/pages/Political-science/104045469631213
- **Conservatism.** www.facebook.com/pages/Conservatism/109489705737023
- **Liberalism.** www.facebook.com/pages/Liberalism/112130355469062

Almost any political party you can think of certainly has its own Facebook page these days, from the Australian Mothers political party to the Dragons Don't Usually Have Wings political party. If you live in the United States, the main two parties are, of course, well represented on Facebook:

- **Democratic Party.** www.facebook.com/democrats
- **Republican Party.** www.facebook.com/GOP

 NOTE In case you're wondering, yes the Tea Party movement has a presence on Facebook. See the Tea Party Patriots page at www.facebook.com/teapartypatriots.

Quote, Unquote: Facebook and the 2008 U.S. Election

The rally was held early in the presidential cycle — the first week of February 2007, a full 21 months before election day — and its guest of honor wasn't yet an actual candidate. But at the Johnson Center on the Fairfax, Virginia, campus of George Mason University, an electric charge was in the air. When Sen. Barack Obama strode onto the stage, shrieks of "I love you!" rang through the hall. Via Facebook, the social-networking Web site invented in 2004 by a Harvard undergraduate, word had already spread among students about the senator and the issues. The news about this campus event went viral in minutes, relegating leaflets and phone calls to the junk pile. — Carl M. Cannon, "The Facebook Election," *Reader's Digest,* June 1, 2008

Canadians can access pages for all five major political parties:

- **Bloc Québécois.** www.facebook.com/pages/Bloc-Quebecois/
  109409415752528
- **Conservative Party of Canada.** www.facebook.com/pages/
  Conservative-Party-of-Canada-Parti-conservateur-du-Canada/
  5661704203
- **Green Party of Canada.** www.facebook.com/GreenPartyofCanada
- **Liberal Party of Canada.** www.facebook.com/LiberalCA
- **New Democratic Party.** www.facebook.com/pages/
  New-Democratic-Party/6052296865

For political junkies of all persuasions, getting their fix means reading the latest political news, applauding (or booing) political opinion pieces, and talking with other people. You can do all of that and much more in the following sampling of Facebook's political resources:

- **Being Conservative.** This is the Facebook page for
  BeingConservative.com, a conservative blog.

  www.facebook.com/beingconservative
- **Being Liberal.** This page offers liberal-focused stories, discussions,
  polls, and more.

  www.facebook.com/pages/Being-Liberal/177486166274
- **CNN Political Ticker.** This page offers political news from the
  political team at CNN (see Figure 5.1).

  www.facebook.com/CNNPoliticalTicker
- **HuffPost Politics.** This page is the Facebook home of the political
  wing of the *Huffington Post*.

  www.facebook.com/HuffPostPolitics
- **OpenSecrets.org: Tracking Money In Politics.** This page is based
  on OpenSecrets.org, the Web site of the Center for Responsive Politics.
  It bills itself as "THE source for nonpartisan information on money in
  politics."

  www.facebook.com/OpenSecrets

5.1 CNN's political arm maintains the CNN Political Ticker page.

Politics Daily. This page offers links to political news stories and opinion pieces written and edited by the journalists at PoliticsDaily.com.

www.facebook.com/PoliticsDaily

Political Humor. This fun page gives you lots of links to political jokes, comedy bits, cartoons, and videos.

www.facebook.com/politicalhumor

Political Wire. This is the Facebook page for the Political Wire blog.

www.facebook.com/Political.Wire

Real Clear Politics. This is the Facebook base for the nonpartisan organization Real Clear Politics. It offers links to stories posted to the RealClearPolitics.com Web site.

www.facebook.com/pages/Real-Clear-Politics/27088225427

Rock the Vote. This page is part of the Rock the Vote organization, which encourages young people to vote and participate in the political process.

www.facebook.com/rockthevote

- **Slate's Political Gabfest.** This page is associated with the weekly Political Gabfest podcast that comes courtesy of *Slate* magazine.

  www.facebook.com/Gabfest

- **U.S. Politics on Facebook.** This page (which is maintained by Facebook) focuses on the use of Facebook by politicians, political parties, political campaigns, and government officials (see Figure 5.2).

  www.facebook.com/uspolitics

- **Washington Post Politics.** This page curates the political stories and op-ed pieces that appear in the *Washington Post* newspaper.

  www.facebook.com/washingtonpostpolitics

5.2 This Facebook-maintained page spotlights how U.S. politicians are using Facebook.

Accessing Government Resources

Government is all about people, and Facebook is all about connecting with people. It's only natural that governments all over the world are starting to use Facebook to connect with the people they serve. In some cases, government agencies are putting up Facebook pages to keep citizens abreast of the latest developments within the agency and to offer links to common services. For example, the California Department of Motor Vehicles maintains a page (see www.facebook.com/CADMV) that offers links to new services, department announcements, and more (see Figure 5.3).

When government agencies want to get information out to citizens, they're increasingly turning to Facebook to disseminate that information. For example, recently the Centers for Disease Control (CDC) wanted to raise awareness about the increasing prevalence of concussions and other traumatic brain injuries (TBIs), so it created a Facebook page called CDC Heads Up — Brain Injury Awareness (www.facebook.com/cdcheadsup; see Figure 5.4), which quickly garnered hundreds of fans.

5.3 The California Department of Motor Vehicles Facebook page offers links to services and information available through its Web site.

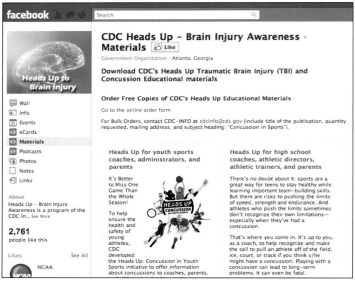

5.4 The Centers for Disease Control created the CDC Heads Up page to raise awareness about the rise of traumatic brain injuries.

Quote, Unquote: Facebook and Government

"It really is [about] the introduction of self-service and [that is] one of the things that we have done with Facebook. Citizens don't have time to come down to city hall, they don't have time to sit and see processes that waste their time; they become very impatient and that's how government gets a bad name. So it's really trying to figure out ways to make those services available any time, any place and make them cheaper to provide. And so when we do things like allow citizens to pay their parking tickets through a Facebook application, you are allowing citizens to be in more control of their interaction with the government rather than government in control of the interactions." — Chris Vein, Chief Information Officer for the City and County of San Francisco, quoted in The Facebook Blog, July 19, 2010

Other government agencies are reaching out to Facebook users for help. For example, recently the U.S. National Archives (see www.facebook.com/usnational archives) posted some old photos of Washington, D.C., monuments and buildings, and it asked people to submit modern-day photos of the same structures (see Figure 5.5).

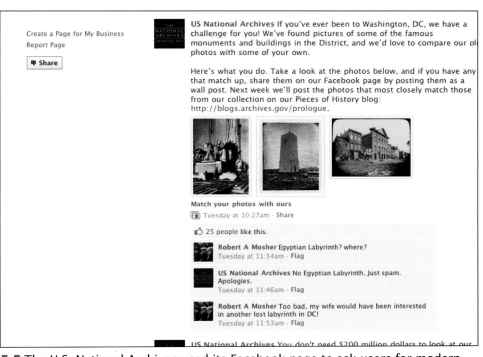

5.5 The U.S. National Archives used its Facebook page to ask users for modern-day photos to match old images of Washington, D.C., monuments and buildings.

In the long run, many government agencies offer services directly through Facebook, mostly by using Facebook applications. For example, Chris Vein, the Chief Information Officer for the City and County of San Francisco, has predicted that soon many government departments will maintain only minimal Web sites and shift services to Facebook.

There are thousands of government-related resources on Facebook, and the best way to find a government department, agency, or official is to use the Facebook Search feature. For your convenience, here's a list of U.S. government Facebook pages that had at least 20,000 fans as of this writing:

- **Arlington National Cemetery.** www.facebook.com/ArlingtonNational Cemetery
- **Centers for Disease Control and Prevention.** www.facebook. com/CDC
- **CO.NX.** www.facebook.com/pages/CoNx/26365096875
- **Department of Defense.** www.facebook.com/DeptofDefense
- **eJournal USA.** www.facebook.com/ejournalUSA
- **Federal Bureau of Investigation.** www.facebook.com/FBI
- **Let's Move!** www.facebook.com/letsmove
- **The Library of Congress.** www.facebook.com/libraryofcongress
- **National Aeronautics and Space Administration.** www.facebook. com/NASA
- **National Oceanic and Atmospheric Administration**. www.facebook. com/usnoaagov
- **National Guard.** www.facebook.com/nationalguard
- **The U.S. Army.** www.facebook.com/USarmy
- **U.S. Census Bureau.** www.facebook.com/uscensusbureau
- **U.S. Coast Guard.** www.facebook.com/UScoastguard
- **U.S. Department of State.** www.facebook.com/usdos
- **U.S. National Weather Service.** www.facebook.com/US.National. Weather.Service.gov
- **U.S. Navy.** www.facebook.com/USNavy
- **United States Air Force.** www.facebook.com/USairforce
- **United States Marine Corps Official Page.** www.facebook.com/ marines
- **Veterans Health Administration.** www.facebook.com/VeteransHealth
- **The White House.** www.facebook.com/WhiteHouse

On a more general level, Facebook maintains a community page related to government:

www.facebook.com/pages/Government/109454222414941

Also, if you want to learn more about how government agencies are using Facebook, see the Facebook and Government page:

www.facebook.com/government

Learning about History

If you're a history buff, you'll find many like-minded people on Facebook, which has a thriving historical community. You can begin at one of Facebook's many community pages related to history, historical studies, and historical periods:

- **History.** www.facebook.com/pages/History/106066639425552
- **Historiography.** www.facebook.com/pages/Historiography/ 105454969487148
- **American History.** www.facebook.com/pages/American-History/ 101879563186878
- **Ancient History.** www.facebook.com/pages/Ancient-history/ 112004385482906
- **Cultural History.** www.facebook.com/pages/Cultural-history/ 109635309062826
- **Military History.** www.facebook.com/pages/Military-history/ 106434036054044
- **Oral History.** www.facebook.com/pages/Oral-history/ 109377989081068
- **Philosophy of History.** www.facebook.com/pages/Philosophy-of-history/108743979149403
- **Renaissance.** www.facebook.com/pages/Renaissance/ 108184865875634
- **Social History.** www.facebook.com/pages/Social-history/ 112617338752401
- **World History.** www.facebook.com/pages/World-History/ 111953518816191

Also, here's a list of resources for some famous museums and other history-related Facebook sites:

- **British Museum.** This page includes information on current events at the museum, a list of new and upcoming exhibitions, photos, and more.

  www.facebook.com/britishmuseum

- **The Field Museum.** This page offers information about the museum, reviews of programs and exhibitions, photos, videos, and more.

  www.facebook.com/fieldmuseum

- **HISTORY Channel.** This page (see Figure 5.6) is the Facebook home for the award-winning HISTORY Channel, which includes This Day in History Wall posts, videos, history discussions, and more.

  www.facebook.com/History

5.6 The HISTORY Channel has a useful and lively Facebook page, which includes This Day in History Wall posts.

- **National Museum of American History.** This page offers history info, links to history articles and blog posts, and more.

  www.facebook.com/americanhistory

- **Natural History Museum, London.** This page gives you information about the museum, a list of upcoming events, photos, and more.

  www.facebook.com/naturalhistorymuseum

- **Rosicrucian Egyptian Museum.** This page includes information on the museum, a list of upcoming events, discussions, videos, and more.

  www.facebook.com/RosicrucianEgyptianMuseum

- **Smithsonian Institution.** This is the main Facebook page for the Smithsonian, and it includes information on current programs, a list of new and upcoming exhibitions, photos, videos, and more.

  www.facebook.com/SmithsonianInstitution

 NOTE Given the diversity and scope of the Smithsonian, it's not at all surprising that the museum also has a diverse presence on Facebook. Besides the main page, you'll also find pages for the National Portrait Gallery (www.facebook.com/npg.smithsonian), the National Museum of African American History and Culture (www.facebook.com/NMAAHC), the National Air and Space Museum (www.facebook.com/airandspace), and the National Museum of Natural History (www.facebook.com/nmnh.fanpage). There's also an app called Smithsonian Gift Collection for sending images of artifacts from the Smithsonian Institution's collection as gifts to your Facebook friends. Run a search on "smithsonian" to see more.

- **United States Holocaust Memorial Museum.** This museum's page includes lively Wall discussions, videos, photos, and more.

  www.facebook.com/holocaustmuseum

- **World History.** This is the Facebook page for WorldHistory.com and it offers historical facts, photos, and discussions.

  www.facebook.com/worldhistory

Facebook and the Environment

Concern for the environment is at an all-time high, and Facebook reflects that interest with lots of resources on environmental issues, climate change, sustainability, and more. You can begin your own research on one of the many community pages related to the environment:

- **Environmentalism.** www.facebook.com/pages/Environmentalism/ 109576845728239
- **Environmental Issues.** www.facebook.com/pages/ Environmental-issues/106073342766403
- **Alternative Energy.** www.facebook.com/pages/Alternative-energy/ 109157292436336
- **Climate Change.** www.facebook.com/pages/Climate-change/ 108011402555363
- **Global Warming.** www.facebook.com/pages/Global-warming/ 108151362545870
- **Greenhouse Effect.** www.facebook.com/pages/Greenhouse-effect/ 112161762133836
- **Greenhouse Gas.** www.facebook.com/pages/Greenhouse-gas/ 107369725959543
- **Green Living.** www.facebook.com/pages/Green-living/ 110343502320337
- **Sustainability.** www.facebook.com/pages/Sustainability/ 105572446142396

For further reading, here's a list of pages related to prominent environmental groups:

- **Alternative Energy.** This nonprofit's goal is to share news stories, discussion forums, photographs, and videos that promote the use of renewable energy technologies.

  www.facebook.com/350.org

- **David Suzuki.** This page includes plenty of announcements on the many activities of the famous Canadian environmentalist and his foundation, The David Suzuki Foundation.

  www.facebook.com/DavidSuzuki

- **Earth Day Network.** This is the official Facebook page for Earth Day Network, the organization driving International Earth Day. Postings on the page vary widely from suggestions on eco-conscious living to ads for eco-friendly products.

  www.facebook.com/EarthDayNetwork

- **Environmental Protection Agency.** On this page, the federal agency responsible for human health and safeguarding the environment releases updates to the public on current topics and activities.

  www.facebook.com/EPA

- **The Environmental Working Group.** This active page includes information and updates on this nonprofit's work to use public information to protect public health and the environment.

  www.facebook.com/pages/Environmental-issues/106073342766403

- **Friends of the Earth U.S.** The page is about the United States branch of the international grassroots organization that advocates for a healthy and just world by focusing on the social and economic causes that lead to environmental problems.

  www.facebook.com/pages/Friends-of-the-Earth-International/106331112736146

- **Greenpeace International.** This page is about the global campaigning organization that seeks to change attitudes and behavior to protect and conserve the environment and promote peace.

  www.facebook.com/greenpeace.international

- **National Wildlife Federation.** This page is about the national organization whose mission is to inspire Americans to protect wildlife for their children's future.

  www.facebook.com/NationalWildlife

- **The Nature Conservancy.** This is the official page of the national organization that works to protect the environment.

  www.facebook.com/thenatureconservancy

- **Sierra Club.** This page (see Figure 5.7) is about America's oldest grassroots environmental organization that works to protect communities, wild places, and the planet.

  www.facebook.com/SierraClub

5.7 The Facebook page for the Sierra Club.

- **World Wildlife Fund.** This page is about the largest multinational nature conservation organization in the world.

  www.facebook.com/worldwildlifefund

Connecting with Charities

As you see in this section, if you're looking to donate money to a worthy cause, Facebook gives you lots of ways to connect with organizations. Facebook also places itself on the cutting edge of charitable giving by offering people and organizations a platform for creating innovative programs and methods.

A great example occurred in 2009 when JPMorgan Chase decided to give away $5 million to various charities. Rather than deciding on the charities in the usual way — that is, putting together a board of directors to oversee the program and having charities submit applications — Chase decided to let the people make the choices. The company created a program called Chase Community Giving, put up a Facebook page (www.facebook.com/ChaseCommunityGiving; see Figure 5.8), created a Facebook application, and asked people to use the app to vote on which charities should get the money.

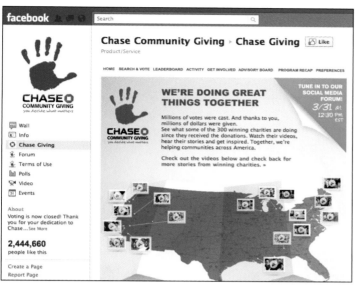

5.8 The Facebook page for the Chase Community Giving program.

Over 2 million people participated; the top 100 charities each received $25,000 and a chance at a second round of voting, where five runners-up each received another $100,000. The winning charity — called Invisible Children; see www. facebook.com/invisiblechildren — received $1 million. (The Chase board also selected a second charity that received $1 million.) In 2010, Chase repeated the program, with more than 2.5 million people choosing 195 charities to receive $20,000, four charities to receive $100,000, and one charity to receive $250,000.

Quote, Unquote: Facebook and Charity

"After the earthquake in Haiti, we shared disaster relief info on our Facebook page from UNICEF reps. Soon, we witnessed the power of our community: Folks spread the word of the urgent needs, and donations started pouring in. Through Facebook, we raised $142,000 for the children of Haiti. Your donations are being put to good use. — E. C., New York, New York

Another uniquely Facebook approach to charitable giving is an application called Causes (www.facebook.com/causes; see Figure 5.9), which has more than 18 million active users. You can use this application to donate directly to a cause, or you can use it to promote a cause and solicit donations for non-profit organizations. For example, when your birthday rolls around, you can ask your friends to donate to a charity of your choice in lieu of presents.

5.9 You can use the Causes application to find, promote, and donate to charities and other causes.

You can start off your explorations of charity on Facebook by reading the related community pages:

- **Charity.** www.facebook.com/pages/Charity/114179368594398
- **Charity Work.** www.facebook.com/pages/Charity-work/108674135829888
- **Fundraising.** www.facebook.com/pages/Fundraising/109592405733713
- **Philanthropy.** www.facebook.com/pages/Philanthropy/105589126140646

Here are several pages for charitable organizations as well as other charity-related resources on Facebook:

- **American Red Cross.** This is the official Facebook page for the national organization.

  www.facebook.com/redcross

- **DonorsChoose.org.** This is the Facebook page for DonorsChoose.org, which enables people to direct learning materials and other resources to classrooms.

  www.facebook.com/DonorsChoose

- **Feed a Child with a Click.** This group is dedicated to obtaining online donations to help prevent hunger.

  www.facebook.com/group.php?gid=8481112831

- **FundRazr.** This application lets you raise money for a cause directly from your Facebook Wall section.

  www.facebook.com/FundRazr

- **Livestrong.** This is the Facebook page for Lance Armstrong's Livestrong Organization.

  www.facebook.com/livestrong

- **March of Dimes.** This is the Facebook home for the March of Dimes.

  www.facebook.com/marchofdimes

- **ONE.** Cofounded by U2's Bono, ONE is an advocacy organization that works against extreme poverty and disease, mainly in Africa.

  www.facebook.com/ONE

- **United Way.** This is the official Facebook page of the worldwide community-based organization that focuses on education, income, and health.

  www.facebook.com/UnitedWay

Finally, if you want to learn more about how nonprofit organizations use Facebook, or if you work with a nonprofit that's thinking about putting up a Facebook page, see the Non-Profits on Facebook page:

www.facebook.com/nonprofits

Quote, Unquote: Facebook and Charity

"Facebook has helped me make new friends around the world who share the same interest and keep me in touch with other related charities who all share the same goal, which has helped us share our support also and connect in order to raise awareness. Without it, I would never have got to meet my kind of people." — J. M., Manchester, England

Volunteering via Facebook

Volunteering has never been easier thanks to the Web, which lets you easily research and sign up for volunteering opportunities that suit your talents or interests. Facebook is leading this wave by becoming *the* place to find volunteer organizations and opportunities, either locally or anywhere in the world.

As usual, Facebook offers a few general references for volunteering in the form of community pages:

- **Volunteering.** www.facebook.com/pages/Volunteering/ 105447916154600

- **Environmental Volunteering.** www.facebook.com/pages/ Environmental-volunteering/114958455182745

- **Virtual Volunteering.** www.facebook.com/pages/Virtual-volunteering/ 110578105631014

But Facebook's real value is in its extensive list of pages, groups, and applications that enable you to find volunteer opportunities of all descriptions:

- **Best Buddies International.** This nonprofit organization is trying to create a worldwide volunteer network to establish relationships with and employment for people with disabilities.

  www.facebook.com/bestbuddies

- **Big Brothers Big Sisters of America.** This is the Facebook home for Big Brothers Big Sisters, which uses adult volunteers to mentor boys and girls.

  www.facebook.com/BigBrothersBigSisters

- **Boy Scouts of America.** This is the Facebook home for the Boy Scouts, who need adult volunteers to lead and mentor boys.

  www.facebook.com/pages/Boy-Scouts-of-America/113441755297

- **Do Something.** This organization is devoted to encouraging teenagers to volunteer and get involved in their communities.

  www.facebook.com/dosomething

- **Erasmus Student Network.** This is the page for Erasmus Student Network, a volunteer student organization.

  www.facebook.com/esn

- **Girl Scouts of the USA.** The Facebook home for the Girl Scouts, who need adult volunteers to lead and mentor girls, is found here.

  www.facebook.com/GirlScoutsUSA

TIP To send a friend a virtual Girl Scout cookie, install the Girl Scout Cookies application: www.facebook.com/GirlScoutCookies.

- **Habitat for Humanity.** This page is the Facebook home for Habitat for Humanity, which uses volunteers to help build homes for people who can't afford them.

  www.facebook.com/habitat

- **National Peace Corps Association.** This page is the Facebook face of the Peace Corps and its volunteers.

  www.facebook.com/PeaceCorpsConnect

- **New York Cares.** A nonprofit organization that connects volunteers and projects in the New York area.

  www.facebook.com/NewYorkCares

- **One World 365.** This group is a directory of volunteer projects from around the world.

  www.facebook.com/group.php?gid=8742846948

- **Operation Gratitude.** This organization sends care packages to military personnel.

  www.facebook.com/OperationGratitude

- **Projects Abroad.** This Facebook page is maintained by an organization that helps young people find volunteer work overseas.

  www.facebook.com/gapyears

- **Remote Area Medical Volunteer Corps.** This page is maintained by Remote Area Medical, which delivers health care to people in remote parts of the world.

  www.facebook.com/RAMUSA.ORG

- **Serve.gov.** This is a government agency that helps people locate volunteering opportunities (see Figure 5.10).

  www.facebook.com/serve

5.10 You can use the Serve.gov page to find volunteer opportunities near where you live.

- **Service Nation.** This nonprofit organization strives to "inspire a new era of voluntary citizen service."

  www.facebook.com/ServiceNation

- **Soldiers' Angels.** This nonprofit uses volunteers to provide letters, blankets, food, care packages, and other comfort items to soldiers and their families.

  www.facebook.com/SoldiersAngelsOfficial

- **The Spirit of Service: Your Daily Stimulus for Making a Difference.** This is an umbrella group that represents more than 500 organizations that help people find volunteer opportunities.

  www.facebook.com/spiritofservice

- **Volunteer Firefighters.** This page is devoted to being a volunteer firefighter.

  www.facebook.com/pages/Volunteer-Firefighters/147799855978

- **VolunteerMatch.** This nonprofit organization lists thousands of volunteer opportunities from around the world.

  www.facebook.com/VolunteerMatch

- **World Vets.** This is the page for World Vets, an organization that uses volunteer vets to provide animal care around the world.

  www.facebook.com/WorldVets

Facebook Activism

Before Facebook came along, if you had a gripe or complaint about something, you probably wrote a letter to the editor of your local paper or perhaps donated some money to a like-minded organization. If you were really involved, you'd sign a petition or even join a protest march. All these forms of activism still exist, of course, but nowadays most people view them as secondary. When spurred to action, their first instinct is to create a Facebook group or put up a Facebook page.

Quote, Unquote: Facebook and Activism

"All I did was make a Facebook page. Anyone who has an opinion could do that and have their opinion heard. I would love to see kids in high school step up and start their own protests and change things in their own way." — Michelle Ryan Lauto, quoted from "In New Jersey, a Civics Lesson in the Internet Age," The New York Times, April 28, 2010

In 2010, student Michelle Ryan Lauto created a Facebook page protesting New Jersey's recent budget cuts for education. She let her 600 friends know about it, and the page quickly amassed 18,000 fans, many of whom later participated in a massive high school walkout that Ms. Lauto organized through her page. In a similar protest, student Will Anderson started a page called Protect Your Bright Futures because Florida was considering a bill that would shift budget money from arts students to math and science students. His page quickly garnered 20,000 fans, and the state senator sponsoring the bill decided to drop it.

The connected nature of Facebook social networks means that a protest message that resonates can attract a remarkably large number of followers in a short time. Journalist David Kirkpatrick calls this the *Facebook effect*, and it works because Facebook makes it easy for a protest message to be seen by millions of people. It might begin humbly enough by promoting your cause to a couple of hundred friends, but if some of those friends pass along your message to a couple of hundred of their own friends, and those friends of friends do the same, a message that connects with people can spread extremely quickly.

For example, a page urging people to boycott BP after that company's disastrous Gulf of Mexico oil spill has more than 800,000 fans (see www.facebook.com/pages/Boycott-BP/119101198107726). In one of the most famous cases of Facebook activism, a page called One Million Voices Against FARC (see www.facebook.com/onemillionvoices) amassed half a million followers and a subsequent event called the National March Against FARC drew over 12 million people around the world. (FARC — which stands for Fuerzas Armadas Revolucionarias de Colombia, or the Revolutionary Armed Forces of Colombia — is a guerrilla organization in Columbia.)

If you want to get started on a more general level, Facebook maintains a few community pages related to activism and protest:

- **Activism.** www.facebook.com/pages/Activism/108190249208655
- **Boycott.** www.facebook.com/pages/Boycott/107604599262180
- **Demonstration.** www.facebook.com/pages/Demonstration/104041706299289
- **Protest.** www.facebook.com/pages/Protest/112109092135301

Quote, Unquote: Facebook and Activism

[Will] Anderson started his "Protect Your Bright Futures" Facebook campaign by inviting 200 friends to join his group. His page listed a synopsis of [state Sen. Jeremy] Ring's proposed scholarship overhaul, which sought to take money from students who, like Anderson, were enrolled in liberal-arts programs, and give it to their counterparts studying math and science…. In 11 days, Anderson's online supporters swelled to almost 20,000, and he got a phone call from state Sen. Jeremy Ring announcing that he had decided to drop the bill seeking the scholarship change. "You can't ignore 20,000 people," Ring, D-Parkland, said later. — Josh Hafenbrack, "Online political action can spark offline change," *South Florida Sun-Sentinel,* April 6, 2008

Getting the most out of activism on Facebook means either becoming a fan of a page or joining a group that promotes a cause you support. And, of course, you can always create your own page or group and pass the word along to your friends. To give you a flavor of the kinds of activism that are popular on Facebook, here's a sampling of pages with at least 50,000 fans:

- **1,000,000 Strong Against Offshore Drilling.** www.facebook.com/dontdrill

- **Amnesty International USA.** www.facebook.com/amnestyusa

- **Make it illegal to protest at military funerals.** www.facebook.com/pages/Make-it-illegal-to-protest-at-military-funerals/109977969025135

- **No H8 Campaign.** www.facebook.com/noh8campaign

- **PETA (People for the Ethical Treatment of Animals).** www.facebook.com/officialpeta

- **Protest against MERALCO electricity price hike.** www.facebook.com/pages/Protest-against-MERALCO-electricity-price-hike/108570395847404

- **Protest Animal Cruelty.** www.facebook.com/dogadoption

- **Protest the Closing of the Largest Islamic Group.** www.facebook.com/weProtest

- **The Red Ribbon Army.** www.facebook.com/TheRedRibbonArmy
- **Smoking doesn't make you cool, sorry.** www.facebook.com/pages/Smoking-doesnt-make-you-cool-sorry/191365587625
- **Stop the UK Petrol Rip-Off, May 2010.** www.facebook.com/pages/Stop-the-UK-Petrol-Rip-off-May-2010-Protest/110748015608987
- **Support the Monk's Protest In Burma.** www.facebook.com/BurmaGlobalActionNetwork
- **Support Our Troops.** www.facebook.com/pages/Support-Our-Troops/61532072931

Campaigning on Facebook

Facebook can be a very powerful tool for communicating a message to the masses. That goes double if you're campaigning for public office. As mentioned earlier in this chapter, President Barack Obama was one of the first politicians to effectively use Facebook to build a strong political following; even now, Obama and his supporters employ Facebook to communicate with the American people and the world beyond.

As an example, consider New Jersey college student Ace Antonio. Frustrated with cuts in state funding for education, Ace launched a campaign for a seat on the Paramus Board of Education. Although Ace had only a limited campaign budget — $300 — he had one clear advantage over his opponent: He understood the power of social media. Ace launched his campaign on Facebook, creating a page that attracted 400 followers on the very first day.

Ace used his campaign's Facebook page to alert followers of campaign events and activities. "I would post what part of the district I was walking through, updating my status every few hours, and I'd have people just show up to walk it with me," Ace says. By the time the election rolled around—which Ace won—Ace's Facebook page had accumulated more than 1,000 followers. "I still use Facebook to communicate to the community that elected me," says Ace. "It is a great way for me to keep everyone informed on the progress we are making in our school district."

chapter 6

Work and Money

Facebook may seem like a place where fun and frivolity rule the roost, but there's a sober side to Facebook that's more suited to a work environment. That is, many people in business — whether they're employees of large corporations or freelancers working for themselves — make use of Facebook features such as Pages, Events, and Groups to enhance and promote their business. On a more personal level, you can also use Facebook's vast resources to help you find a job, save money, become a savvy shopper, and keep your personal finances in good shape. And even if you've left the world of work for the world of retirement, Facebook has plenty of resources to also help you get the most out of that stage of your life.

Enhancing Your Business with Facebook

Facebook started off as a way for college students to connect with each other. Even when Facebook opened its servers to anyone over the age of 13, most people used it to keep up with friends and share their lives. It didn't take long, however, for companies to realize that Facebook comes with a unique set of tools that can help promote products and brands, create goodwill in the community, get customer feedback, and improve internal processes.

Using Pages to promote a product or brand

The old way of marketing a product, service, or brand was to work up some creative copy — such as a print ad, a TV spot, or a flyer — and then get that copy in front of as many eyeballs as possible. This is *one-way street* marketing, where you send out your message and see what happens.

Nowadays, the best marketing has a social component, where you not only get out a message that promotes a product, service, brand, or cause, but you also listen to and engage your would-be customers, fans, or followers. This is *two-way street* marketing, where there's an exchange of ideas, information, and feedback between the marketer and the potential customer.

Facebook makes it easy to engage in two-way street marketing because you can create a Page for a particular product, service, brand, or cause. A typical Page gives you many ways to interact with potential buyers and existing customers:

- Use the About box to briefly explain the Page topic.
- Use the Info page to describe your product or service, provide a company overview, create a link to your Web site, and more.
- Use the Wall page to display messages about your product, link to Web pages related to your product, and post product pictures and videos. You can also configure the Wall section to allow people who "like" the Page to post their own content.
- You can use the Notes page to create longer posts related to your product.
- You can use the Discussions page to ask for feedback, answer questions, troubleshoot problems, and communicate directly with customers and potential customers.

Quote, Unquote: Pages and Promotion

"I have been a realtor for over 8 years and have always been very tech savvy, or so I have been told. So when the market crashed I decided to start my own virtual assistance company. I have grown from 0 clients to over 100 in 6 months and I have not spent one dime in marketing. I have used my contacts in the real estate world, my reputation, and the Facebook Business Page. This is an incredible free tool!" — S. S., Douglasville, Georgia

Your first task is to select the type of Page you're creating:

- **Local Business or Place.** Click this option if you're creating a Page for a resource in your area, particularly a business or public location, then use the Choose a Category list to select the type of business or location, as shown in Figure 6.1.

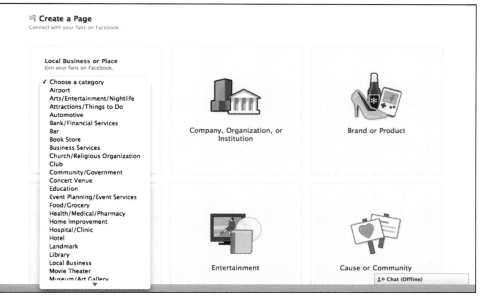

6.1 If you're promoting a resource in your area, click Local Business or Place and then choose the type of business or place.

- **Company, Organization, or Institution.** Click this option if you're promoting your company, an organization such as a non-profit or a government agency, or an institution such as a school, then use the Choose a Category list to select a type.

- **Brand or Product.** Click this option if you're promoting a brand, a product or a service, then use the Choose a Category list to select a type, as shown in Figure 6.2.

6.2 If you're promoting your brand, product, or service, click the Brand or Product option and then choose a category.

- **Artist, Band, or Public Figure.** Click this option if you're creating a Page for an artist, a singer or musical group, or a famous person, then use the Choose a Category list to select the type, as shown in Figure 6.3.

- **Entertainment.** Click this option if you're creating a Page for anything related to the entertainment field, including a book, fictional character, music album, movie, or TV show, then use the Choose a Category list to select the type.

- **Cause or Community.** Click this option if you're creating a Page for a cause, movement, activism, or a community of like-minded people.

Fill in the fields (the fields you see depend on the Page type you chose), select the I agree to Facebook Pages Terms check box, then click Get Started. Facebook builds the new Page and displays it. To complete the Page, click Edit Page and then do the following:

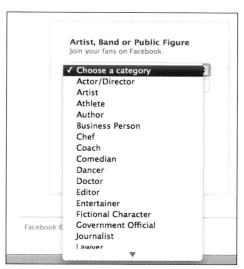

- Click Profile Picture to add an image for the Page.

- Click Basic Information and then use the About box to briefly describe your Page topic.

6.3 If you're promoting an artist, musical group, or famous person group, click Artist, Band, or Public Figure and then choose the category.

- Click Basic Information to edit the rest of the Page info.

- Add more apps to the Page. Click Edit Page and then click Apps to display the list of available apps (see Figure 6.4), then click the app you want to add.

Quote, Unquote: Pages and Promotion

"Facebook has provided my company a new area to really reach and communicate with customers, to not yell but to really effectively communicate our brands." — D. A., Kuala Lampur, Malaysia

6.4 Depending on the type of Page you created, Facebook offers a large selection of apps you can add to the Page.

Sending out Page invitations

Once your Page is ready to be shown to the world, you can invite your friends to come take a look and, hopefully, "like" your Page. Open the Page, then click the Suggest to Friends link that appears on the right side of the Page under the Admins section. When Facebook displays your list of friends, choose the friends you want to invite, then click Send Recommendations.

Each friend then sees a Page suggestion link in the Requests area of his or her Facebook Home page, as shown in Figure 6.5. The friend can then visit the Page and return to the suggestion and click Confirm to like the page, or Ignore to remove the suggestion.

Most of your friends will also get an e-mail message alerting them to your invitation.

6.5 When you send out invitations to your friends, each person sees a Page suggestion link in the Requests section of his or her Home page.

Adding an application to your page

One of the most useful aspects of Pages is that you can enhance them with applications. For example, you can add Facebook's Photos application if you want to display images associated with your product or brand.

To add an application, follow these steps:

1. **Display your page.**

2. **Click Edit Page.**

3. **In the Apps section, click Browse more applications to open the Applications Directory.**

4. **Locate the application you want to use, and then open the application's Page.**

5. **Click Wall or Info, then click Add to My Page.**

6. **If you have multiple Pages, click the Add to Page button beside the Page you're configuring (see Figure 6.6), then click Close.**

6.6 If you maintain multiple Pages, choose the Page to which you want to add the application.

Adding a Page administrator

If your company is small or you're a freelancer, then chances are you're the only person who makes changes to the page and performs other administrative chores. For larger teams, however, it makes sense to share some of the burden by designating one or more other people to be Page administrators.

NOTE It's much easier to add a Page administrator if that person is friends with you on Facebook, so go ahead and connect with the other person if you haven't done so already.

To add a Page admin (as Facebook calls such a person), follow these steps:

1. **Display your page.**
2. **Click Edit Page.**
3. **In the Manage Admins section, start typing the name of the friend you want to add, and then click the friend (or friends) you want to set up as administrators.**
4. **Click Save Change.** Your friend is added as an admin of the page.

Creating a friendly username for your Page

One big problem you might have noticed with your Page is that Facebook gives it a very long and unmemorable address that looks something like this:

www.facebook.com/pages/The-Name-of-Your-Page/12345678901234

Try telling that to someone at a cocktail party! To makes things easier, you can replace this long-winded address with a much shorter one that's easier to remember. You do this by applying a username to the Page, which is a short word (or a phrase with the spaces removed) that you create yourself. For example, if you choose the username MyGreatProduct, then the address of the Facebook Page will now look like this:

www.facebook.com/MyGreatProduct

NOTE Before you can register a username with Facebook, you must verify your Facebook account. Go to www.facebook.com/confirmphone.php, type your cell phone number, and then click Confirm. Facebook sends a code as a text message to your phone. Return to Facebook (which should now show the Confirm Your Phone page), type the confirmation code, and then click Confirm.

Quote, Unquote: Facebook and Business

"Living in Iceland, Facebook has been a great tool to promote my business all over the world. I have gotten a lot of new great personal business contacts from using Facebook." — M. C., Reykjavik, Iceland

---

Assuming your Page has at least 25 fans, you're eligible for a username. To create your Page username, go to www.facebook.com/username/, and then click the Set a username for your Pages link. Use the Page Name list to choose your Page, type your desired username as shown in Figure 6.7, and then click Check availability. If Facebook tells you the username is available, click Confirm to set it.

6.7 If your Page has at least 25 fans, you can set up a username to make it easier to navigate to the Page.

Using Events to set up meetings and conferences

You might think that Facebook Events are only useful for planning birthday parties, anniversary celebrations, and other social gatherings, but there's no reason you can't branch out. For example, if you want to schedule a meeting with coworkers or a conference with clients, the Events application has everything you need. This works best if all the attendees are on Facebook and you're friends with them, but you can also invite people via e-mail.

To schedule your meeting, click Home to display your Facebook Home page, click Events in the Navigation area, and then click Create an Event. You then use the Create an Event page to specify the particulars of the meeting:

- Use the When? controls to set the date of the meeting and the time it starts. Also, be sure to click the Add end time link to specify when the meeting ends.

- Use the More info? text box to describe the purpose of the meeting as well as any special instructions.

- The attendees can consist of Facebook friends as well as coworkers (or clients or whoever) who are not on Facebook. To create the list of attendees, click Select Guests to open the Select Guests dialog box, then use the list of friends to click each person you want to invite. For people not on Facebook, type their e-mail addresses in the Invite by E-mail Address text box, separating each address with a comma.

- To prevent anyone else from seeing the meeting Event, be sure to deselect the Anyone can view and RSVP check box. This means that your meeting will be a private event that's viewable only by the people you invite.

Figure 6.8 shows a meeting Event ready to go.

6.8 Use the Create an Event page to specify the details of your meeting.

Using Groups to help team members stay in touch

If you're part of a team at work, you know that communication among team members is crucial. Facebook can help your team stay in touch with each other by having each member join a Group. This is particularly useful if you have team members who work in other offices, other cities, or other countries. Members can send messages via the Group Wall; discuss various team-related topics using the Group discussion board; share photos, videos, or links; and the Group administrator (that is, the person who created the Group) can send messages to everyone in the Group.

To set up your Group, click Home to open your Home page, and then click Create Group. You then use the Create Group screen to specify the Group info:

- The Group name should be the name that your team uses at work, to avoid confusion.

- To populate the Group, click inside the Members box. For each person you want to add, type the first letter of the person's name, then click the person in the list of names that appears.

- For the Privacy setting, in most cases, you'll want to keep this Group private, particularly if you'll be discussing proprietary business infor- mation. To ensure that no one sees the Group (either in a Group search or in the profiles of each Group member), select the Secret option. If you only want to keep the Group's content private (while leaving the group's members public), choose Closed instead.

Figure 6.9 shows an example of a Create a Group screen, ready to go. Click Create Group to proceed.

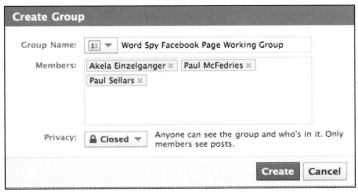

6.9 Use the Create a Group screen to specify the details of your Group.

Quote, Unquote: Pages and Promotion

"I live in Colombia but work with clients from around the world. Facebook has helped us communicate with people, our fan page is growing, and we use every single feature." — A. R., Bogota, Colombia

Advertising on Facebook

If you want to get the word out about a product or service, a Facebook Page is a great way to go. The only problem with that approach by itself is that you're relying on people to find your Page. Sure, you can tell people about your Page on your company Web site, but if you want to generate new business, then you need to get new Facebook people to view and ideally like your Page. Similarly, if you have a product or service that has its own Web site instead of a Facebook Page, you might still want to get more people to the site.

How can you generate more traffic either to a Facebook Page or to a Web site? In most cases, you can drive all kinds of people to your Page or Web site by using a *Facebook ad*. A Facebook ad is a small, mostly text-based message (you're allowed a small image) that appears in the right sidebar of many Facebook Pages, including user profiles. The awesome thing about Facebook ads is that you can easily target the ads to people who might be interested in your product or service. Nobody likes seeing irrelevant advertisements, and Facebook tries to prevent this by giving you multiple ways to target your audience:

You have a couple of ways to get started:

- If you're advertising a product that has a Facebook Page, click Home, click Ads and Pages, and then click the Advertise Page link that appears beside the page you want to promote. In the Advertise on Facebook page that appears, the name of your Page appears automatically in the Facebook Content list.

- If you're advertising a product that has a Web site, click the Advertising link that appears at the bottom of all Facebook Pages, and then click Create an Ad. In the Advertise on Facebook page that appears, use the Destination URL field to enter the address of the product's Web site.

> ### Quote, Unquote: Facebook and Advertising
>
> "Facebook is a dream come true for my social media clients in Abu Dhabi, and Dubai, United Arab Emirates. Businesses affected by the recession have less to spend on advertising. Yet they need customers visiting their Web sites, walking into their stores, using their services. With Facebook, my clients are getting exposure at a fraction of the cost of conventional advertising. — F. N., Abu Dhabi, United Arab Emirates

As for the rest of the Advertise on Facebook page, you use the Title text box to fill in the ad title, which is the link that users click to go to your Page or Web site; you use the Body Text box to type the ad copy, up to a maximum of 130 characters; and you use the Image control to choose an image to appear in the ad.

Figure 6.10 shows an ad for a Facebook Page ready to go. Notice that Facebook shows a preview of the ad below the info you entered.

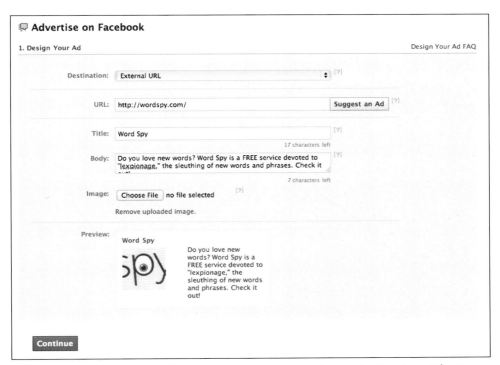

6.10 Use the Advertise on Facebook page to set up the ad destination, title, text, and image.

Click Continue to display the Targeting section, where you tell Facebook who you want to see the ad. There are five main sections (note that you need to click Show Advanced Targeting Options to see some of the options mentioned here):

- **Location.** Use this text box to type the names of one or more countries. Facebook targets your ad at people who currently reside in these countries. If you want to target a more specific geographic area, select a single country, and then select either a state or province, or a city within that country. If you select a city, you can also specify a target radius (say, within 20 miles).

  NOTE Unfortunately, Facebook doesn't offer an "All" option to target an ad at the entire Facebook community. If you leave the Country field blank, Facebook just considers the targeting to be invalid.

- **Demographics.** You use these controls to target your ad by age, sex, birthday, relationship interests, current relationship status, and language.

- **Likes & Interests.** You use this text box to select one or more things that Facebook users have liked or have identified as an interest. This is probably the most crucial part of the targeting process, because by choosing likes and interests that closely match your product, you can be reasonably sure that a high percentage of the people who see your ad will be interested in your product.

- **Education & Work.** You use this section to target users by education (such as College Grad or In College), and by workplace (that is, you type the names of one or more workplaces you want to target).

As you make your targeting choices, Facebook uses the right column to show a running total of the *estimated reach*, which is the approximate number of Facebook users who will see your ad. Figure 6.11 shows an example of a completed targeting section, and you can see that Facebook's estimated reach for this ad is well over 1 million people.

When your targeting is complete, to see the Campaigns, Pricing and Scheduling section (see Figure 6.12). You use this section to select a currency, a time zone, a campaign name, and the daily maximum you want to spend. You can also set up a schedule for the ad to run. Facebook also tells you the estimated *cost per click*, which is the amount Facebook charges you each time a person clicks your ad.

Click Review Ad, make sure everything is set up correctly, and then click Place Order. From here, you supply your credit card info or a PayPal authorization, and your ad is live within minutes. To track your ad, click Home, click Ads and Pages, and then click the ad name under the Campaigns heading.

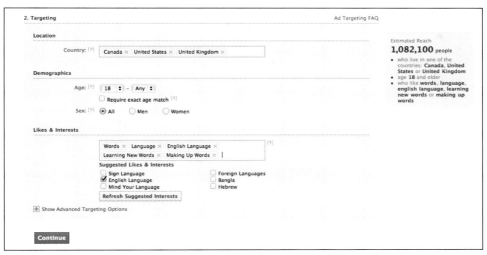

6.11 Use the Targeting section to specify your target audience for the ad, and watch the Estimated Reach number on the right.

6.12 Use the Campaigns, Pricing and Scheduling section to finalize your ad campaign.

Using Facebook to Find a Job

There's no shortage of people looking for jobs these days, as evidenced by the U.S. unemployment rate, which stood at 9.6 percent in June 2010 (more than double what it was five years earlier). To make matters worse, all those people seem to be chasing fewer and fewer job openings as companies tighten their budgets and hunker down until the economy shows signs of life.

And it's not just the unemployed who are looking for work. The ranks of job seekers also include people who are underemployed, workers who are bored or disillusioned with their current jobs, ambitious folks looking for new challenges, and people who are simply looking for a change.

Then there's the considerable cohort of people in their 50s and up who are just entering the workforce or reentering after a long timeout. Perhaps their kids are now grown up or off to college and they're looking to fill a suddenly large block of free time; perhaps a spouse has been let go or given a pay cut or reduced hours and there is a need to pick up the financial slack; or perhaps it's just a simple desire to get out into the working world and do something useful or interesting.

All of this means that looking for a job is as tough as it has ever been. If you're in that boat, you can certainly start your search the old-fashioned way by looking at want ads in your local paper (or even the new-fashioned way by looking at want ads on Craigslist.com). Of course, anyone can do that, so you need an edge: some way of separating yourself from the herd of other job seekers.

That's where Facebook comes in. If you're looking for work, be sure to leverage the power of your network to solicit help from your friends. For example, if there's a particular field you're interested in, send out a status update asking for information about that field. Similarly, if you'd like to work for a particular company, ask your friends if they've had any experience dealing with the company.

TIP Are you aware of any friends on Facebook who are also looking for a job? If so, consider starting a Facebook support group where you can share leads, tips, and inspiration.

Quote, Unquote: Finding a Job on Facebook

"Facebook was the key component in how I landed the best job at the most brilliant interactive agency. Thanks, Facebook, for striving to connect the world through this awesome site and for connecting me to the best coworkers, colleagues, and clients anyone could ask for! " — M. E., Spokane, Washington

Many savvy job seekers are wielding Facebook's other social tools to take their work search to a higher level. Not only are companies and employment agencies actively recruiting on Facebook, but you've also got a great vehicle to promote yourself — your Facebook profile — and a great mechanism for getting the word out to potential employers — Facebook ads.

Using Facebook ads to get yourself in front of potential employers usually involves four main tasks:

- **Constructing the ad itself.** Facebook ads are small (135 characters max), so you don't have room for your entire résumé. However, to be effective, a good Facebook want ad must include the following six things:

  - Your name (just your first name will do)
  - Your picture
  - One awesome thing about you
  - What you want (a job!)
  - What industry you want to work in
  - Something that speaks directly to the reader.

  That's a lot to fit into a small space, so you need to be short, concise, and to the point. For example, "Hi, I'm Ellen. I'm an award-winning graphic designer. My dream is to work in new media design. Can you help me? Click to see my resume." Or, "My name is John and I am an editor with 20 years' experience. I am looking for a job in publishing. Can you help? Click for my resume."

- **Targeting the ad.** This is a crucial step because it takes advantage of the information that Facebook knows about its users. For example, if you want a job in your city, then you need to target people who live (and presumably work) in that city (say, within a 25-mile radius). For likes and interests, you should use keywords that apply to the industry and job you're looking for. If you're targeting a particular company, be sure to include that company's name so that people who have liked the company will see your ad. Finally, for education, be sure to select College Grad, because almost all hiring managers will have a college education.

- **Creating a landing page.** When people click your ad link, they should land on a page that acts as your online resume (hence why it's called a landing page). So construct your page with a view to impressing anyone who drops by. Also, make sure you give people plenty of ways to contact you (phone, e-mail, Facebook, and so on).

- **Cleaning up (and showing off) your Facebook profile.** Nowadays, it's routine for hiring managers to check out the Facebook profiles of prospective employees. Those managers are looking for deal breakers — sloppy writing, bad communication skills, inappropriate photos, and so on — that would weed out a candidate right away. However, they're also looking for deal *makers*: signs that you are an intelligent, thoughtful, hard-working, professional, and social person. So take some time to spruce up your profile to show yourself in your best light and to set your activities and interests so they align with (or, at least, don't contradict) the type of job you want. Having done that, make sure you also tweak your profile privacy settings to ensure that potential employers can see them.

Do Facebook job ads work? They did for Ian Greenleigh, a social media specialist who wanted to work for a particular social media marketing company in his hometown. A recruiter saw his ad and got him an interview at the company. The company's chief marketing officer also saw the ad and was impressed enough to bring Ian back for a second interview, and he ended up getting the job.

Ads aren't the only Facebook tool you can use in your job search. Here are a few other suggestions:

- Become a fan of any companies that you're targeting. At the very least this keeps you updated on the activities of the organization, plus they may list jobs or post information on job fairs.

- Join a Group of other professionals in your field. For example, if you are a graphic artist, you might want to join the following Groups:

NOTE There are many Facebook addresses in this section. All of them are case sensitive, and some of them quite long. Rather than typing the addresses by hand, see the Facebook page for this series: www.facebook.com/FBGseries. Alternatively, you can type a page's name in Facebook's Search box to locate it. Please note that Facebook does not endorse the sites listed in this book.

- **Graphic Design.** www.facebook.com/group.php?gid=2205267915
- **I ♥ Graphic Design.** www.facebook.com/group.php?gid=2344101144
- **Digital Art, Illustration, Painting, Graphic Design.** www.facebook.com/group.php?gid=2212111981

- Look for Pages that are related to your field and become a fan. The Page might occasionally post job openings, but a more promising avenue is the Discussions tab (if the Page has one), which could talk about job prospects.

- Regularly search Facebook Events to see if there are workshops or job fairs in your field happening in your geographic area.

- If you have your own business or are a freelancer or self-employed, create a Page for your business and have happy customers become fans of the page.

Besides these tools, Facebook also offers some useful resources for the job hunter:

- **About.com Job Searching.** This page (see Figure 6.13) has About. com's handy job searching tips and advice.

  www.facebook.com/aboutjobsearch

- **Career Builder.** This is the Facebook home of the online career site, CareerBuilder.com.

  www.facebook.com/careerbuilder

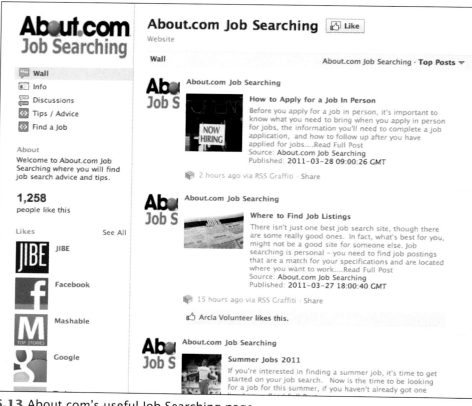

6.13 About.com's useful Job Searching page.

- **Career Network.** This Page is the Facebook face of the Career Network job board.

  www.facebook.com/TheCareerNetwork

- **Simply Hired.** This Page is devoted to the Simply Hired job search engine.

  www.facebook.com/simplyhired

- **Facebook Marketplace.** This Facebook application has a Jobs section that can show you available jobs in your current location.

  apps.facebook.com/marketplace

- **LiveCareer Resume Builder.** This application makes writing a resume fast and easy. With just one click, you can choose a professional design for your resume, and tune your text using hundreds of expert-written examples.

  www.facebook.com/apps/application.php?id=130939360270350

"Facebook is becoming an important way to source new employees. More companies are creating Facebook Fan sites to start a dialogue with potential new hires." — Jeanne Meister, author of *The 2020 Workplace: How Innovative Companies Attract, Develop & Keep Tomorrow's Employees Today*

Money-Related Resources on Facebook

They say you can never be too rich. Facebook may be able to help there, too. Facebook is loaded with useful and practical resources relating to money: shopping, saving money, personal finance, taxes, and more. The next few sections provide you with the details.

Becoming a savvy shopper

You can't buy things on Facebook, at least not yet. (I should say you can't buy *real* things on Facebook; you can use Facebook Credits to buy *virtual* things, such as supplies in the Facebook game FarmVille, or premium items in the Hallmark Social Calendar application.) However, you *can* use Facebook to make your online or offline shopping easier and more productive.

If you're interested in a particular product or brand, chances are it has a Facebook page. If so, you should become a fan of that page, which means you'll hear about updates and other news about the product. Many product pages also come with a Reviews tab that enables you to see what other people think about the product, as well as a Discussions tab that people use to talk about the product.

As a savvy consumer, you know that you need to do your homework before heading to the mall (either offline or online). Facebook can help here by offering lots of resources related to product research, price comparisons, user reviews, and more. Here are a few to check out:

- **Become.com.** This is the Facebook page for Become.com, which is a product research site.
  www.facebook.com/pages/Becomecom/25597601080

- **Consumer Guide Automotive.** This page is devoted to reviews and reports on new and used cars and trucks.

  www.facebook.com/cgautomotive

- **Consumer Reports.** This is the Facebook home of the famous product testing magazine (see Figure 6.14).

  www.facebook.com/ConsumerReports

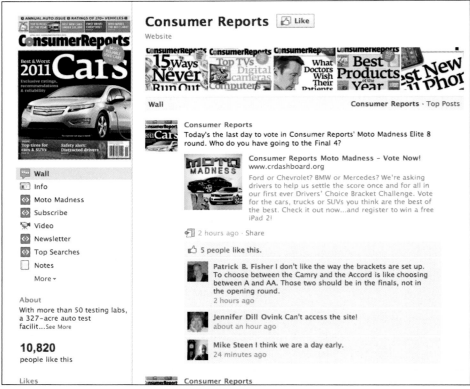

6.14 The Facebook page for *Consumer Reports* magazine.

- **eBay.** This page lets you know about what's happening on eBay, the famous online auction site.

  www.facebook.com/eBay

- **Edmunds.com**. This is the Facebook page for Edmunds.com, which provides automotive pricing guides and other consumer information on cars and trucks.

  www.facebook.com/Edmunds

- **Epinions.com.** This page offers reviews and evaluations of consumer products.

   www.facebook.com/Epinions

- **PriceGrabber.com.** This page offers links to items on PriceGrabber. com, the popular shopping portal that gives you price comparisons, user reviews, seller ratings, and more.

   www.facebook.com/PriceGrabber

- **Shopping.com.** This is the Facebook home of Shopping.com, an online source for comparative shopping and product reviews.

   www.facebook.com/shopping.com

- **Yahoo! Shopping.** This page has links to the Shopping section of Yahoo!, which gives you price comparisons, product specifications, user ratings, and more.

   www.facebook.com/yahooshopping

Saving money: freebies, bargains, coupons, and more

Is there anyone who doesn't love getting a good deal? Whether you get a thrill out of finding a bargain, are an avid coupon user, or just prefer to live frugally, Facebook has tons of practical resources that can help you save money on just about anything.

A good way to start is to become a fan of a company's, product's, or brand's page. This will give you the inside scoop on that entity. Once you're a fan of a page, you may also receive special offers — such as discounts, free gifts, or coupons — not available to nonfans. You may also be tapped for more marketing. For example, the Starbucks page (www.facebook.com/Starbucks) currently includes a Starbucks Card app (see Figure 6.15) that lets you reload a friend's Starbucks reward card, and even manage your own card, all within Facebook.

Liking company or product Pages is also a good idea if you're in the market for a major purchase, such as a computer or appliance. Not only will you hear about special offers, but you may receive coupons and information about various products that will help you narrow your product search.

You should also search for a Page or Group related to your local neighborhood. Such Groups or Pages often share news of local bargains, plus local businesses may announce sales, discounts, or specials offers. It's also a good idea to search Facebook Events for workshops on saving money in your area.

6.15 Use the Starbucks Card app to reload a friend's card and manage your own card.

You should also check whether your geographic area has a Facebook resource of free things to do, like the Page Free Things to Do in Chicago (www.facebook.com/FreeThingstoDoinChicago), or the Group Free and Cheap Cool Things to Do in Kansas City (www.facebook.com/group.php?gid=78155506788).

Of course, you could also start your own Page related to bargains in your neighborhood. A good model to follow is the Page created by the writer Faye Penn. It's called Brokelyn (www.facebook.com/pages/Brokelyn/99105377269), and it deals with "living big on small change in Brooklyn, NY" (see Figure 6.16).

Facebook is also home to a rather astounding number of resources devoted to finding deals and living frugally. Here's a sampling:

- **BradsDeals.com.** This is the Facebook home of BradsDeals, which tells you about great deals, coupons, and more.

  www.facebook.com/bradsdeals

- **Coupons for Fans.** You can use this application to create your own coupons for use on your own Facebook Pages.

  www.facebook.com/apps/application.php?id=224396475227

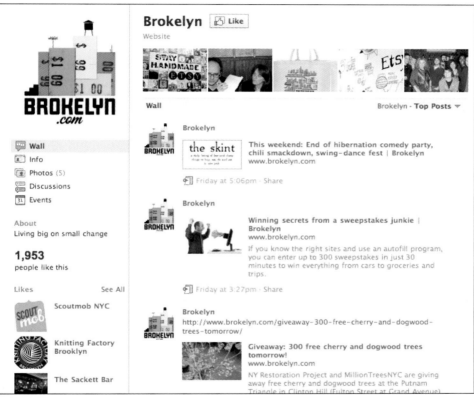

6.16 Writer Faye Penn's Brokelyn page is a great example of a page dedicated to living cheaply in a particular neighborhood.

- **Coupon Mom.** Famous snip and clip mom Stephanie Nelson's Facebook Page continues to dish out the same advice she gives on her Web site, *Oprah*, and *The Today Show*.

  www.facebook.com/couponmom

- **Coupon Shack.** Coupons and money-saving advice from this popular Web site are now on Facebook.

  www.facebook.com/couponshack

- **Deal Seeking Mom.** She's a mom and she's seeking deals by sharing information on coupons, giveaways, and various other money-saving tips.

  www.facebook.com/DealSeekingMom

- **Frugal Dad.** This Page offers lots of practical advice on how to achieve financial independence through frugal living.

  www.facebook.com/frugaldad

- **The Frugal Girls.** This Facebook Page offers tons of useful advice on saving money by using coupons, looking for freebies, and cooking with thrifty recipes.

  www.facebook.com/thefrugalgirls

- **Gilt Groupe.** You can follow this popular invitation-only (membership free) Web site on Facebook. The site offers luxury women's, men's and children's fashion at 70 percent off.

  www.facebook.com/GiltGroupe

- **GoRecommend.** This handy application lets you leverage your friends. By recommending your favorite places to your friends you can forward them coupons and other offers. In return, you may even win $1,000 in a daily draw.

  www.facebook.com/gorecommend

- **Grocery Coupon Network.** Created by coupon lovers for coupon lovers, this is the official Facebook Page of the popular Web site that dispenses oodles of coupons and other money-saving tips.

  www.facebook.com/pages/Grocery-Coupon-Network/187379439313

- **Groupon.** This is the Facebook home of the famous group coupon service that has become so popular. Like the Groupon Page to get access to Facebook-exclusive deals, contests, and giveaways.

  www.facebook.com/groupon

- **Money Saving Mom.** This is the official Facebook page for the popular Web site Money Saving Mom, which lists plenty of deals for kids' stuff and coupons that grandparents may be interested in.

  www.facebook.com/MoneySavingMom

- **Penny Drop.** This application is a game that allows users to bid on discounted products.

  www.facebook.com/apps/application.php ?id=230486256138

- **RetailMeNot.** This popular Web site that aggregates national coupons has an active Facebook Page.

  www.facebook.com/RetailMeNot

- **Wise Bread.** This Page shows you how to "live large on a small budget."

  www.facebook.com/pages/Wise-Bread/26830741467

Tracking your personal finances

Given the current state of the economy, keeping your financial affairs in order has never been more important. Fortunately, Facebook can help. First, Facebook is completely free (and always will be), so it adds no further strain to your budget. Second, Facebook connects you to a wealth of useful and practical financial information, tips, and advice.

If you're just getting started with personal finance, the concepts and terms might be unfamiliar to you. To help out, Facebook offers a wide selection of finance-related Community Pages. Here are the main ones to check out:

- **Bond.** www.facebook.com/pages/Bond/106642839375957
- **Finance.** www.facebook.com/pages/Finance/107870585903083
- **Interest.** www.facebook.com/pages/Interest/113191845361739
- **Investing.** www.facebook.com/pages/Investing/108691492495284
- **Loan.** www.facebook.com/pages/Loan/104028499633525
- **Money.** www.facebook.com/pages/Money/112422112103820
- **Money Market.** www.facebook.com/pages/Money-market/103128886393984
- **Mortgage.** www.facebook.com/pages/Mortgage/113390172007818
- **Mutual Funds.** www.facebook.com/pages/Mutual-funds/108080909225884
- **Personal Budget.** www.facebook.com/pages/Personal-budget/110371768984143
- **Personal Finance.** www.facebook.com/pages/Personal-finance/110115959011619
- **Real Estate.** www.facebook.com/pages/Real-estate/105771509455243

- **Stock Market.** www.facebook.com/pages/Stock-market/
  107726235917388
- **Stocks.** www.facebook.com/pages/Stocks/108248902529362

If you're looking for practical advice and tips, you've come to the right place. Facebook is home to dozens of resources that offer smart, useful, and timely advice on loans, mortgages, investing, and much more. Here's a sampling:

- **CBS MoneyWatch.** This is the Facebook home of the popular personal finance Web site (www.moneywatch.com).

  www.facebook.com/CBSMoneyWatch

- **David Bach.** This is the Facebook Page for personal finance guru David Bach.

  www.facebook.com/DavidBach

- **Get Rich Slowly.** This Page is based on the popular Get Rich Slowly blog, and it offers tips and techniques for "sensible personal finance."

  www.facebook.com/GetRichSlowly

- **Kiplinger's Personal Finance magazine.** This Page (see Figure 6.17) is the Facebook face of the magazine *Kiplinger's Personal Finance*, and it offers personal finance tips, links to personal finance articles, and more.

  www.facebook.com/pages/Kiplingers-Personal-Finance-magazine/
  65904782836

- **LearnVest.** This Page offers financial tips, checklists, and other advice for personal finance.

  www.facebook.com/learnvest

- **MainStreet.** This is a personal finance Page created by the same people who bring you TheStreet (shown later in this list).

  www.facebook.com/pages/MainStreet/59696903893

- **Mint.com.** This is the Facebook home of the popular Mint.com Web site, which enables you to manage your money online.

  www.facebook.com/mint

- **Money College.** This Page focuses on saving money while in college, so you might find it useful if you have kids or grandkids in school.

  www.facebook.com/MoneyCollege

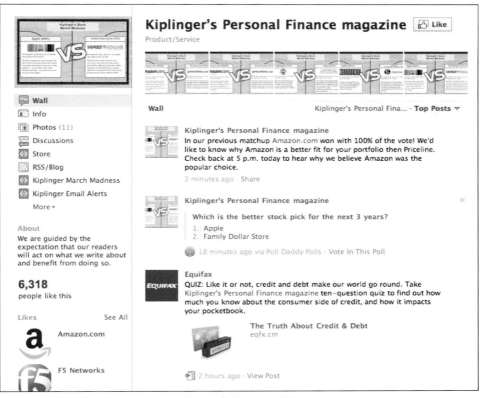

6.17 The Facebook page for *Kiplinger's Personal Finance* magazine.

- **Money Girl.** This Page offers lots of practical financial advice.

  www.facebook.com/MoneyGirlQDT

- **Money-Rates.com.** This Page specializes in interest rates and banking.

  www.facebook.com/MoneyRatesdotcom

- **The Motley Fool.** This is the Facebook home of the popular Motley Fool financial advice Web site.

  www.facebook.com/themotleyfool

- **Rob Carrick — Personal Finance.** This Page is maintained by the *Globe and Mail*'s popular personal finance columnist, so it's mostly suited for Canadians.

  www.facebook.com/robcarrickfinance

- **SmartMoney.** This is the Facebook home of *SmartMoney* magazine, which specializes in personal finance and investing.

  www.facebook.com/SmartMoney

- **TheStreet.com.** This Page is maintained by TheStreet, a popular investment advice company.

  www.facebook.com/TheStreet

- **WalletPop.com.** This is the Facebook Page for WalletPop.com, a popular personal finance Web site.

  www.facebook.com/walletpop

Learning about taxes

If you're looking for information about taxes, tax policy, and tax codes, Facebook offers a few useful resources, particularly if you looking for info on U.S. taxes. First, here are some Community Pages to check out:

- **Income Tax.** www.facebook.com/pages/Income-tax/109370642415053

- **Taxes.** www.facebook.com/pages/Taxes/115185091827016

- **Internal Revenue Service.** www.facebook.com/pages/Internal-Revenue-Service/107968832558644

Other tax-related resources on Facebook are dominated by people and organizations who want lower taxes or who are against taxes altogether. Most of these are rabidly partisan, but here are some nonprofits that take a more cool-headed approach to the subject:

- **Americans for Tax Reform.** This organization "opposes all tax increases as a matter of principle."

  www.facebook.com/americansfortaxreform

- **National Taxpayers Union.** This organization is devoted to lower taxes and smaller government.

  www.facebook.com/NationalTaxpayersUnion

- **Tax Foundation.** This nonprofit organization focuses on information about tax policy in the U.S.

  www.facebook.com/taxfoundation

Facebook and Retirement

If you're retired, you can use Facebook to find other retirees and to learn more about getting the most out of your post-work phase. If you're planning on retiring in the not-too-distant future, Facebook can connect you with resources that help you prepare, both mentally and financially. And of course, your Facebook friends can help usher you through this major life change.

Some good places to start are the Facebook Community Pages devoted to some basic retirement finance topics:

- **Annuity.** www.facebook.com/pages/Life-annuity/106869786019157
- **Pension.** www.facebook.com/pages/Pensions/114696798542721
- **Retirement.** www.facebook.com/pages/Retirement/104024849634960
- **Social Security.** www.facebook.com/pages/Social-security/ 104160556287381

You'll also find several resources devoted to retirement planning:

- **National Alliance for a Better Retirement.** This nonprofit advocacy Group offers information to help people achieve a financially secure retirement.

  www.facebook.com/pages/National-Alliance-for-a-Better-Retirement/ 115001806635

- **National Institute on Retirement Security.** This nonprofit organization focuses on educating people and companies about the role of pensions in the economy.

  www.facebook.com/pages/National-Institute-on-Retirement-Security/ 124385032312

- **Putnam Investments.** The Facebook Page for this investment firm contains lots of useful links to articles and blog posts related to retirement planning.

  www.facebook.com/PutnamInvestments

- **TIAA-CREF.** This Page for the Teachers Insurance and Annuity Association, College Retirement Equities Fund includes an application called the Nest Egg Challenge (see Figure 6.18), which enables you to challenge your friends in areas such as increasing your savings or reducing your bills.

  www.facebook.com/tiaa-cref

6.18 The TIAA-CREF Nest Egg Challenge application helps you save for retirement by challenging your friends.

A great way to spend at least part of your retirement is using Facebook to make new friends, and a great way to do that is to search Facebook for your peers. In addition to using Facebook's built-in tools to locate your friends, as discussed in previous chapters, you can try searching for Pages or Groups related to any professional associations you may have belonged to (or are still a member of, for that matter). For example, if you're a retired teacher in Missouri, you can join the Missouri Retired Teachers Association on Facebook at www.facebook.com/pages/Missouri-Retired-Teachers-Association/ 106169873024.

As another example, if you do a search for "retired police officers on Facebook," you'll see things can get pretty specific. How about the Retired Westen (sic) New York Law Enforcement Officers in Florida Page? (See www.facebook. com/pages/Retired-Westen-New-York-Law-Enforcement-Officers-in-Florida/ 204098032563.)

Quote, Unquote: Facebook and Retirement

"Would like to thank all my special friends for helping me enjoy my retirement. Love you all." — L. N., Newbury, England

Similarly, you can also search for Pages or Groups devoted to people who used to work at your company. For example, there's the Hewlett Packard Alumni Group at www.facebook.com/group.php?gid=2450210642. Another example is the Group called Manhattan (Kansas, that is) Fire Department Retirees; see www.facebook.com/pages/Manhattan-Fire-Department-Retirees/ 59833898285.

Also, here's a selection of useful resources on Facebook related to retirement:

- **AARP.** This is the Facebook home of the Association for the Advancement of Retired People (AARP), a nonprofit organization devoted to people aged 50 and up (see Figure 6.19).

  www.facebook.com/AARP

 TIP Besides the national organization Page, AARP also maintains state-level Pages, such as AARP Montana (www.facebook.com/ AARPMontana) and AARP California (www.facebook.com/ aarpcalifornia).

- **AARP Advocates.** This Page is devoted to the lobbying arm of AARP.

  www.facebook.com/AARPadvocates

- **AARP Bulletin Today.** This Page offers a daily news bulletin from AARP that covers "health and health policy, Medicare, Social Security, consumer protection, personal finance, livable communities, and AARP state and national news."

  www.facebook.com/aarpbulletintoday

- **AARP the Magazine.** This Page offers links to articles from *AARP the Magazine*, which is AARP's monthly magazine.

  www.facebook.com/aarpmag

Quote, Unquote: Facebook and Retirement

"Too old for MySpace. Too young for a retirement home. Here I am on Facebook!" — K. C., Pensacola, Florida

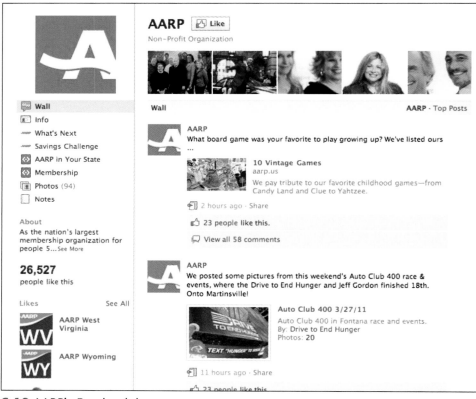

6.19 AARP's Facebook home.

- **The American Association of Retirement Communities.** This non-profit association focuses on showing communities how to attract retirees.

  www.facebook.com/pages/The-American-Association-of-Retirement-Communities/130492160448

- **Baby Boomers Rock.** If you were born between the years 1946 and 1964, check out this page to share and interact with other baby boomers.

  www.facebook.com/boomerbabies

- **RLTV (Retirement Living TV).** This is the Facebook home of Retirement Living TV, a cable network that offers programs aimed at people who are 50 and older.

  www.facebook.com/pages/RLTV-Retirement-Living-TV/87635644059

- **Social Security Administration.** This government page offers information about U.S. Social Security, brought to you by the Social Security Administration.

  www.facebook.com/socialsecurity

Wall | Info | Photos | Notes

Fitness and Health

According to most experts on aging, the four keys to a healthy and vibrant second half of life are having lots of social connections, keeping your mind active, eating well, and exercising regularly. How does Facebook fit into all this? It can certainly help maintain and strengthen your social ties, but it's also mentally stimulating, has lots of great info on nutrition (as you see in Chapter 10), and can help motivate you to exercise more regularly (for example, by seeing pictures of how great your friends look). If you do end up with health problems (as most of us will), Facebook can also help by offering lots of useful information on medical conditions, access to support groups, and more.

Facebook and Fitness

When you're over 50, maintaining or improving your fitness — particularly your flexibility, strength, balance, and cardiovascular health — is crucial. Good overall fitness gives you more energy, a sharper mind, more stamina, and more independence (because you have the strength and agility to do more things on your own), and has been shown in study after study to reduce the risk of many diseases and to prolong life.

If you're just getting started, the second thing you should do is check out Facebook's Community Pages on exercise and the various activities you can perform to get in shape. (The *first* thing you should do is see your doctor and get a thorough physical.)

NOTE There are many Facebook addresses in this section. All of them are case sensitive, and some of them quite long. Rather than typing the addresses by hand, see the Facebook page for this series: www.facebook.com/FBGseries. Alternatively, you can type a page's name in Facebook's Search box to locate it. Please note that Facebook does not endorse the sites listed in this book.

- **Fitness.** www.facebook.com/pages/Fitness/107760395922439
- **Exercise.** www.facebook.com/pages/Exercise/108612699169124
- **Aerobic exercise.** www.facebook.com/pages/Aerobic-exercise/ 109562195729781
- **Cycling.** www.facebook.com/pages/Cycling/114031331940797
- **Pilates.** www.facebook.com/pages/Pilates/112101572139886
- **Running.** www.facebook.com/pages/Running/109368782422374
- **Speed walking.** www.facebook.com/pages/Speed-walking/10650791 9385078
- **Strength training.** www.facebook.com/pages/Strength-training/ 112037055478468
- **Stretching.** www.facebook.com/pages/Stretching/108015655894153
- **Swimming.** www.facebook.com/pages/Swimming/105788652787522
- **Triathlon.** www.facebook.com/pages/Triathlon/108027592558903
- **Walking.** www.facebook.com/pages/Walking/108364105854575

- **Weight training.** www.facebook.com/pages/Weight-training/ 103280426370878
- **Yoga.** www.facebook.com/pages/Yoga/111987425484572

Next up, I highly recommend the Facebook Page for the American Senior Fitness Association (www.facebook.com/SeniorFitness; see Figure 7.1), which offers tons of fitness advice as well as fitness programs for would-be instructors.

7.1 The Facebook Page for the American Senior Fitness Association has lots of good info geared to older exercisers.

Another good general fitness Page is Active.com (www.facebook.com/ Activecom), which offers advice, tips, and training plans for a wide variety of activities.

Fitness magazines are prominent on Facebook, and some of the better Pages to check out are the following:

- *Fitness.* www.facebook.com/fitnessmag

- ⚙ *Max Sports & Fitness.* www.facebook.com/pages/
  Max-Sports-Fitness-Magazine/229547965050
- ⚙ *Men's Fitness.* www.facebook.com/MensFitnessMagazine
- ⚙ *Muscle & Fitness.* www.facebook.com/pages/Muscle-Fitness-magazine/
  115322465646
- ⚙ *Natural Muscle.* www.facebook.com/naturalmusclemag
- ⚙ *Oxygen.* www.facebook.com/pages/Oxygen-Magazine/77249939369
- ⚙ *Shape.* www.facebook.com/SHAPEmagazine
- ⚙ *Women's Fitness.* www.facebook.com/pages/
  Womens-Fitness-magazine/39580498392

If you're already a member of a gym, use the Facebook Search feature to see whether you can find a Page or other resource for your club. There are lots of gyms on Facebook — including Gold's Gym, as shown in Figure 7.2 (see www. facebook.com/goldsgym) — so there's a good chance yours will be, too. This is a great way to stay up to date on new classes and happenings at the gym, plus connect with other members.

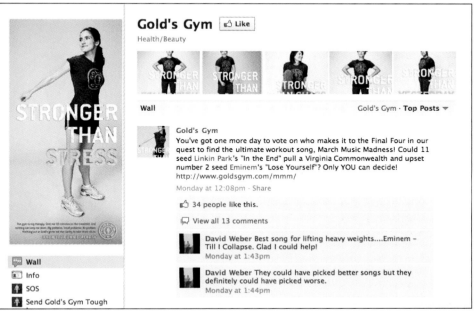

7.2 There are many gyms on Facebook, including the world-famous Gold's Gym.

Many celebrity trainers maintain strong presences on Facebook, including Jillian Michaels, the famous trainer from the reality show *The Biggest Loser* (www.facebook.com/jillianmichaels). If there's a celebrity trainer you follow, use Facebook search to see whether he or she has a Facebook Page.

Finally, Facebook is also home to lots of great fitness-related applications. You can do an application search for programs in your area of interest, but here are a few to give you an idea of what's available:

- **Cardio Trainer.** This application enables you to track your workouts using GPS on your Android smartphone.

  www.facebook.com/cardiotrainer

- **Fit-ify! Exercise Tracker.** You can use this application to track your fitness goals.

  www.facebook.com/apps/application.php?id=8209307103

- **Map My Run.** You use this application to map your run, share that run, and have others comment on the route. And it's not just for runners; cyclists and walkers can use it, too.

  www.facebook.com/mapmyrun

- **My Countdown.** This application enables you to set goals and share them with the world, which therefore gives you some motivation to reach those goals.

  www.facebook.com/mycountdowns

Facebook for Runners

Running is one of the most popular (and one of the most healthy) fitness activities, particularly with so-called *masters* runners aged 40 and up. Facebook has a thriving running community, with many Pages, Groups, Events, and applications devoted to running, training, racing, and connecting with other runners.

For example, many running clubs have a home on Facebook, including the New York Road Runners (www.facebook.com/NewYorkRoadRunners; see

Figure 7.3) and the Hash House Harriers (www.facebook.com/hashing). When searching for running clubs, you can speed things up considerably by choosing the Sports & Recreation category, and then the Fitness & Exercise subcategory.

Note, too, that many races have their own Pages, including the ING New York City Marathon (www.facebook.com/ingnycm) and the Bay to Breakers 12K (www.facebook.com/baytobreakers), so use the Facebook search feature to look for Pages associated with any race you want to run or are already registered to run. Not surprisingly, many races are also set up as Events. However, be sure to look for official Events created by the race organizers, and not unofficial Events created by Groups or organizations whose members are planning to attend the race.

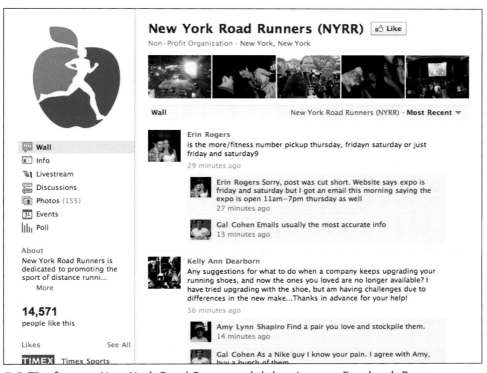

7.3 The famous New York Road Runners club has its own Facebook Page.

If you're looking for running advice, training tips, nutrition info, gear reviews, or running-related stories, running magazines are your best bet, and the major publications all have homes on Facebook. These include the following:

- **Canadian Running.** www.facebook.com/CanadianRunningMagazine

- **Runner's World.** www.facebook.com/runnersworldmagazine; see Figure 7.4

- **Running Times.** www.facebook.com/pages/Running-Times-Magazine/ 23403427089

- **Track & Field News.** www.facebook.com/pages/Track-Field-News/ 84526083332

- **Trail Runner.** www.facebook.com/pages/Trail-Runner-magazine/ 52704825212

- **Women's Running.** www.facebook.com/womensrunning

7.4 The Facebook Page for *Runner's World* magazine.

If you want to commune with your fellow runners and get more tips and advice, there are many other resources on Facebook for you. Here's a sampling:

- **Cool Running.** This Page offers tons of great running advice for training, race strategies, equipment, and more.

  www.facebook.com/pages/CoolRunning/89260269536

- **Couch-to-5K Running Plan.** This Page (brought to you by the Cool Running people; see previous entry) offers a training plan that gets beginners running 5 kilometers (about 3 miles) in just two months.

  www.facebook.com/C25Kplan

- **i am runner.** This useful Page offers tons of tips and advice for runners of all levels.

  www.facebook.com/iamrunner

- **LogYourRun.** You can use this application to share your running routes and workout times from LogYourRun.com with your Facebook friends.

  www.facebook.com/pages/LogYourRun/6387221403

- **National Running Day.** This is mostly about National Running Day, but also offers general tips and advice on running.

  www.facebook.com/runningday

- **Running.** This is a general running Page for anyone who loves to run, and it offers a busy Wall section, lively discussions, and an application that enables you to share your favorite running routes.

  www.facebook.com/pages/Running/93961945054

TIP   The Running Page application that enables you to share running routes with your friends is called Social Running Map, and you can find it directly by navigating to www.facebook.com/running.map.

- **The Running Trail.** This popular Page is devoted to trail running.

  www.facebook.com/RunningTrail

- **Ultra Running.** This Page focuses on ultramarathons and similar tests of super-endurance.

  www.facebook.com/pages/Ultra-Running/92624365889

Finally, most runners are fanatical about their shoes, and that often means being fanatical about a particular shoe *company*. If you fall into that category, you might want to become a fan of that company to keep up with the latest news. Here are the Facebook Pages of some of the major running shoe manufacturers:

- **adidas.** www.facebook.com/adidas.running
- **Asics.** www.facebook.com/pages/ASICS/175882623116
- **Brooks.** www.facebook.com/brooksrunning
- **Montrail.** www.facebook.com/Montrail
- **New Balance.** www.facebook.com/Newbalance
- **Nike.** www.facebook.com/nikerunning
- **Puma.** www.facebook.com/PUMARunning
- **Reebok (men).** www.facebook.com/reebokmen
- **Reebok (women).** www.facebook.com/reebokwomen
- **Salomon.** www.facebook.com/salomonrunning
- **Saucony.** www.facebook.com/Saucony

Weight Loss and Facebook

If you're looking to lose some weight, there are resources on Facebook that can help you get there, not only by offering lots of useful resources, but also by helping you motivate yourself. For example, a popular way of using Facebook for weight loss is to use status updates to harness your family and friends for support. The idea is that you post your current weight or your target weight, as well as your efforts to meet your goal, and everyone cheers you on.

Quote, Unquote: Facebook and Weight Loss

"I had an idea in March to simply post my weight as sort of a string on my finger to keep me on a diet. I posted '359' the first day and a friend put a '?'. I told her what I was doing and she became the first of my many cheerleaders. Long story short, with the support of my FB family I am 301." — N. T., Middletown, Rhode Island

Next up are the Community Pages related to weight loss, dieting, and eating healthfully:

- **Calorie Restriction.** www.facebook.com/pages/Calorie-restriction/ 105651952802818

- **Cooking Healthy.** www.facebook.com/pages/Cooking-Healthy/ 376201741739

- **Dieting.** www.facebook.com/pages/Dieting/108090125879204

- **Eating Healthy.** www.facebook.com/pages/Eating-Healthy/ 10150150119710580

- **Low-Carbohydrate Diet.** www.facebook.com/pages/ Low-carbohydrate-diet/105590539474668

- **Low-Fat Diet.** www.facebook.com/pages/Low-fat-diet/ 110932485603035

- **Weight Loss.** www.facebook.com/pages/Weight-loss/109525879073785

TIP Do you have a collection of friends or family members who are also trying to lose weight? Why not start a Facebook support group where you can share inspiration and tips?

If you're following a particular weight-loss program, look for it on Facebook where you'll likely find extra health tips and a community of like-minded fat fighters. For example, Facebook is home to the Weight Watchers program (www.facebook.com/weightwatchers; see Figure 7.5) as well as Jenny Craig (www.facebook.com/jennycraig).

Another good idea is to search Facebook Events for weight-loss Events in your area. Search the Events category using terms such as *weight loss*, *diet*, and *healthy cooking*.

CAUTION Facebook does have lots of useful and practical information on weight loss and healthy eating. However, despite the site's best efforts to remove pages and applications that do not comply with its terms of use, Facebook is also home to various fly-by-night operators who'll try to sell you unproven or even bogus information, programs, pills, or supplements. So when you're searching for weight-loss info on Facebook, bear in mind that if it sounds too good to be true, it almost certainly is.

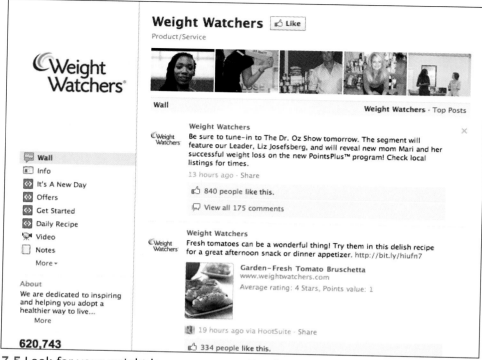

7.5 Look for your weight-loss program on Facebook, such as the Weight Watchers Page.

Here's a list of some Pages and applications that you might find useful:

- **Hungry Girl.** This is the Facebook home (see Figure 7.6) for the popular Web site Hungrygirl.com. The site is run by Lisa Lillien, a successful weight-loss story herself, who started Hungrygirl.com to share inspiration, recipes, and tips with others.

  www.facebook.com/HungryGirl

- **Never Say Diet.com.** This Page focuses on helping women make changes to reach their ideal size.

  www.facebook.com/pages/NeverSayDietcom/67807840906

- **My Diet.** This application has a food diary and various other fat tackling applications, and it also keeps track of your progress in relation to your friends.

  www.facebook.com/fatsecret

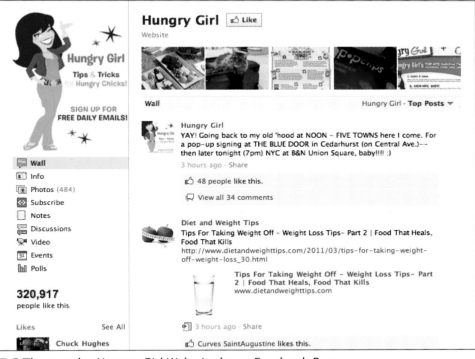

7.6 The popular Hungry Girl Web site has a Facebook Page.

Learning about Medical Conditions

If you suffer from a medical condition, there are resources on Facebook that can help you get through it. Not only can you use Facebook to keep your family and closest friends apprised of your condition, you can also join Facebook support groups (see the next section for more on this). Facebook also plays host to several excellent resources for researching medical conditions.

Some good general references Pages to get you started are the following:

- **Centers for Disease Control and Prevention.** www.facebook.com/ CDC

- **Mayo Clinic.** www.facebook.com/MayoClinic; see Figure 7.7

- **National Institute for Mental Health.** www.facebook.com/nimhgov

- **Public Health Agency of Canada.** www.facebook.com/pages/
  Public-Health-Agency-of-Canada/10860597051
- **Veterans Health Administration.** www.facebook.com/
  VeteransHealth

7.7 The Facebook Page for the famous Mayo Clinic.

Although the U.S. Department of Health and Human Services doesn't have a Facebook presence as I write this (although you can check www.hhs.gov/open/getinvolved/facebook.html for a list of HHS-related Pages on Facebook), many state health departments are on Facebook, including the Michigan Department of Community Health (www.facebook.com/pages/Michigan-Department-of-Community-Health-MDCH/51057276745) and the Alaska Department of Health and Social Services (www.facebook.com/Alaska-Department-of-Health-and-Social-Services/99962144928).

Your community public health service may also be on Facebook. Examples include Carson City (Nevada) Health and Human Services (www.facebook.com/CCHHS) and the City of Hartford (Connecticut) Department of Health and Human Services (www.facebook.com/HartfordHealth).

You see in this section that Facebook has a great deal of useful and objective information on medical conditions. Unfortunately, Facebook also has a great deal of snake-oil salesmen who'll try to sell you bogus information or untested cures. If you're using Facebook to search for information about a particular condition or disease, don't believe everything you see, and don't share too much information with strangers.

If you have a condition that has a foundation, there's a very good chance that the foundation has a Facebook Page or Group. On these Pages, you'll find plenty of information and plenty of stories from people coping with the same ailment. Here are some examples:

- **Alzheimer's Association.** www.facebook.com/actionalz
- **American Cancer Society.** www.facebook.com/AmericanCancerSociety
- **American Diabetes Association.** www.facebook.com/AmericanDiabetesAssociation
- **American Lung Association.** www.facebook.com/lungusa
- **Arthritis Foundation.** www.facebook.com/Arthritis.org
- **Canadian Cancer Society.** www.facebook.com/CanadianCancerSociety
- **Canadian Diabetes Association.** www.facebook.com/pages/Canadian-Diabetes-Association/103776256327151
- **Heart & Stroke Foundation of Canada.** www.facebook.com/heartandstroke
- **National Rheumatoid Arthritis Society.** www.facebook.com/nationalrheumatoidarthritissociety
- **National Stroke Association.** www.facebook.com/NationalStrokeAssociation

There might be an advocacy Group that is working on research on your condition that you want to follow. Two examples are the Michael J. Fox Foundation for Parkinson's Research (www.facebook.com/michaeljfoxfoundation; see Figure 7.8) and the Christopher and Dana Reeve Foundation (www.facebook.com/ReeveFoundation).

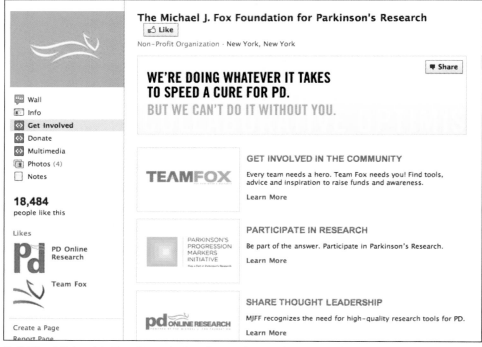

7.8 The Michael J. Fox Foundation for Parkinson's Research is on Facebook.

Note, too, that even if you have a rare condition, a search may reveal a Page or Group that focuses on that same condition. For example, a search on *albinism* reveals the National Organization for Albinism and Hypopigmentation (www.facebook.com/pages/National-Organization-for-Albinism-and-Hypopigmentation/133455076055), the Albinism Page (www.facebook.com/Albinism), and a Page called Under the Same Sun (www.facebook.com/pages/Under-the-Same-Sun/26902533275), which is a nonprofit founded to advocate for human rights for people with albinism in Tanzania, where those afflicted with the genetic disorder are often the targets of violence and discrimination.

If you have a particular disease, illness, or health problem, do a search on "living with *condition*" (where *condition* is the name of the medical condition). For example, a search on "living with diabetes" reveals Pages for local organizations, such as the greater Cincinnati Families Living with Diabetes Page (www.facebook.com/pages/Families-Living-with-Diabetes/199538933635). You can also search for your condition and your local area. For example, a search on "Cancer New York" reveals a couple of Pages and a Group:

- **National Cervical Cancer Coalition – NCCC – New York Chapter.** www.facebook.com/pages/National-Cervical-Cancer-Coalition-NCCCNew-York-Chapter/125881538617

- **American Cancer Society DetermiNation – New York and New Jersey.** www.facebook.com/pages/American-Cancer-Society-DetermiNation-New-York-and-New-Jersey/112548008775688

- **Running for Cancer in New York.** www.facebook.com/group.php?gid=2375098253

You can also do an Event search to find local fundraising or support group meetings. For active organizations with national networks (such as multiple sclerosis), a search can return dozens of Events in large and small communities across the continent. Even conditions that don't have large networks still run Events.

For example, a recent search on *mood disorders* returned the Mood Disorder Association of Manitoba's 3rd annual Rock 'n Roll Marathon, as well as a free Event titled "Music and Mood Disorders: Tchaikovsky," in San Antonio, Texas. For smaller locales, the results may vary, though they can change if someone lists an Event. For example, "Portland Cancer" currently returns one Page result, but the Events will change as the calendar does.

NOTE Unfortunately, Facebook isn't a great resource for information on medications. Yes, there are plenty of medication-related resources on the site, but most of them are marketing pitches for various nostrums and unproven supplements. And although many legitimate drug companies do maintain a presence on Facebook, most of their pages highlight the benefits of their products without prominently explaining the risks.

Locating Support Groups

Living with a disease, illness, or health problem can be traumatic, disorienting, and frightening. Surrounding yourself with friends and family can help, and many people find that Facebook's social connections are instrumental in helping them deal with a medical problem. However, living with a condition is also frequently a lonely experience, because no matter how much love and support you get from those close to you, they can never really understand what you're going through.

Perhaps the best way to combat the feelings of isolation that a disease creates is to seek out other people who understand or are living with the same condition. Facebook can really help here because it's home to all kinds of support groups for various conditions, and I introduce you to some of them in this section.

As you might imagine, most support groups are actually Facebook Groups, so the best way to locate a support group is to run a search on the name of your condition, and then restrict the search results to just Groups.

 Many of the support groups you find on Facebook are run by caring individuals who understand your disease, and the members are mostly people who have the disease now, or who've had it in the past (or know someone who has been through it). However, as with many other aspects of Facebook, some support groups exist only to disseminate controversial or unproven information, or to sell dubious products and programs. So before joining any Group, check out the Wall posts, Group info, and discussions, as well as any Web site associated with the Group.

Quote, Unquote: Facebook and Support Groups

"After being diagnosed with a brain disorder called Chiari Malformation in January 2007, Facebook has allowed me to connect to thousands of other 'Chiarians' to share stories and offer support for one another. When you are diagnosed with a disorder that has limited awareness, it is great to find others that share your experiences and allow you to not feel alone."
—J. S., Orland Park, Illinois

For example, a Group search on heart disease returns the following Groups (see Figure 7.9 for an example of a Group):

- **Womens Heart Disease.** www.facebook.com/group.php?gid=2452805792

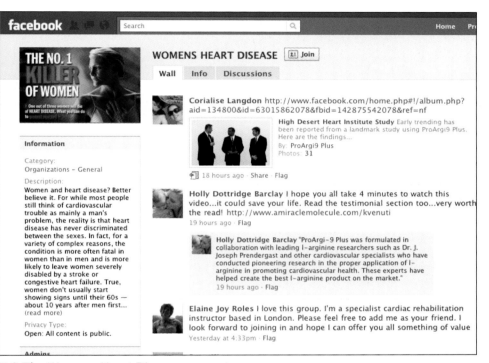

7.9 The Womens Heart Disease support group.

- **Fight Against Heart Disease <3.** www.facebook.com/group.php?gid=47584378996

- **Women Fighting Heart Disease.** www.facebook.com/group.php?gid=38876638364

- **WomenHeart The National Coalition for Women with Heart Disease.** www.facebook.com/group.php?gid=31347782363

- **Heart Disease.** www.facebook.com/group.php?gid=2242854526

Similarly, a Group search on strokes returns the following:

- **Brain Stem Support Group.** www.facebook.com/group. php?gid=22623750832
- **Stroke: Support Group for People Suffering from this Illness.** www.facebook.com/group.php?gid=14867705050
- **National Stroke Association.** www.facebook.com/group. php?gid=27244248463

Note, however, that many Facebook Pages also function as support Groups. For example, the top cancer support Groups on Facebook are a mixture of Groups and Pages (see Figure 7.10 for an example Page):

- **Lung Cancer Support Alliance.** www.facebook.com/group. php?gid=21715275735

7.10 The Facebook Page for the Prostate Cancer Foundation.

- **CancerCompass.** www.facebook.com/pages/Cancer-Compass/ 167555892394

- **The Skin Cancer Foundation.** www.facebook.com/ skincancerfoundation

- **Skin Cancer.** www.facebook.com/group.php?gid=83390463156

- **Supporting prostate cancer.** www.facebook.com/group. php?gid=19931699064

- **Prostate Cancer Foundation.** www.facebook.com/PCF.org

- **Colon Cancer Canada.** www.facebook.com/coloncancercda

- **Susan Cohan Kasdas Colon Cancer Foundation, Susie's Cause.** www.facebook.com/ColonCancerFoundation

- **Colon Cancer Alliance.** www.facebook.com/group. php?gid=29075372469

- **Abolish Colon Cancer.** www.facebook.com/group. php?gid=2212168476

Learning about Aging and Longevity

If you're interested in the aging process and in current research on antiaging medicines and longevity, Facebook is home to a few good resources that should satisfy your curiosity. You can start with the Community Pages, which offer lots of excellent content on these topics:

- **Aging.** www.facebook.com/pages/Aging/107926462574844

- **Gerontology.** www.facebook.com/pages/Gerontology/ 109320372428124

- **Geriatrics.** www.facebook.com/pages/Geriatrics/103818856324046

- **Life Extension.** www.facebook.com/pages/Life-extension/ 108351759189466

- **Longevity.** www.facebook.com/pages/Longevity/112452115433356

You can also take a look at the following Facebook resources:

- **The American Academy of Anti-Aging Medicine (A4M).** This Page focuses on current research into ways to retard the aging process.

  www.facebook.com/pages/The-American-Academy-of-Anti-Aging-Medicine-A4M/59538112786

- **The Art of Aging.** This Facebook Page was created by artist Sophie Lumen to encourage women to embrace the aging process (see Figure 7.11).

  www.facebook.com/pages/The-Art-of-Aging/123159131029916

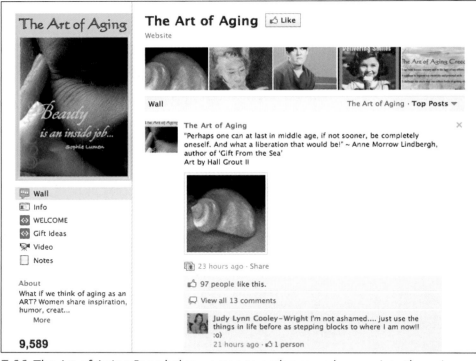

7.11 The Art of Aging Page helps women to embrace and appreciate the aging process.

- **California Health and Longevity Institute.** This Page offers lots of links to articles and blog posts on all aspects of healthier lifestyle choices to promote a longer life.

  www.facebook.com/pages/California-Health-Longevity-Institute/104049172923

- **The CR Way Longevity Center.** This is the Facebook Page for the CR Way program, which espouses a low-calorie lifestyle for longer life.

  www.facebook.com/pages/The-CR-Way-Longevity-Center/ 63382918141

- **Instant Health: The Shaolin Qigong Workout for Longevity.** This Page is dedicated to the Qigong workout program.

  www.facebook.com/pages/Instant-Health-The-Shaolin-Qigong-Workout-For-Longevity/173239604543

- **Longevity Conference.** This Page is dedicated to spreading the most recent information on living a longer life.

  www.facebook.com/longevityconference

- ***Longevity* Magazine.** This is the Facebook home of *Longevity*, a magazine dedicated to healthy living (see Figure 7.12).

  www.facebook.com/pages/Longevity-Magazine/10584341758

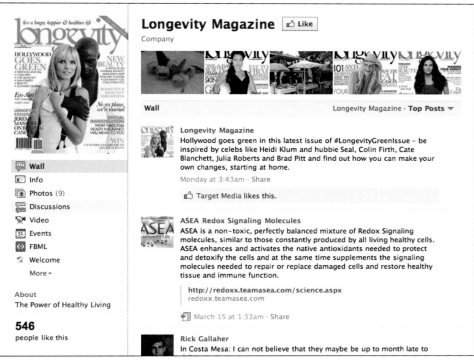

7.12 The Facebook Page for *Longevity* magazine.

● **Success in Aging.** This Page offers lots of tips and articles on successful aging and is maintained by Diane Alexander Patterson, who has a master's degree in gerontology and is the founder of the AgeWise Web site (www.agewise.tv/).

www.facebook.com/successinaging

Researching Doctors and Hospitals

If you need to research a doctor or hospital, there are a few Facebook resources that can help you get started. For example, the HealthGrades Page (www.facebook.com/HealthGrades; see Figure 7.13) is the Facebook home of the leading independent healthcare rating organization, which rates hospitals, doctors, nursing homes, and more.

7.13 The Facebook Page for the HealthGrades healthcare rating organization.

If you have a medical condition and know of a hospital that excels or specializes in treatment of that ailment, look for it on Facebook. For example, Sunnybrook Health Sciences Centre in Toronto specializes in a variety of areas, such as high-risk pregnancies, cardiovascular disease, neurological disorders, and orthopedic and arthritic conditions, among many others. Its Facebook Page (www.facebook.com/SunnybrookHSC; see Figure 7.14) offers plenty of current research, information on new equipment, treatment options, fundraising, and so on.

7.14 The Facebook home of the world-renowned Sunnybrook Health Sciences Centre.

To find the hospital you're looking for, you must be sure to search for the official name, not the hospital's common name. For example, it's Sunnybrook Health Sciences Centre not Sunnybrook Hospital.

Here's a list of some of the top hospitals in North America and their Facebook Pages:

- **Cleveland Clinic.** www.facebook.com/ClevelandClinic
- **Duke University Medical Center.** www.facebook.com/pages/ Duke-University-Medical-Center/46075864559?ref=search
- **Johns Hopkins.** www.facebook.com/Johns.Hopkins.Medicine
- **Massachusetts General.** www.facebook.com/massgeneral
- **Mayo Clinic.** www.facebook.com/MayoClinic
- **Memorial Sloan-Kettering Cancer Center.** www.facebook.com/ sloankettering.
- **Ronald Reagan UCLA Medical Center.** www.facebook.com/pages/ Ronald-Reagan-UCLA-Medical-Center/397785675088
- **Stanford Hospital.** www.facebook.com/StanfordHospital
- **Yale-New Haven Hospital.** www.facebook.com/ yalenewhavenhospital

Keeping Up with Medical News and Research

The fields of healthcare and medicine are in constant flux with new studies, new technologies, and new scientific findings. If you're curious about the latest news on health and medicine, there are lots of resources on Facebook to help you keep up.

For example, the famous cardiothoracic surgeon and author Dr. Mehmet Oz is a fount of health news, and he maintains a very popular Facebook Page (www. facebook.com/droz; see Figure 7.15).

Another terrific source of health news is the Medicues Health News Page (www. facebook.com/pages/Medicues-Health-News/113684101900; see Figure 7.16), which offers links to many health-related news articles on the medicues.com Web site.

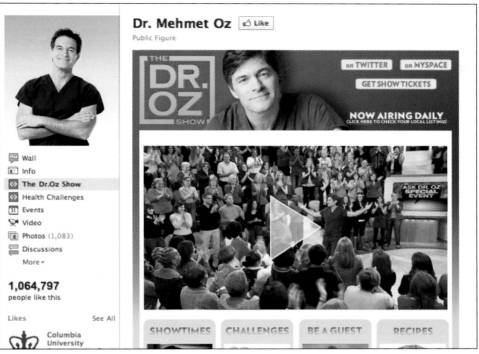

7.15 The Facebook Page for Dr. Mehmet Oz has lots of information on the latest health findings.

Here are a few other Facebook resources you can use to stay current on the state of health and medicine:

- **Breast Cancer Medical News with Dr. Tabor.** This Page focuses on the latest findings in breast cancer research.

  www.facebook.com/BreastCancerNews

- **Dr. Joseph Mercola.** This is the Facebook Page for the famous Mercola.com, the Web site founded by Dr. Joseph Mercola to disseminate the latest health news and research.

  www.facebook.com/doctor.health

- **Medical News Today.** This application enables users to receive up-to-date health science news.

  www.facebook.com/apps/application.php?id=38124346174

7.16 The Medicues Health News Page is chock full of links to articles on the latest health news and research.

- **NIH News in Health.** This Page is maintained by the National Institutes of Health (NIH) and focuses on the latest health and medical research conducted by NIH scientists.

  www.facebook.com/newsinhealth

- **Quality Health.** This Page offers links to articles related to health news.

  www.facebook.com/QualityHealth

If you already know quite a bit about health science and medicine, you can take your research up a notch by perusing these physician-focused Facebook resources:

- **American Academy of Family Physicians (AAFP).** This Page is the AAFP's Facebook base and it offers news and commentary on the latest health industry topics.

  www.facebook.com/familymed

- **American Medical Association (AMA).** This Page is home to the AMA, and it offers mostly links to policy articles, but it does offer news on the latest research.

  www.facebook.com/AmericanMedicalAssociation

- **American Medical News.** This is the Facebook Page for *American Medical News*, a newspaper for physicians.

  www.facebook.com/amednews

- **BeWell.com.** This Page is the Facebook home of the BeWell.com Web site, a social network that focuses on the latest health news and research.

  www.facebook.com/pages/BeWellcom/73373359264

- **Diabetes News Hound.** This Page offers news on the latest findings in diabetic research.

  www.facebook.com/pages/Diabetes-News-Hound/83262406093

- **The Doctor's Channel.** This Page contains links to videos covering the latest medical research.

  www.facebook.com/thedoctorschannel

- **MD Consult.** This Page has links to the latest medical research, albeit geared to physicians and other medical professionals.

  www.facebook.com/mdconsult

- **Medscape.** This busy Page offers many links to articles on the latest health and medical news.

  www.facebook.com/medscape

TIP Medscape also offers Pages related to specific medical disciplines, including Medscape Emergency Medicine (www.facebook.com/medscapeemergencymedicine), Medscape Neurology (www.facebook.com/medscapeneurology), Medscape Oncology (www.facebook.com/medscapeoncology), and Medscape Pediatrics (www.facebook.com/medscapepediatrics).

- **Physician's First Watch.** This busy Page is primarily aimed at physicians and it offers lots of links to the latest medical research.

  www.facebook.com/pages/Physicians-First-Watch/123553070098

Finally, you can see the cutting edge of medical research by checking out the various medical journals that have Facebook homes:

- *American Journal of Nursing.* www.facebook.com/AJNfans
- *Archives of Internal Medicine.* www.facebook.com/pages/Archives-of-Internal-Medicine/114116793520
- *Archives of Dermatology.* www.facebook.com/pages/Archives-of-Dermatology/117506346528
- *Archives of Neurology.* www.facebook.com/pages/Archives-of-Neurology/100679858757
- *Archives of Ophthalmology.* www.facebook.com/pages/Archives-of-Ophthalmology/100265333750
- *British Journal of Medical Practitioners.* www.facebook.com/BritishJournalofMedicalPractitioners
- *Clinical Geriatrics.* www.facebook.com/pages/Clinical-Geriatrics/177493570815
- *Emergency Medicine Journal.* www.facebook.com/EMJournal
- *Gastroenterology.* www.facebook.com/gastrojournal
- *Journal of the American Medical Association.* www.facebook.com/pages/JAMA-Journal-of-the-American-Medical-Association/87087958340
- *Journal of Cell Biology.* www.facebook.com/JCellBiol

- ***Journal of Medical Ethics.*** www.facebook.com/pages/ Journal-of-Medical-Ethics/46580332857
- ***The Lancet.*** www.facebook.com/TheLancetMedicalJournal
- ***New England Journal of Medicine.*** www.facebook.com/ TheNewEnglandJournalofMedicine
- ***Neurology.*** www.facebook.com/NeurologyJournal

8 chapter

Arts and Media

Most of the Facebook topics you've explored so far in the book have been topical (such as politics and the environment), practical (such as job hunting and personal finances), or good for you (such as fitness and weight loss). In this chapter, you take a break from these more serious and sober topics to focus on a few subjects that, while still fascinating and useful, lie more on the fun and entertainment side of the scale. I speak of the arts and media, and in this chapter you learn how to use your social connections to get more out of books, music, movies, theater, television, and the visual arts.

Getting More Out of Books

There has been much debate of late about whether the Internet in general, and social networking sites such as Facebook and Twitter in particular, are causing a general trend away from long-form reading. That is, are we gradually losing our ability to concentrate long enough to read a book, and is that ability being replaced by a need for rapid, short bursts of information, such as status updates and blog posts?

Lots of big thinkers believe this to be true, but the fact is that people still read books, lots of books. According to the Association of American Publishers (AAP), U.S. book publishers had total sales of $23.9 billion in 2009. Admittedly, that's a bit off from the $24.3 billion sold in 2008, but it still represents a huge market. Also, the AAP announced in July 2010 that year-to-date sales for 2010 were up a very healthy 11.6 percent from the same period in 2009, so there's lots of life left in the publishing industry.

That's good news for those of us who love books, and it helps explain why Facebook has a thriving community of readers, authors, and publishers. The easiest way to get in on the fun is to update your Facebook profile to include your favorite books. Click Profile, click Edit Profile, and then click Arts and Entertainment. In the Books text box, type the title of a favorite book. As you type, Facebook displays a list of books that match what you've typed, as shown in Figure 8.1. If you see the book you want to add, click it in the list. Repeat for your other favorite books, and then click Save Changes.

8.1 As you type a book title, Facebook displays a list of matching titles.

NOTE You can also use the Books text box to type the names of your favorite authors and the names of your favorite publishers.

In most cases, Facebook sets up the book in your Profile page as a link to the book's associated Community Page. Click the link to see the book's Wikipedia entry (if it has one) and to see what other Facebookers are saying about the book.

TIP Want to see who else among your friends likes your favorite book? Simply visit that book's Facebook Page. Any friends who also cite that book as a favorite will appear in the box on the upper right of the Page labeled You and *Name of Book*.

Most books are set up as Community Pages, but more and more publishers are seeing the wisdom of using a regular Facebook Page not only as marketing vehicles for a book, but also to connect with people who are fans of the book. These book Pages often have book excerpts; extra content such as notes, photos, and videos related to the book; lists of events such as book signings; and more. For example, Figure 8.2 shows the Facebook Page for the book *Facebook Marketing: An Hour a Day*.

NOTE In case you're wondering, yes, this series does have its own Facebook Page. To check it out, see www.facebook.com/ FBGseries.

Facebook is a social network, and the most social thing you can do with a book is join a book club, so it's no surprise that Facebook is loaded with online book clubs. Almost all of them have "book club" somewhere in the name, so searching on that phrase will lead to a bounty. If you're searching Groups, you can narrow things down by selecting Entertainment & Arts as the main category, and Books & Literature as the subcategory. Many book clubs also exist on Facebook as Pages, so be sure to search through Pages, as well. Here are a few Groups and Pages devoted to discussing books:

- **Book Club.** www.facebook.com/pages/Book-Club/193558430461
- **Chapter-a-Week Book Club.** www.facebook.com/pages/Chapter-a-Week-Book-Club/48456973308

8.2 Many books now come with their own Facebook Pages.

NOTE There are many Facebook addresses in this section. All of them are case sensitive, and some of them quite long. Rather than typing the addresses by hand, see the Facebook page for this series: www.facebook.com/FBGseries. Alternatively, you can type a page's name in Facebook's Search box to locate it. Please note that Facebook does not endorse the sites listed in this book.

- **Elite Literary Guild Book Club.** www.facebook.com/pages/Elite-Literary-Guild-Book-Club/209965084525

- **Princeton Book Review.** www.facebook.com/pages/Princeton-Book-Review/73532562757

- **Science Fiction Book Club.** www.facebook.com/ScienceFictionBookClub

- **Victorious Book Club.** www.facebook.com/pages/Victorious-Book-club/231089674406

- **Young Adult Book Club.** www.facebook.com/youngadultbookclub

TIP If you're a book person, chances are lots of your Facebook friends are too. Why not use Facebook to start a virtual book club with your fellow readers? The group could be a formal one, with strict protocols for choosing new selections on a regular basis, or simply a gathering place for friends to share news about what they're reading. Alternatively, if you participate in a book club offline, you could create a Facebook group for the members of that club to facilitate communication about book picks and the like. And of course, you can use Facebook Events to schedule any club-related activities!

If you're looking for book reviews, Facebook is the place to be. For starters, Facebook is home to many official book review publications, including the following:

- *New York Review of Books* (www.facebook.com/nybooks), which includes links to reviews and essays (see Figure 8.3)

- The *New York Review of Books*' companion Page called New York Review Books (www.facebook.com/NYRB.Classics), which focuses on book reviews from the NYRB and from around the Web.

- *The Nation* Books & Arts (www.facebook.com/pages/The-Nation-Books-Arts/272154794004), which has links to reviews in *The Nation.*

- *Times Literary Supplement* (www.facebook.com/pages/Times-Literary-Supplement/221115152587)

- *London Review of Books* (www.facebook.com/LondonReviewOfBooks)

- *Paris Review* (www.facebook.com/parisreview)

- *Edinburgh Review* (www.facebook.com/pages/Edinburgh-Review/202034306209).

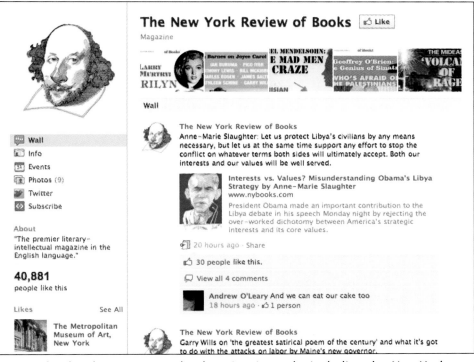

8.3 Facebook is home to many book review journals, including the *New York Review of Books*.

If you can tear yourself away from your latest read, or if you're looking for suggestions for your next read, Facebook is loaded with book- and reading-related resources. Here's a sampling:

- **1001 Books You Must Read Before You Die.** This Group focuses on discussing 1,001 of the best books of all time.

  www.facebook.com/group.php?gid=12693542393

- **Avid Readers Unite.** This busy Page focuses on books and book reviews.

  www.facebook.com/AvidReadersUnite

- **BBC World Book Club.** This is the Facebook Page for the popular BBC radio program called World Book Club.

  www.facebook.com/bbcworldbookclub

- **The Book Studio.** This Page features book reviews, author interviews, book giveaways, and more.

  www.facebook.com/pages/The-Book-Studio/178933895931

- **CBC Book Club.** This Facebook Page is maintained by the Canadian Broadcasting Corporation and is devoted to monthly discussions on a particular topic.

  www.facebook.com/cbcbookclub

- **I Actually Read Books because I Want to.** This Group is devoted to books and the people who love reading them.

  www.facebook.com/group.php?gid=2204747257

- **I Love Reading.** This Page features lively reading-related discussions centered around questions posed by the Page administrator.

  www.facebook.com/pages/I-Love-Reading/74517523505

- **International Reading Association.** This is the Facebook Page for the International Reading Association, which is devoted to spreading literacy worldwide.

  www.facebook.com/pages/International-Reading-Association/
  81491751082

- **The Reader's Catalog.** This Page features gift ideas for book lovers.

  www.facebook.com/pages/The-Readers-Catalog/120942384618099

- **The Reader's Nook.** This very popular Page enables book readers to connect and share their favorite reads.

  www.facebook.com/readersnook

- **Reading Books.** This Page, maintained by the Public Libraries Web site (publiclibrairies.com), is all about the love of reading books.

  www.facebook.com/pages/Reading-Books/61208776359

- **Reading Is Fundamental (RIF).** This is the Facebook Page of RIF, an organization devoted to encouraging children to read.

  www.facebook.com/ReadingIsFundamental

- **The Reading Room.** This popular Page offers book recommendations, book discussions, and book reviews.

  www.facebook.com/thereadingroomonline

- **Reading to Kids.** This is the Facebook Page for Reading to Kids, an organization that aims to inspire a love of reading in children.

  www.facebook.com/readingtokids

Finally, you'll also find quite a few applications on Facebook that you can use to share what you're reading with your friends, rate and review the books you've read, and see which books your friends have on their bedside tables. Here are the four most popular applications:

- **Goodreads Books.** www.facebook.com/apps/application. php?id=2415071772
- **I'm Reading.** www.facebook.com/apps/application. php?id=2397701323
- **Visual Bookshelf.** www.facebook.com/apps/application. php?id=2481647302
- **weRead.** www.facebook.com/apps/application.php?id=2406120893

TIP Looking for personalized book recommendations? Check out Scribd (www.scribd.com), a Web site that suggests books based on your Facebook likes and interests and on what books your friends like.

Connecting with Other Music Fans

Music, which is easily digitized and easily downloaded to your computer or streamed (that is, played in real time), has found a natural home on the Web. Bands and musicians also love the Web because it enables them to connect directly with their fans to promote their latest releases and advertise events such as upcoming tour dates. And for music lovers, the Web has been an incredible boon that enables them to find out more about bands they like, find new bands, and learn more about music genres, the music industry, and the latest music news.

Unfortunately, it's not always easy to take advantage of this bounty because it resides on multiple sites scattered around the Web. Fortunately, many bands and musicians have established bases on Facebook, which also offers tons of other music-related resources, so you can get your music fix right on the Facebook site.

The fastest way to get started is to modify your Facebook profile to include your favorite bands and musicians. Click Profile, click Edit Profile, and then click Arts and Entertainment. In the Music text box, type the name of a favorite artist. As you type, Facebook displays a list of artists that match what you've typed, as shown in Figure 8.4. If you see the name of the artist you want to add, click it in the list. Repeat for your other favorite artists, and then click Save Changes.

8.4 As you type the name of a band or musician, Facebook displays a list of matching artists.

 You can also use the Music text box to type the names of your favorite music genres, and the names of your favorite music labels.

 If you're interested in seeing who among your friends shares your musical tastes, try visiting one of your favorite recording artists' Facebook page. Any friends who also cite that artist as a favorite will appear in the box on the upper right of the Page labeled You and *Name of Artist*.

If the musician you added is very obscure, or if the band doesn't have its own Facebook Page, Facebook sets up the artist in your Profile page as a link to the associated Community Page. Click the link to see the artist's Wikipedia entry (if any) and to see what other Facebookers are saying about the artist.

However, many bands, singers, and other musicians have set up their own Facebook Pages not only as marketing vehicles for albums, tours, and T-shirts, but also to connect with their fans. These musician Pages often have sample songs, artist photos and videos, lists of upcoming events (such as tour dates), and more. For example, Figure 8.5 shows the Facebook Page for the band Fleet Foxes.

8.5 Many bands and musicians now have their own Facebook Pages.

Facebook's Discover Facebook Pages section (www.facebook.com/pages/ browser.php) displays some of the most popular Pages, and it has a Music sub-section, where you can quickly become a fan of your favorite artists (hover your mouse over each musician and then click Like).

A number of music publications are established on Facebook, and they're a great place to start if you want to keep up with the latest music news. Most are aimed at a (much) younger demographic, but some good general interest examples include *Billboard* (www.facebook.com/BillboardMagazine), *Rolling Stone* (www.facebook.com/rollingstone), *BBC Music Magazine* (www.facebook. com/pages/BBC-Music-Magazine/466438365514), and *Gramophone* (www. facebook.com/GramophoneMagazine; see Figure 8.6).

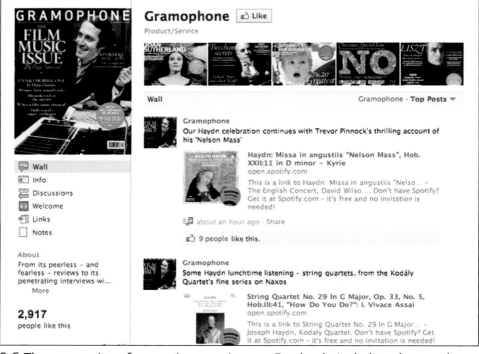

8.6 There are quite a few music magazines on Facebook, including the popular *Gramophone,* which caters to classical music aficionados.

If you have a favorite musical genre, a good place to learn more about it is the genre's community page. Facebook has Community Pages for just about every music genre you can imagine (and quite a few that you *can't* imagine), but here are just a few of the more popular ones:

- **Adult Contemporary.** www.facebook.com/pages/Adult-contemporary-music/104035312965417
- **Bluegrass.** www.facebook.com/pages/Bluegrass/103761669662270
- **Blues.** www.facebook.com/pages/Blues/108090439218250
- **Classical.** www.facebook.com/pages/Classical/111978298819671
- **Country.** www.facebook.com/pages/Country-music/103738639665231
- **Folk.** www.facebook.com/pages/Folk-music/111635295519570
- **Jazz.** www.facebook.com/pages/Jazz/108166409205738

- **Opera.** www.facebook.com/pages/Opera/109558099062698
- **Reggae.** www.facebook.com/pages/Reggae/103804356324465
- **Show Tunes.** www.facebook.com/pages/Show-tunes/111007178919329
- **World.** www.facebook.com/pages/World-music/111950032154573

Facebook has a thriving music community, although the musical tastes tend to skew a bit on the young side. Fortunately, you'll also find plenty of music resources for all ages. Here's a small taste:

- **Billboard.** This is the Facebook home of Billboard.com, the online version of *Billboard* magazine, and it offers links to music news, charts, reviews, and more.

  www.facebook.com/Billboard

- **Free on iTunes.** If you're a fan of the iTunes Page (see a little later in the list), you can use this application to access free iTunes content.

  www.facebook.com/apps/application.php?id=42894731102

- **I Love Music!** This popular and lively Page focuses on discussions about any and all aspects of music.

  www.facebook.com/pages/I-Love-Music/62584727474

Quote, Unquote: Facebook and Music

Richard Whennell, a music teacher in the English town of Bracknell, had wanted to start a community choir for years... Along with his wife Melissa, also a musician and teacher, Richard started thinking about the best way to promote the group.... Melissa suggested they try a Facebook group, and the initial response was exciting. Within 24 hours, the Bracknell Glee Club group (www.facebook.com/group.php?gid=130921190282925) had almost 40 members... The group is still attracting people on Facebook and now has more than 200 members. "It's lovely to feel like the group exists the whole week long, rather than just the 2 hours that we get together on a Thursday evening," Richard explained. Added Melissa, "We feel really blessed to be living in a time of such great technology." — "English Town Embraces Facebook Glee Club," The Facebook Blog, June 9, 2010

● **iTunes.** This Page displays information about new content on the iTunes Store, special offers, and more (see Figure 8.7).

www.facebook.com/iTunes

NOTE The address www.facebook.com/iTunes displays the U.S. version of the iTunes Page. If you live in another country, you need to access your country's version of the Page, such as iTunes Canada (www.facebook.com/iTunesCA) or iTunes UK (www.facebook.com/iTunesUK).

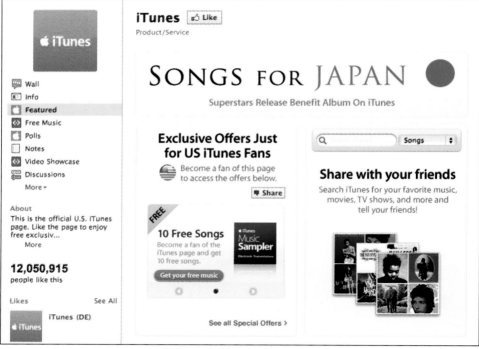

8.7 If you get your music from iTunes, check out the iTunes Page for alerts on special offers, new content, and more.

● **Pandora (page).** This Page offers tips and articles about using the Pandora online radio site.

www.facebook.com/PROJECTOPANDORARTP

● **Pandora (application).** If you have a Pandora account, you can use this application to play music right from your Facebook profile.

www.facebook.com/apps/application.php?id=2409304917

- **SoundHound.** If you use the SoundHound music recognition app on your iPhone or other mobile device, you can use this Facebook application to share recognized music with your friends.

  www.facebook.com/SoundHoundApp

If you want to share music with your friends, the easiest way to do it is to post a link, where the link connects to an online MP3 file. (Note that many sites don't allow third-party links such as this, so your link might not work.) Once you add the link, Facebook gives you an Artist field and an Album field that you can fill in, as shown in Figure 8.8. When you post the link, your friends can see it in their News Feeds, and they can click the Play button to listen to the song.

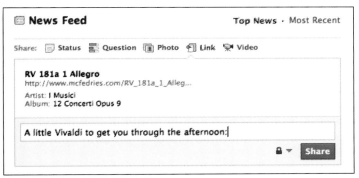

8.8 When you link to an MP3 file, you can specify the artist name and album title.

TIP No doubt, if you love music, you have loads of Facebook friends who share your passion. You can create a group to connect these friends—a sure-fire way to foster discussions on the topic, share leads on new bands, and so on. Alternatively, consider creating a group for Facebook friends in your area who are devotees of local music. That way, you can keep abreast of upcoming shows. And of course, you can use Facebook Events to arrange to meet up at your favorite venue the next time your favorite act comes through town!

Facebook also offers lots of applications that enable you to add music to your profile. Here are the most popular applications in this category:

- **Last.fm Profile.** www.facebook.com/apps/application. php?id=56988796213

Quote, Unquote: Facebook and Music

"Facebook is helping me to create awareness for Chords for Change, a charity teaching kids to play music in Capetown, South Africa. Currently I am competing in a competition to raise $10,000 dollars for CFC." — J. L., Gauteng, South Africa

- **MixPod Music Playlist.** www.facebook.com/mixpod
- **Music (iLike).** www.facebook.com/iLike
- **Music (Burst).** www.facebook.com/apps/application. php?id=2436915755
- **Profile Song.** www.facebook.com/apps/application. php?id=18489293024
- **ReverbNation.** www.facebook.com/m.player
- **Songs.** www.facebook.com/Playlists

Finally, Facebook is home to a number of music-related games that you play to test your music knowledge and compare your results with your friends:

- **Billboard Music Challenge.** www.facebook.com/apps/application. php?id=119411738078884
- **Crazy Cow Music Quiz.** www.facebook.com/apps/application. php?id=168640034863
- **Ken Bruce's PopMaster.** www.facebook.com/apps/application. php?id=128381093563
- **Massive Music Quiz.** www.facebook.com/apps/application. php?id=8414456434
- **Music Challenge.** www.facebook.com/apps/application. php?id=57220127280
- **Music Challenger.** www.facebook.com/apps/application. php?id=2784127156

TIP Interested in finding new music? Visit the Pandora Web site (www.pandora.com), which has partnered with Facebook to enable you to share your musical discoveries with your Facebook friends and vice versa.

Learning about Theater

If you're a theater buff, then you know that there are few pleasures in life that are as intense, engaging, and satisfying as a night out watching a good play that has been well directed and well acted. That passion for plays is evident on Facebook, which has a small but fervent theater community.

If you're just getting started, check out the community pages related to theater:

- **Theatre.** www.facebook.com/pages/Theatre/111721232174401
- **Theater.** www.facebook.com/pages/Theater/106255402747201

 NOTE The Theatre and Theater community pages display the same Wikipedia entry, but the related posts displayed on each page are different because of the spelling difference between theater (the common spelling in the United States) and theatre (the common spelling in the rest of the English-speaking world, although also seen in the U.S.). Of the two, the Theatre page is by far the more popular.

- **Playwright.** www.facebook.com/pages/Playwright/104013429633972
- **Playwriting.** www.facebook.com/pages/Playwriting/108218739212335
- **Dramaturgy.** www.facebook.com/pages/Dramaturgy/112122895471174

There are also lots of community pages devoted to famous playwrights, including the following:

- **Arthur Miller.** www.facebook.com/pages/Arthur-Miller/109521105741400
- **David Mamet.** www.facebook.com/pages/David-Mamet/112086088807462
- **Edward Albee.** www.facebook.com/pages/Edward-Albee/104115166291682
- **Eugene O'Neill.** www.facebook.com/pages/Eugene-ONeill/108103879218035
- **Harold Pinter.** www.facebook.com/pages/Harold-Pinter/105520236147510

- **Neil Simon.** www.facebook.com/pages/Neil-Simon/
105422679491210

- **Oscar Wilde.** www.facebook.com/pages/Oscar-Wilde/
108050589215954

- **Samuel Beckett.** www.facebook.com/pages/Samuel-Beckett/
112334062111134

- **Tennessee Williams.** www.facebook.com/pages/Tennessee-Williams/
105549182811621

Not surprisingly, William Shakespeare is well represented on Facebook, not only with a popular Community Page (www.facebook.com/pages/William-Shakespeare/ 105608322805571), but with many regular Pages that people have set up in The Bard's honor, where fans discuss their favorite plays, trade quotations, review local productions, and more (see Figure 8.9):

8.9 One of the many Facebook pages devoted to William Shakespeare.

- **Shakespeare.** www.facebook.com/pages/Shakespeare/15564111210
- **Shakespeare.** www.facebook.com/pages/Shakespeare/41910597070
- **Shakespeare William.** www.facebook.com/W.Shakespeare
- **William Shakespeare, Infamous Poet and Playwright.** www.facebook.com/WilliamShakespeare1

If you're interested in researching specific plays, run a Page search on the play's title. The more famous plays should each have their own Community Pages. See, for example, *A Streetcar Named Desire* (www.facebook.com/pages/A-Streetcar-Named-Desire/109529079073387), *Waiting for Godot* (www.facebook.com/pages/Waiting-for-Godot/107748882587709), and *Rosencrantz and Guildenstern Are Dead* (www.facebook.com/pages/Rosencrantz-and-Guildenstern-Are-Dead/106252339405036).

> Many famous plays have been turned into movies, so when you search, be sure to click the result that comes from the Book category, not the Movie category.

If there's a particular theater company that you like to follow, chances are it has a Facebook presence that should tell you about the upcoming season, special events, reviews, and more. Examples include Chicago's famous Steppenwolf Theatre Company (www.facebook.com/SteppenwolfTheatre), New York's Roundabout Theatre Company (www.facebook.com/RoundaboutTheatreCompany), and Toronto's Soulpepper Theatre Company (www.facebook.com/SoulpepperTheatre).

Don't worry if you're in a small community, because plenty of small theaters are on Facebook, such as the Milwaukee Repertory Theater (www.facebook.com/MilwRep). Also, search your community to see if there is a Group of like-minded theater lovers such as those in the Vancouver Theatre Group (www.facebook.com/group.php?gid=2217747859) or the Philadelphia Theatre Group (www.facebook.com/group.php?gid=2243769150).

> If you enjoy performing in community theater productions, why not use Facebook to set up a group for the cast members of a particular production? Members could use the group to communicate schedule changes, set up gatherings to run lines, and offer support. Don't' forget to use Facebook Events when you're planning the cast party!

There might be an annual festival in your area that you want to keep up to date on. For example, the Idaho Shakespeare Festival has a Facebook home (www.facebook.com/IdahoShakespeareFestival), as does the Stratford Shakespeare Festival (www.facebook.com/StratfordFestival). There's also a Facebook Page for the world's largest theater festival, The New York City International Fringe Festival (www.facebook.com/NYCFringe), as well as the Edinburgh Festival Fringe Society (www.facebook.com/edfringe; see Figure 8.10).

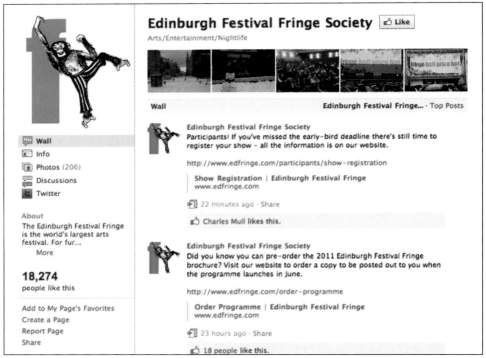

8.10 The Facebook Page for the famous Edinburgh Festival Fringe Society.

Finally, here are a few other theater-related Facebook Pages you can check out:

- **Theater / *The New York Times*.** This is the Facebook Page for the theater section of *The New York Times*, where you'll find reviews, news, and other tidbits on the theater scene.

   www.facebook.com/nytimestheater

- ***Playbill*.** This is the Facebook home for the magazine that discusses all things theater.

   www.facebook.com/playbill

- **Theatre.** This is a Page for theater lovers from all around the world.

  www.facebook.com/theatreonline

- **The Tony Awards.** This is the Facebook Page for the famous Tony Awards, which recognize excellence in theater.

  www.facebook.com/TheTonyAwards

Making Movies Social

Whether you're a cinephile, a cineaste, or just a plain old movie buff, you'll find plenty of Facebook resources to whet your appetite for movie news, information, and trivia, and to connect with other people who share your cinematic interests.

The easiest way to get started is to edit your profile to add your favorite movies. Click Profile, click Edit Profile, and then click Arts and Entertainment. In the Movies text box, type the title of a favorite movie. As you type, Facebook displays a list of movies that match what you're typing, as shown in Figure 8.11. If you see the movie you want to add, click it in the list. Repeat for your other favorite movies, and then click Save Changes.

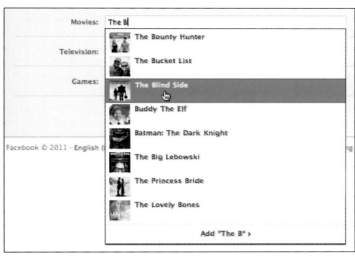

8.11 As you type the name of a movie, Facebook displays a list of matching films.

NOTE You can also use the Movies text box to type the names of your favorite actors, directors, movie genres, and movie studios.

TIP Find out which of your friends like the same movies you do by navigating to the Facebook page for one of your favorite films. Any friends who cite that film as a favorite will appear in the box on the upper right of the page labeled You and *Name of Film*.

If the movie you added is old, or if the movie doesn't have its own Facebook Page, Facebook sets up the movie in your Profile page as a link to the associated Community Page. Click the link to see the movie's Wikipedia entry (if any) and to see what other people are saying about the movie.

Many recent and current movies have their own Facebook Pages not only as marketing vehicles for movie tickets, DVDs, and movie tie-ins, but also to connect with their fans. These movie Pages often have discussions, reviews, news (such as DVD release announcements), commentary, and more. For example, Figure 8.12 shows the Facebook page for the movie *The Blind Side*.

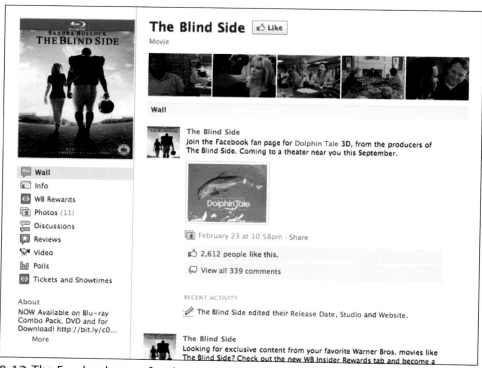

8.12 The Facebook page for the movie *The Blind Side*.

If you're more interested in older films, most reasonably popular movies have an associated Community Page that includes a Wikipedia entry and recent posts that mention the movie. Examples include:

- **Casablanca.** www.facebook.com/pages/Casablanca/113671328643333
- **Gone With the Wind.** www.facebook.com/pages/Gone-with-the-Wind/106121319419152
- **It's a Wonderful Life.** www.facebook.com/pages/Its-a-wonderful-life/110796785612226
- **Titanic.** www.facebook.com/pages/Titanic/103780066327309

In addition, you'll occasionally see a regular Page (that is, one that isn't automatically generated to include a Wikipedia entry or Facebook-wide posts, but rather an official page, maintained by the movie company) for an old movie, such as *The Sound of Music* (www.facebook.com/TheSoundOfMusic) and *The Lord of the Rings* (www.facebook.com/lordoftheringstrilogy).

TIP Many movies (such as *Gone with the Wind* and *The Lord of the Rings*) were adapted from books, so when you search, be sure to click the result that comes from the Movie category, not the Book category.

Also, you may know that the Discover Facebook Pages section (www.facebook.com/pages/browser.php) displays a list of the Pages that have the most Facebook fans, but it also has a Movies subsection, where you can see which movies and movie studios are the most popular. From there, you can become a fan of a movie by hovering your mouse over the film icon and clicking Like, or you can click through to a favorite movie.

TIP Do you love to talk movies? In that case, creating a Facebook group for all your film-buff friends is a great way to foster film talk. Another idea might be to create a group for movie fans in your area; then, use the Facebook Events to set up real-world outings to your local cinema.

Do you have a favorite actor or director that you follow? Run a Facebook search for that person, and you should find at least a community Page to read. For example, a search for Clint Eastwood (an actor and director) returns the Clint Eastwood Page (www.facebook.com/pages/Clint-Eastwood/105658626135269), the Clint Eastwood Westerns Page (www.facebook.com/pages/Clint-Eastwood-Westerns/101979616507675), as well as Pages for the movies *Million Dollar Baby* (www.facebook.com/pages/Million-Dollar-Baby/105521156147471) and *Gran Torino* (www.facebook.com/pages/Gran-Torino/108244742529425).

If you want to research a particular genre of movies, you should be able to find related Community Pages. See for example the Romantic Comedies page (www.facebook.com/pages/Romantic-Comedies/115164288494616), Musicals (www.facebook.com/pages/Musicals/105821596124331), the Action page (www.facebook.com/pages/Action-film/105504132816737), and the Foreign Films page (www.facebook.com/pages/Foreign-films/106023152771806).

Do you like film festivals? Most of the major fests have a Facebook presence where you can get information, dates, trailers, and more. Here are a few to check out:

- **Berlin International Film Festival.** www.facebook.com/pages/ Berlin-International-Film-Festival/8843624347
- **Cannes.** www.facebook.com/cannes
- **Montreal World Film Festival.** www.facebook.com/pages/Montreal-World-Film-Festival-Festival-des-Films-du-Monde-de-Montreal-FFM/ 87227321447
- **Sundance Film Festival.** www.facebook.com/sundance
- **Telluride Film Festival.** www.facebook.com/pages/ Telluride-Film-Festival/19893653854
- **Toronto International Film Festival.** www.facebook.com/TIFF
- **Tribeca Film Festival.** www.facebook.com/TribecaFilm
- **Venice Film Festival.** www.facebook.com/pages/ Venice-Film-Festival/41340329462

If you're just a film festival junkie, then you should join the International Film Festivals Group (www.facebook.com/group.php?gid=4202612955), which is attempting to compile a complete list of the world's film festivals. Another popular Group is Film Festivals (www.facebook.com/group.php?gid=2950805157), which includes a large list of U.S., Canadian, and international festivals.

If you want to keep up with the latest news about the major studios, producers, and distributors, most have Facebook Pages you can check out. Here's a sampling:

- **Disney Movies.** www.facebook.com/DisneyMovies

- **Lionsgate.** www.facebook.com/lionsgate
- **Overture Films**. www.facebook.com/OvertureFilms
- **Paramount.** www.facebook.com/Paramount
- **Sony Pictures.** www.facebook.com/SonySpotlight
- **Warner Bros.** www.facebook.com/warnerbrosent
- **The Weinstein Company.** www.facebook.com/weinsteinco

Facebook is loaded with tons of other movie-related resources. To give you an idea what else is out there, here's a variety of Pages and Groups that you can check out:

- **The Academy of Motion Picture Arts and Sciences / The Oscars.**
  This is the Facebook home of the Oscars, and it includes Oscar-related news, polls, videos, and discussions (see Figure 8.13).

  www.facebook.com/TheAcademy

8.13 The Facebook Page for the Oscars and the Academy of Motion Picture Arts and Sciences.

- **BoxOfficeMojo.** This Page (which is run by the same people who run the Internet Movie Database; see later in the list) focuses on the daily box office returns for current movies as well as box office news and analysis.

  www.facebook.com/BoxOfficeMojo

- **Criticker.** This Page is the Facebook version of the Criticker Web site (www.criticker.com/), which aims to connect people who share the same taste in movies.

  www.facebook.com/pages/Criticker/7978515094

- **/Film.** This Page offers movie reviews, news, discussions, interviews, and commentary.

  www.facebook.com/pages/Film/183439626150

- **Flickchart.** This is the Facebook Page for Flickchart, which ranks movies by having users compare two movies at a time and asking which they think is better.

  www.facebook.com/Flickchart

- **I Heart Movies.** This is the Facebook Page for the Web site (www.iheart movies.com/) that aims to be the "best DVD organizer on the web."

  www.facebook.com/IHeartMovies

- **IMDb.** This is the Facebook home of the famous Internet Movie Database (imdb.com/), where you'll find lots of movie-related news and discussions.

  www.facebook.com/imdb

- **Independent and Foreign Films Rock.** This popular Group focuses on independent and foreign films.

  www.facebook.com/group.php?gid=2205294535

- **Movies!** This Page includes discussions and links related to recent movies.

  www.facebook.com/newmovies

- **Roger Ebert.** This is the Facebook Page for the famous movie critic, and it includes links to his reviews.

  www.facebook.com/RogerEbert

- **Rotten Tomatoes.** This Page offers movie reviews, trailers, and commentary.

  www.facebook.com/rottentomatoes

- **Spout.** This Facebook Page is devoted to sharing favorite movies and discovering great movies you might have missed.

  www.facebook.com/spout

Finally, if you want to share your movies with your Facebook friends, there are a couple of applications you can use:

Flixster. www.facebook.com/flixster

Netflix Updates. www.facebook.com/apps/application.php?id= 36046502195

Netflix's Web site (www.netflix.com) also supports Facebook connections, which means you can log in to your Netflix account and then connect your account to Facebook. This enables you to rate and review movies, and then post that data to your Facebook Wall section for your friends to see. Another site, Rotten Tomatoes (www.rottentomatoes.com), offers similar functionality.

Exploring Social TV

Many pundits have been predicting the death of traditional TV for years now, but according to the latest data, reports on the demise of TV have been greatly exaggerated. For example, a recent Nielsen Company report showed that Americans watched an average of about 158 hours of TV per month in the first quarter of 2010, an *increase* of about two hours from the same period in 2009. Clearly, even in this era of the Web and YouTube, our appetite for TV is greater than ever.

So it's slightly surprising that Facebook has a thriving and active community of TV fans. After all, if our TV watching is increasing, who has time to talk about TV on a social networking site? One explanation is that according to many critics (and many TV watchers), TV shows have never been better. With shows such as *Mad Men,* TV shows now rival (and perhaps even surpass) the quality of most movies, and that creates passionate viewers who want to talk about these great shows.

Another explanation is that back in the day when there were only a few channels, great chunks of the population all watched the same shows, and we'd all discuss those shows around the water cooler the next day. The TV landscape is much larger and much more fractured today, so finding people who watch the same shows as you is getting increasingly difficult. Facebook solves that by making it a snap to find like-minded viewers.

The best way to get going is to modify your profile to add your favorite TV shows. Click Profile, click Edit Profile, and then click Arts and Entertainment. In the Television text box, type the title of a favorite show. As you type, Facebook displays a list of shows that match, as shown in Figure 8.14. If you see the show you want to add, click it in the list. Repeat for your other favorite shows, and then click Save Changes.

8.14 As you type the name of a TV show, Facebook displays a list of matching shows.

NOTE You can also use the Television text box to type the name of your favorite TV actors, TV show genres, and TV networks.

TIP Wonder if any of your Facebook friends have listed your most-loved show among their favorites? To find out, open the Facebook page for the show; friends who have indicated that they "like" it will appear in the upper right corner of the page, labeled You and *Name of Show*.

If the TV show you added is old, or if the show doesn't have its own Facebook Page, Facebook sets up the show in your Profile page as a link to the associated Community Page. Click the link to see the show's Wikipedia entry (if any) and to see what other people are posting about the show.

Many recent and current TV shows have their own Facebook Pages that feature show clips, discussions, news, and more. For example, Figure 8.15 shows the Facebook Page for the TV show *Mad Men.*

If you're more interested in older shows, many of the more popular ones have an associated Community Page, which include a Wikipedia entry (if one exists) and recent posts that mention the show. Examples include:

- *All in the Family* (www.facebook.com/pages/All-in-the-Family/ 112078725470379)
- *Cheers* (www.facebook.com/Cheers)
- *I Love Lucy* (www.facebook.com/I.Love.Lucy)
- *M*A*S*H* (www.facebook.com/pages/MASH/109785492374599)
- *The Mary Tyler Moore Show* (www.facebook.com/pages/ Mary-Tyler-Moore-Show/112030778816405).

8.15 The Facebook Page for the *Mad Men* TV show.

However, sometimes you do see a regular Page for an old show, such as *Seinfeld* (www.facebook.com/seinfeld).

You might be familiar with the Discover Facebook's Pages section (www.facebook.com/pages/browser.php), which shows a list of the most popular Facebook Pages, but it also has a Television subsection that lists some popular shows. From there, you can become a fan of a show by hovering your mouse over the show's icon and clicking Like, or you can click through to a favorite show.

Dozens of TV shows also come with their own Facebook applications that enable you to read episode summaries, play games, connect with other show fans, and in some cases even watch full episodes. An easy way to connect to these applications is by using the TV Shows on Facebook application (apps.facebook.com/addtvshows; see Figure 8.16), which includes links to every TV show application on Facebook.

8.16 The TV Shows on Facebook application maintains a massive list of TV show applications.

If you're interested in TV-related news, articles, and commentary, check out the Facebook home of TV.com (www.facebook.com/tvcom). If you want to add TV show badges to your Facebook profile, connect with the TV Show Badges and Chat application (www.facebook.com/apps/application.php?id=2486598929).

Facebook is also home to all the big networks, of course. Here's the list:

- **A & E.** www.facebook.com/AETV
- **ABC.** www.facebook.com/pages/ABC/107334982289
- **ABC News.** www.facebook.com/abcnews
- **CBS.** www.facebook.com/CBS
- **CBS News.** www.facebook.com/CBSNews
- **CNN.** www.facebook.com/cnn
- **Comedy Central.** www.facebook.com/ComedyCentral
- **C-SPAN.** www.facebook.com/CSPAN
- **Discover Channel.** www.facebook.com/DiscoveryChannel
- **ESPN.** www.facebook.com/ESPN
- **Fox.** www.facebook.com/FOXBroadcasting
- **Fox News.** www.facebook.com/FoxNews
- **HBO.** www.facebook.com/HBO
- **History Channel.** www.facebook.com/pages/History-Channel/ 132248903470929
- **Lifetime.** www.facebook.com/lifetime
- **Lifetime Movie Network.** www.facebook.com/lifetimemovienetwork
- **MSNBC.** www.facebook.com/msnbc
- **NBC.** www.facebook.com/nbc
- **PBS.** www.facebook.com/pbs
- **Weather Channel.** www.facebook.com/TheWeatherChannel

The latest trend in TV is what some people are calling *social* TV, where you no longer watch TV alone or with your family, but with your Facebook friends, too. For example, ABC.com connected with Facebook to give viewers a live view of Michael Jackson's funeral, where they could post comments to their friends in real time. The Jackson funeral garnered ABC.com its highest Nielsen rating ever. And you may find ever-increasing numbers of your friends using Facebook to comment on TV shows while they watch them.

TIP If several members of your set enjoy the same TV show, consider creating a group centered around that show and inviting them to join. Then, you can log in during the broadcast of your show to interact with all your Facebook buddies in the group. It's as if all your friends are together, right in your living room!

TV.com (which I mentioned earlier as a good place for TV news) also connects with Facebook to allow you to interact with your Facebook friends, and NBC. com has been experimenting with social TV, too. The tvClickr application (www.facebook.com/tvClickr) implements social TV by having you click whatever show you're currently watching on TV, and you can then chat with friends who are also watching the show, make comments about the show, answer trivia questions, and more.

Appreciating Art

If you're interested in art in general, and the visual arts in particular, you can use Facebook to connect with people who have similar interests and who can help you learn more about nearly any topic you want to explore, from architecture to painting to sculpture.

As always, you can get yourself off to a fine start by visiting one of Facebook's art-related Community Pages, each of which offers a Wikipedia entry on the topic as well as the latest Facebook posts on the subject. Here are a few to check out:

- **Animation.** www.facebook.com/pages/Animation/107786229244841
- **Architecture.** www.facebook.com/pages/Architecture/ 107709299252611
- **Art.** www.facebook.com/pages/Art/112230005457685
- **Arts and Crafts.** www.facebook.com/pages/Arts-and-crafts/ 109400172411628
- **Collage.** www.facebook.com/pages/Collage/109272742424437
- **Drawing.** www.facebook.com/pages/Drawing/112608815418540
- **Graphic Design.** www.facebook.com/pages/Graphic-design/ 109803049037749
- **Illustration.** www.facebook.com/pages/Illustration/104086106293169

- **Painting.** www.facebook.com/pages/Painting/111925778823301

- **Printmaking.** www.facebook.com/pages/Printmaking/105553976143730

- **Sculpture.** www.facebook.com/pages/Sculpture/108034949225192

- **Typography.** www.facebook.com/pages/Typography/112773058736924

Art museums and galleries are incredible resources for learning about and connecting with art, and the good news is that many of the best museums and galleries have Facebook Pages where you can learn about current or upcoming programs or exhibits, get links to articles, and talk about art with like-minded people.

Some prime examples of art museums and galleries on Facebook are the Metropolitan Museum of Art (www.facebook.com/metmuseum; see Figure 8.17), the Louvre (www.facebook.com/museedulouvre), the Getty Museum (www.facebook.com/gettymuseum), and The Museum of Modern Art (MoMA; www.facebook.com/MuseumofModernArt).

8.17 The Facebook home of the Metropolitan Museum of Art.

Here are a few other art museums and galleries to check out:

- **Art Gallery of Ontario.** www.facebook.com/AGOToronto
- **Cooper-Hewitt, National Design Museum.** www.facebook.com/cooperhewitt
- **Design Museum.** www.facebook.com/designmuseum
- **Hermitage Museum.** www.facebook.com/hermitage.museum.russia
- **Musée d'Orsay.** www.facebook.com/pages/Musee-dOrsay/112753340462
- **National Gallery.** www.facebook.com/thenationalgallery
- **National Gallery of Art.** www.facebook.com/nationalgalleryofart
- **National Portrait Gallery.** www.facebook.com/npg.smithsonian
- **Salvador Dali Museum.** www.facebook.com/theDaliMuseum
- **Smithsonian American Art Museum.** www.facebook.com/americanart
- **Solomon R. Guggenheim Museum.** www.facebook.com/guggenheimmuseum
- **The Tate.** www.facebook.com/tategallery
- **Uffizi Gallery.** www.facebook.com/pages/Galleria-degli-Uffizi/125439825281
- **Van Gogh Museum.** www.facebook.com/VanGoghMuseum
- **Victoria and Albert Museum.** www.facebook.com/victoriaandalbertmuseum
- **Whitney Museum of Modern Art.** www.facebook.com/whitneymuseum

TIP Creating a group for your arty friends is a great way to stay connected. It's especially handy if everyone in the group is local; you can trade info on upcoming openings. And of course, you can use Facebook Events to plan excursions into the real-world art world.

Looking for more? I suspected as much. Here's a list of some popular Facebook Pages that focus on the visual arts:

- **American Illustration.** This Page features the work of some of the best illustrators working in America today.

  www.facebook.com/pages/American-Illustration/241908030433

- **Animation Magazine.** This is the Facebook Page for *Animation Magazine*, which covers the animation industry.

  www.facebook.com/AnimationMagazine

- **Architecture.** This popular Page focuses on architectural images and discussions.

  www.facebook.com/pages/Architecture/101355203101

- **ArchitectureLinked.com.** This Page is devoted to architectural links, news, and discussions.

  www.facebook.com/pages/ArchitectureLinkedcom/216104237063

- **Drawing.** This Page features drawings posted by users.

  www.facebook.com/pages/Drawing/148855870163

- **Drawing.** On this Facebook Page you get links to drawing resources on the Web, as well as drawings posted by users.

  www.facebook.com/pages/Drawing/74758298741

- **Drawn! The Illustration and Cartooning Blog.** This is the Facebook home of Drawn!, a Web site (see www.drawn.ca/) devoted to illustrators, cartoonists, and anyone who enjoys drawing.

  www.facebook.com/drawn.ca

- **DreamWorks Animation.** This is the official Facebook Page for the DreamWorks animation division.

  www.facebook.com/DreamWorksAnimation

- **Graphic Design.** This Page includes links and discussions related to graphic design, and a Graffiti tab where people create and post images.

  www.facebook.com/pages/Graphic-Design/12767141754

- **Graphic Design.** This Facebook Page features links to graphic design samples, as well as designs posted by users.

  www.facebook.com/graphicarts

- **Painting.** This popular Page offers discussions about and links to paintings.

  www.facebook.com/painting

- **The Painting Experience.** This Page offers painting-related Notes and Events, as well as links to painting articles.

  www.facebook.com/paintingexperience

- **Sculpture.** This Page features sculpture-related discussions and links, as well as photos of users' sculpting efforts.

  www.facebook.com/pages/Sculpture/77150108647

- **Sculpture Network.** This nonprofit's goal is to support and promote the "three-dimensional art."

  www.facebook.com/sculpture.network

- **Walt Disney Animation Studios.** This is the Facebook home of the famous Walt Disney animation team (see Figure 8.18), and it includes trailers for current projects, archival footage, behind-the-scenes videos, and much more.

  www.facebook.com/DisneyAnimation

8.18 The Facebook home of Walt Disney Animation Studios.

chapter 9

Wall | **Info** | **Photos** | **Notes**

Hobbies and Leisure

If you're like most people over 50, you almost certainly enjoy any number of hobbies and leisure activities. These could range from redecorating, gardening, needlecraft, crosswords, or creative writing, to camping, hiking, or any kind of sport. When pursuing any of these activities, you're almost certainly not on Facebook, but that doesn't mean that Facebook can't play a supporting role. For any hobby or leisure pursuit that interests you, there are thousands — perhaps even millions — of people on Facebook who share your passion. Using Facebook, you can connect with some of those people to share ideas, get tips, and learn more.

Getting Home Improvement Tips and Techniques

If you enjoy interior design and decorating, you've got lots of company on Facebook because this is one of the most popular topics among Facebookers. For example, as I write this, more than one 100,000 people list Interior Design as an interest on their Facebook profile (with another 50,000 or so listing the very similar Interior Decorating). So the Interior Design Community Page (www. facebook.com/pages/Interior-design/112517512096835) has not only an interesting and useful Wikipedia entry, but also lots of posts from people talking about these topics.

People who love interior design also tend to love interior design magazines, and these are well represented on Facebook. Here are just a few examples:

 NOTE There are lots of Facebook addresses in this chapter, and some of them are quite long. Rather than typing the addresses by hand, see the Facebook page for this series: www.facebook. com/FBGseries. Alternatively, you can type a page's name in Facebook's Search box to locate it.

- *Architectural Digest.* www.facebook.com/architecturaldigest
- *Better Homes and Gardens.* www.facebook.com/mybhg
- *Interior Design.* www.facebook.com/InteriorDesignMagazine
- *House Beautiful.* www.facebook.com/HouseBeautiful
- *Style at Home.* www.facebook.com/Style-at-Home/74723918518
- *Dwell.* www.facebook.com/pages/Dwell-Magazine/12773906654

Do you have a decorating diva you like to follow? Chances are she's on Facebook, so take a look. Examples include the following:

- **Candice Olson.** www.facebook.com/pages/Divine-Design-with-Candice-Olson/316108916551
- **Debbie Travis.** www.facebook.com/pages/Debbie-Travis/315146386516
- **Genevieve Gorder.** www.facebook.com/pages/Genevieve-Gorder/102166819088
- **Martha Stewart.** www.facebook.com/MarthaStewartLiving; see Figure 9.1

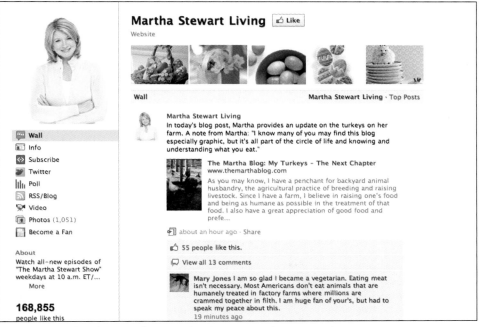

9.1 The Facebook page for *Martha Stewart Living* magazine.

- **Sabrina Soto.** www.facebook.com/pages/Sabrina-Soto/73052852392
- **Sarah Richardson.** www.facebook.com/sarahrichardson.design

Sources for inspiration

If you're looking for inspiration, you'll find loads of Facebook pages that are rife with great ideas and tips. A great place to start is the Facebook page for the International Interior Design Association (IIDA; see www.facebook.com/IIDAHQ and Figure 9.2), which is teeming with fantastic design ideas. Also check out Home Designing (www.facebook.com/homedesigning) and Home Design Ideas (www.facebook.com/pages/Home-Design-Ideas/104049876269).

Many manufacturers also have a presence on Facebook, and these pages are often useful for decorating ideas, new product announcements, sale alerts, and more. For paint, for example, check out Benjamin Moore (www.facebook.com/benjaminmoorepaints) and Sherwin Williams (www.facebook.com/Sherwin WilliamsforYourHome). Similarly, for bath and kitchen fixtures, see Kohler (www.facebook.com/Kohler) and Moen (www.facebook.com/moen).

9.2 The Facebook page for the IIDA has lots of fun and interesting interior design ideas.

Here are a few other Facebook resources devoted to interior design and decorating:

- **Apartment Therapy.** This Facebook page is based on a popular blog that aims to help create lovely environments and connect people to the resources they need to make that happen.

  www.facebook.com/apartmenttherapy

- **designboom**. This page focuses on the interactions between architecture, art, and design.

  www.facebook.com/pages/designboom/53252542178

- **HGTV**. This is the Facebook home of the Home and Garden TV network.

  www.facebook.com/HGTV

- **HGTV Canada.** This is the Facebook home of the Canadian version of HGTV.

  www.facebook.com/hgtv.ca

- **Interior Decorating.** This is a popular and helpful page put together by interior designer Lisa Young.

  www.facebook.com/pages/Interior-Decorating/66011811049

- **Linda Longo @ Home Lighting & Accessories Magazine.** This is a terrific Facebook page for keeping up to date with the latest in lighting.

  www.facebook.com/pages Linda-Longo-Home-Lighting-Accessories-magazine/257579659665

- **Oh Joy!** This fun page is maintained by the Oh Joy! design studio.

  www.facebook.com/ohjoystudio

Sources for DIY

The 1950s were a hobbyist's paradise with magazines such as *Mechanix Illustrated* and *Popular Mechanics* showing the do-it-yourselfer how to build a go-kart for the kids and how to soup up his lawnmower with an actual motor! In fact, the term *do-it-yourself* didn't enter the language until the early '50s, and the abbreviation DIY soon followed. Fifty years later, we're now firmly entrenched in what some people are calling the DIY renaissance, where people are building, modifying, and repairing things on their own.

Facebook fully reflects this trend with quite a few useful and practical resources you can check out if you're a do-it-yourselfer. Begin with the Do It Yourself Community Page (www.facebook.com/pages/Do-it-yourself/105598099473599), which offers a fascinating look at the new DIY scene and features lots of DIY-related posts.

DIY-related magazines on Facebook include *Make* (www.facebook.com/make magazine; see Figure 9.3); *Popular Mechanics* (www.facebook.com/popular mechanics), *Fine Homebuilding* (www.facebook.com/FineHomebuildingMagazine), *Old House Journal* (www.facebook.com/oldhousejournal), and *ReadyMade* (www.facebook.com/readymadeonline).

I also recommend Would Mike Holmes Approve of Your Work? (www.facebook.com/pages/Would-Mike-Holmes-Approve-of-your-work/234356256306) and the DIY Network (www.facebook.com/DIYNetwork). For major retailers, check out Home Depot (www.facebook.com/homedepot) and Lowes (www.facebook.com/lowes).

9.3 *Make* magazine's Facebook home.

TIP

If you're about to launch a big DIY project—painting your living room, tiling your shower, or what have you—and you could use a little help, why not create an Event on Facebook and invite your friends to pitch in? You just might get a few extra hands.

Facebook for Gardeners

If your idea of pure bliss involves sticking your hands in rich, loamy soil, and if talking to flowers and shrubs seems perfectly normal to you, then you are almost certainly a gardener. No doubt you prefer to be outside communing with your garden, but if it's raining or night has fallen, then you can turn to Facebook to connect with your fellow horticulturists. And, believe me, there are a *lot* of them. Gardening is amazingly popular among Facebook users!

To get started, check out the Gardening Community Page (www.facebook.com/pages/Gardening/105975426100728), which includes a wonderfully comprehensive Wikipedia article, and tons of gardening-related posts from Facebook folk. Here are some other useful Community Pages to peruse:

- **Botany.** www.facebook.com/pages/Botany/107790042577534
- **Flowers.** www.facebook.com/pages/Flowers/114937881856580
- **Horticulture.** www.facebook.com/pages/Horticulture/108067345888755
- **Organic Gardening.** www.facebook.com/pages/Organic-Gardening/110839778945025
- **Plants.** www.facebook.com/pages/Plants/114300575253539
- **Shrubs.** www.facebook.com/pages/Shrubs/110613558959962
- **Vegetables.** www.facebook.com/pages/Vegetables/110532125640919
- **Vegetable Gardening.** www.facebook.com/pages/Vegetable-Gardening/401558996150

Gardening magazines are a great way to get growing tips, see wonderful pictures of gardens, and learn useful garden lore. Many of them now have Facebook Pages, including the following:

- *Fine Gardening.* www.facebook.com/pages/Fine-Gardening-Magazine/18412536066
- *Canadian Gardening.* www.facebook.com/canadiangardening
- *Country Gardens.* www.facebook.com/CountryGardensMagazine
- *Garden Design.* www.facebook.com/gardendesignmag
- *Horticulture.* www.facebook.com/HorticultureMagazine; see Figure 9.4
- *Organic Gardening.* www.facebook.com/OrganicGardening
- *The Herb Companion.* www.facebook.com/theherbcompanion

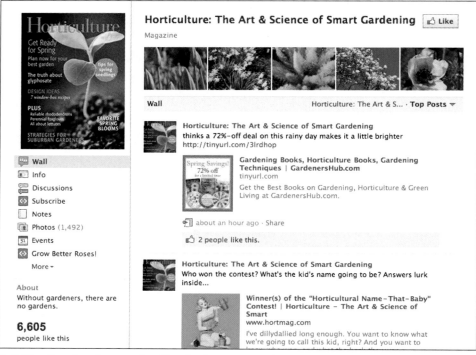

9.4 The Facebook page for *Horticulture* magazine.

Gardening associations and societies can be great sources of information, not only about gardening, but also about horticultural events and news, and you usually get lots of great photos. Facebook examples include the National Gardening Association (www.facebook.com/pages/The-National-Gardening-Association/55400939034) and The American Horticulture Society (www.facebook.com/americanhorticulturalsociety).

TIP If you do a Google search for "master gardeners on Facebook," the results will include plenty of local master gardener associations.

If you have a favorite botanical garden, search for it on Facebook because many now have their own Pages. Examples include the New York Botanical Garden (www.facebook.com/NYBotanicalGarden) and the Toronto Botanical Garden (www.facebook.com/pages/Toronto-Botanical-Garden/140359549334415). Most of these Pages offer announcements of upcoming events and the latest garden news.

You should also look to see whether your favorite gardening show has a Facebook presence. Many do, including the longest-running gardening show on TV, PBS's *Victory Garden* (www.facebook.com/VictoryGarden), *Dig In* (www.facebook.com/pages/Dig-In/108986349134976), and *Desperate Landscapes* (www.facebook.com/pages/Desperate-Landscapes/226577784985).

For most growers, gardening is their favorite activity, but their second favorite activity is *talking* about gardening. Perhaps that's why there are some lively and useful gardening-related Groups on Facebook. Here are a few to check out:

- **Garden Rant.** This lively Group features rants against the perfect gardens portrayed in gardening magazines. Contributors include several popular gardening writers, including Amy Stewart.

  www.facebook.com/group.php?gid=11288464172

- **Guerrilla Gardening.org.** This is where guerrilla gardeners come together to share ideas and experiences.

  www.facebook.com/group.php?gid=2341197575

- **Organic Gardening.** This popular Group is devoted to gardening using organic materials and techniques.

  www.facebook.com/group.php?gid=2354132780

Quote, Unquote: Guerilla Gardening Defined

"guerrilla gardening n. The surreptitious or unauthorized planting of flowers, shrubs, vegetables, and other flora in a public space. Today's guerrilla gardeners are an activist bunch who view their politicized plants as symbols for reconnecting with the land in the face of urban blight and as a way of green-thumbing their collective noses at The Man. The planting-as-protest began in the 1970s with a New York group called the Green Guerrillas. These urban horticulturalists started off crudely by lobbing seed grenades (Christmas tree ornaments filled with soil and wildflower seeds) into abandoned, debris-filled lots, but eventually converted hundreds of these lots into flower- and vegetable-filled community gardens. The movement has since spread around the world (one slogan: "Resistance Is Fertile") and now operates under the more general rubric of guerrilla gardening."
— From WordSpy.com (wordspy.com/words/guerrillagardening.asp)

- **Seed Swap.** This Group features gardeners looking to swap seeds.

  www.facebook.com/group.php?gid=381796355711

- **You Grow Girl.** Started by the gardening writer and photographer Gayla Trail, this Group (see Figure 9.5) is a community of laid-back gardening types that focus mainly on food and container gardening.

  www.facebook.com/group.php?gid=2369021275

> **TIP** Of course, there's nothing to stop you from creating a group for anyone in your circle of Facebook friends who has been blessed with a green thumb. It's a great way to foster discussion on gardening!

Facebook is also a great place to find gardening-related events in your area. For example, run a search on the phrase "seed swap" and you'll find plenty of swaps happening across the country. (You can also try searching on "seed share" and "plant swap.") If you enjoy poking around in other people's gardens, run a search on the phrase "garden tour" and (depending on the time of year, of course) lots of events in the United States and Canada come up. Other garden-related event searches to try are "plant sale" and "gardening seminar."

> **TIP** If you find that your own garden has been overrun by perennials, why not create an Event of your own and invite friends to dig up your spare plants for their own plots (under your supervision, of course)?

When winter kicks in and the garden is covered in snow, what's a forlorn gardener to do? Three words: mail-order catalogs! Nothing beats the winter blahs like perusing a bright and colorful catalog to look for interesting seeds, bulbs, or whatever. If you have a favorite mail-order catalog (and I know you do), check to see if it's on Facebook. Here are a few that are:

- **High Country Gardens.** www.facebook.com/hcg4fans
- **Territorial Seed Company.** www.facebook.com/ TerritorialSeedCompany
- **Baker Creek Heirloom Seed Company.** www.facebook.com/pages/ Baker-Creek-Heirloom-Seed-Company/155935376162

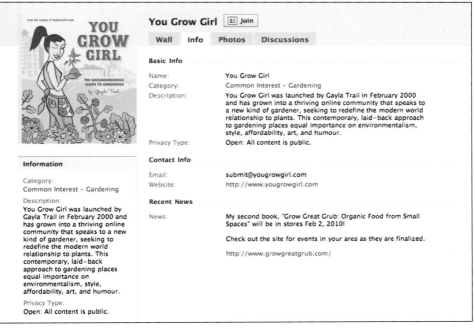

9.5 You Grow Girl is a popular Facebook Group.

Finally, here are three other very useful and informative gardening resources that you might want to spend some time with:

- **Garden Naturally Group.** This Group is dedicated to gardening without chemicals.

  www.facebook.com/pages/Garden-Naturally-Group/245120832263

- **Vegetable Gardening.** This Page is devoted to all things vegetable and offers seeds as well as information and tips on growing.

  www.facebook.com/VeggieGardening

- **Wildlife Garden.** This Page is for people who love the natural world in their gardens.

  www.facebook.com/WildlifeGarden

Finding Fans of Sewing and Needlecraft

If you're into sewing, knitting, quilting, and any other kind of needlecraft, be prepared to make lots of new friends who share your interest! Vast numbers of needle-happy Facebook folk have interests such as sewing, knitting, quilting, crochet, cross stitch, embroidery, and needlepoint on their Facebook profiles, so like-minded souls are never far away.

The Community Pages for all these needlecrafts each come with a useful and interesting Wikipedia entry, plus lots of Facebook posts related to the craft. Here they are:

- **Sewing.** www.facebook.com/pages/Sewing/109188022434549
- **Knitting.** www.facebook.com/pages/Knitting/108407175850402
- **Quilting.** www.facebook.com/pages/Quilting/108414005849724
- **Crochet.** www.facebook.com/pages/Crocheting/115617785119520
- **Cross stitch.** www.facebook.com/pages/Cross-stitch/
106070389425031
- **Embroidery.** www.facebook.com/pages/Embroidery/
108088149211949
- **Needlepoint.** www.facebook.com/pages/Needlepoint/
113226288690924

There are lots of magazines devoted to several (or even all) of these needle-crafts, and many of those are on Facebook. Two to check out are *Craft* (www.facebook.com/craftzine) and *Living Crafts* (www.facebook.com/pages/Living-Crafts-Magazine/139331741421).

If you're looking for patterns, Facebook can help there, too. Take a peek at the following:

- **Simplicity Patterns.** www.facebook.com/simplicitypatterns
- **Kwik Sew Patterns.** www.facebook.com/KWIKSEW

- **Lazy Girl Designs Quilting and Sewing Patterns.** www.facebook. com/lazygirl
- **e-Patterns Central.** www.facebook.com/ePatternsCentral
- **Magpie Patterns.** www.facebook.com/pages/Magpie-Patterns/ 294687840108

If sewing is your thing, start with the sewing publications that have Facebook homes:

- *Sew Beautiful.* www.facebook.com/SewBeautifulMag
- *SewStylish.* www.facebook.com/pages/SewStylish/149903751433
- *Stitch.* www.facebook.com/StitchMagazine
- *Threads.* www.facebook.com/pages/Threads-Magazine/86313676529

For general sewing interest and to connect with fellow sewers, check out the American Sewing Guild (www.facebook.com/sewingguild; see Figure 9.6) and the Sewing Page (www.facebook.com/pages/Sewing/10884133218). Note, too, that Singer, the manufacturer of sewing machines, is also on Facebook (www. facebook.com/pages/Singer-Sewing-Company/45056394921).

Facebook is also home to lots of sewing-related Groups. Here's a few to get you started:

- **EXTREME sewing!** This Group's description says it all: "Because sewing can be so much more INTENSE than one might think!"

  www.facebook.com/group.php?gid=2253475937
- **Lazy Girl Design Sewing and Quilt Patterns.** This Group is run by Lazy Girl Designs, the pattern company that I mentioned earlier.

  www.facebook.com/group.php?gid=7523938139
- **Sewing.** This popular and lively Group is devoted to all things sewing.

  www.facebook.com/group.php?gid=2413823996
- **Sewing Mamas.** This is the Facebook home for SewingMamas.com.

  www.facebook.com/group.php?gid=54944719225

9.6 Hang out with sewers, sewists, and seamstresses, on the American Sewing Guild Page.

If you love to knit, you'll find lots of fellow knitters all over Facebook. Many of them congregate on the Facebook Pages for knitting-themed magazines, including the following:

- **Knitty.** www.facebook.com/pages/Knitty/12716861602
- **Vogue Knitting.** www.facebook.com/pages/Vogue-Knitting/ 91533205498
- **Knit Simple.** www.facebook.com/pages/Knit-Simple/150556797606
- **Creative Knitting.** www.facebook.com/CreativeKnittingMagazine

If you're just looking to hang out with knitters, learn more about knitting techniques, and see some examples of knitting work, lots of people on Facebook have put up general-interest knitting Pages. I suggest the Knitting Guild Association (www.facebook.com/TKGA.CastOn), Knitting (www.facebook.com/pages/Knitting/23250125453), Knitting Daily (www.facebook.com/KnittingDaily), and Knitting Daily TV (www.facebook.com/KnittingDailyTV). Also, consider joining the popular Facebook Groups Addicted to Knitting (www.facebook.com/group.php?gid=2221050980) and Knitting (www.facebook.com/group.php?gid=23541384636).

Quilting is amazingly popular on Facebook, with well over 130,000 people including it as an interest on their profile. That's probably why you find lots of quilting magazines on Facebook, including the following:

- *Quilting Arts.* www.facebook.com/QuiltingArts
- *American Patchwork & Quilting.* www.facebook.com/apqmagazine
- *Fons & Porter's Love of Quilting.* www.facebook.com/FonsandPorter
- *Popular Patchwork.* www.facebook.com/pages/Popular-Patchwork-Magazine/54696104804

A terrific quilting resource is Womenfolk: The Art of Quilting (www.facebook.com/pages/Womenfolk-The-Art-of-Quilting/45147863567; see Figure 9.7), which is dedicated to the historical art of quilting and the women who quilted in the past. Two popular and lively Pages are the American Quilter's Society (www.facebook.com/pages/American-Quilters-Society/117671499395) and the Quilters Club of America (www.facebook.com/pages/Quilters-Club-of-America/62941380670). If you're looking to improve your quilting skills, look no further than Quilt University (www.facebook.com/pages/Quilt-University/190956227203), which offers online classes.

Here are a few other quilting-related resources that are worth a peek:

- **International Quilt Festival.** This is the Facebook home of the world's largest quilting festival.

   www.facebook.com/QuiltFestival

- **Pat Sloan's Quilting Place.** This is a popular Group dedicated to "Quilting fun and mayhem."

   www.facebook.com/group.php?gid=45564533357

- **The Quilt Show.com with Alex Anderson and Ricky Tims.** This Page features lots of quilting tips, examples, and ideas.

   www.facebook.com/pages/The-Quilt-Showcom-with-Alex-Anderson-and-Ricky-Tims/78053794421

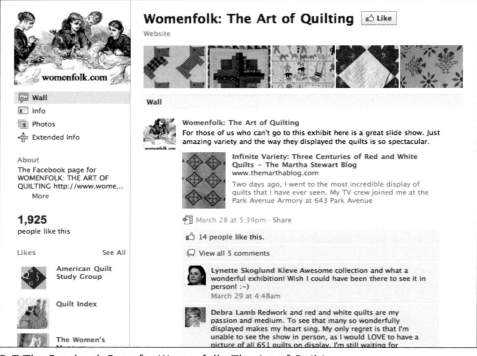

Womenfolk: The Art of Quilting 👍 Like
Website

womenfolk.com

- 🖼 Wall
- ℹ️ Info
- 📷 Photos
- ➕ Extended Info

About
The Facebook page for WOMENFOLK: THE ART OF QUILTING http://www.wome...
More

1,925
people like this

Likes   See All

American Quilt
Study Group

Quilt Index

The Women's
Museum

Wall

Womenfolk: The Art of Quilting
For those of us who can't go to this exhibit here is a great slide show. Just amazing variety and the way they displayed the quilts is so spectacular.

Infinite Variety: Three Centuries of Red and White Quilts – The Martha Stewart Blog
www.themarthablog.com
Two days ago, I went to the most incredible display of quilts that I have ever seen. My TV crew joined me at the Park Avenue Armory at 643 Park Avenue

📅 March 28 at 5:39pm · Share

👍 14 people like this.

💬 View all 5 comments

Lynette Skoglund Kleve Awesome collection and what a wonderful exhibition! Wish I could have been there to see it in person! :-)
March 29 at 4:48am

Debra Lamb Redwork and red and white quilts are my passion and medium. To see that many so wonderfully displayed makes my heart sing. My only regret is that I'm unable to see the show in person, as I would LOVE to have a picture of all 651 quilts on display. I'm still waiting for

9.7 The Facebook Page for Womenfolk: The Art of Quilting.

- **Quilting Bee.** This lively Group is for "serious quilters" who are "addicted to quilting."

  www.facebook.com/group.php?gid=2215810305

- **Quilting Bloggers directory from the Quilting Gallery.** This is the Facebook Page of an online group that maintains a list of over 4,000 people with blogs related to quilting.

  www.facebook.com/Quilting.Bloggers

If you're hooked on crocheting (sorry, I couldn't resist), you'll find more than 200,000 like-minded people on Facebook. Lots of them gather at the Page set up by the magazine *Crochet!* (www.facebook.com/CrochetMagazine), which, according to its own description, "isn't the same old magazine that your grandmother had." Another crochet magazine with a Facebook home is *Crochet World* (www.facebook.com/CrochetWorldMag).

Other notable places where crocheters congregate on Facebook are the following:

- **The Art of Crochet by Theresa.** www.facebook.com/Crochetmania
- **Crochet Me.** www.facebook.com/CrochetMe
- **Crochetville.** www.facebook.com/Crochetville
- **Crochet Guild of America.** www.facebook.com/CrochetGuild OfAmerica
- **Runway Crochet.** www.facebook.com/runwaycrochet.fans

If you're itching to talk about crochet and ask (or answer) questions, here are two popular Groups that should scratch that itch: Crochet (www.facebook.com/group.php?gid=73203893322) and Crochet Addict (www.facebook.com/group.php?gid=6979547797).

Finally, I would be remiss if I didn't also mention a Page called Yarn Bombing (www.facebook.com/yarnbombing; see Figure 9.8), which is devoted to the guerrilla art of *yarn bombing*, the surreptitious or unauthorized placement of knitted objects on statues, posts, and other public structures.

TIP Those of us over 50 are known for our rebellious streak—after all, we lived through the 1960s. While we may have mellowed, yarn bombing can serve as a great outlet for our unruly side. Why not form your own yarn-bombing group for like-minded Facebook friends, using Facebook's Events feature to organize group bombings — er, outings?

Sewing, knitting, quilting, and crocheting are the most popular needlecrafts on Facebook, but that doesn't mean the other needle arts don't have thriving Facebook communities. Here are some resources to check out if you're into embroidery, cross stitch, or needlepoint:

- **Embroidery, Cross-stitch and Needlepoint.** This is a Group dedicated to needle types.
  www.facebook.com/group.php?gid=2316774208
- **Embroidery.** This is a Group for people who enjoy embroidery.
  www.facebook.com/group.php?gid=3036186190

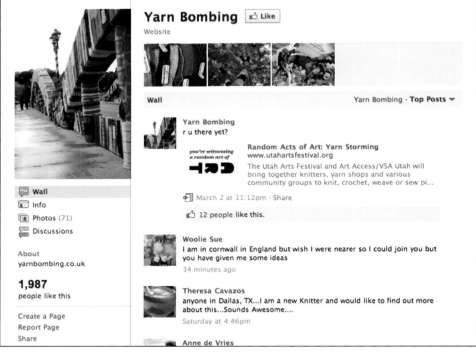

9.8 Yarn bombing has a home on Facebook.

- **Embroidery Garden.** This is the Facebook Page for a Web site that offers embroidery designs, appliques, and projects.

  www.facebook.com/pages/Embroidery-Garden/143334308826

- **Cross Stitch Crazy.** This is the Facebook home of *Cross Stitch Crazy* magazine.

  www.facebook.com/crossstitchcrazy

- **About Cross Stitch.** This is About.com's cross stitch Page.

  www.facebook.com/About.comCrossStitch

- **Heart of Cross Stitch.** This is a Group for cross stitchers to share patterns, ideas, and more.

  www.facebook.com/group.php?gid=82095529763

- **The American Needlepoint Guild.** This the Facebook Page for the ANG, a nonprofit dedicated to encouraging interest in needlepoint.

  www.facebook.com/pages/ANG-The-American-Needlepoint-Guild-Inc/126036324107064

- **Not your Grandma's Needlepoint.** This Page showcases "unique, whimsical, one of a kind needlepoint pieces inspired by pop culture and sixties psychedelia."

  www.facebook.com/pages/Not-your-Grandmas-Needlepoint/ 90453855753

TIP — As a member of the over-50 set, you're no doubt familiar with the concept of a quilting bee. With Facebook groups, you can create a new type of quilting (or knitting, or crocheting, or stitching — you get the idea) bee, and invite all your needle-crazy friends to join. Your Facebook bee might include discussions about techniques or photos of current projects. You can even use Facebook Events to invite group members to a real-world bee.

Crosswords and Puzzles on Facebook

Crosswords are quite popular on Facebook. However, despite that popularity, crossword-related resources are relatively rare on Facebook. One notable exception is the Crosswords Community Page (www.facebook.com/pages/Crosswords/106502649387233), which features a fascinating and in-depth Wikipedia article and lots of Facebook posts. If cryptic crosswords are more your style (or if you'd like to figure out how to solve them), check out the Cryptic Crosswords Community Page (www.facebook.com/pages/Cryptic-crosswords/106134896091344).

Lots of Facebook crossword fans meet at the Crossword Puzzles Page (www.facebook.com/CrosswordPuzzles), which is probably the best general crossword resource on Facebook. Strangely, despite the huge popularity of *The New York Times* puzzles, the New York Times Crossword Puzzle Page on Facebook (www.facebook.com/NYTcrossword) has (at least as I write this) very little content. Perhaps by the time you read this it will be a bit more lively.

If Facebook doesn't have much in the way of crossword-related Pages or Groups, perhaps it's because people prefer to do crosswords rather than talk about them. So, not surprisingly, you'll find lots of games that have crossword themes. Here are a few that have received high ratings from players:

- **Crossword Fun.** www.facebook.com/apps/application. php?id=111285206546

- **Cryptic Crossword.** www.facebook.com/apps/application. php?id=13639818094

- **Daily Crossword.** www.facebook.com/apps/application. php?id=2674676070

- **The Hindu Crossword.** www.facebook.com/thehinducrossword

- **Team Crossword.** www.facebook.com/teamcrossword

- **Photo Crossword.** www.facebook.com/apps/application. php?id=115379418484

TIP Can't come up with that seven-letter word for "shaded passageway" on your own? Why not ask your Facebook friends for help? No doubt, one of your wordy friends will supply the correct answer in no time flat.

Scrabble fans have lots of company on Facebook, because tens of thousands of people have added Scrabble as an interest on their profiles, and hundreds of thousands of people play the official Scrabble game. To learn more about Scrabble, visit the official Scrabble Page (www.facebook.com/Scrabble). There's also the popular Scrabble(TM) Page for fans (www.facebook.com/pages/ScrabbleTM/9639213585). The official game comes in two versions, one for players in the United States and Canada (see Figure 9.9), and one for the rest of the world:

- **Scrabble (U.S. and Canada).** www.facebook.com/ScrabbleEA
- **Scrabble Worldwide (excluding U.S., and Canada).** www.facebook.com/apps/application.php?id=7730584433

9.9 A Facebook Scrabble game in progress.

Hundreds of thousands of people also play Lexulous (www.facebook.com/apps/application.php?id=3052170175), which is a Scrabble clone that uses slightly different rules.

If you're into Sudoku, you can visit its Community Page (www.facebook.com/pages/Sudoku/107966615898575) to learn more about the game and techniques for solving it. There are also a couple of popular Sudoku applications:

- **Mister Sudoku.** www.facebook.com/apps/application.php?id=329612764889
- **Action Sudoku.** www.facebook.com/ActionSudoku
- **Zebra Sudoku.** www.facebook.com/zebrasudoku

One of my favorite games is Kakuro, a game of logic where you fill in numbers to make sections of the puzzle add up to predefined sums, and it's on Facebook in the form of a Community Page (www.facebook.com/pages/Kakuro/105636469471005) and an application (www.facebook.com/KakuroConquest).

There are tons of word- and puzzle-related games on Facebook, so I can't list them all. Here's a sampling of some highly rated games you might want to check out:

- **Classic Word Games.** www.facebook.com/classicwordgames
- **KenKen.** www.facebook.com/apps/application.php?id=183437650359
- **Mind Games.** www.facebook.com/MindGames
- **MindJolt Games.** www.facebook.com/mindjolt
- **Word Challenge.** www.facebook.com/wordchallenge
- **Word Twist.** www.facebook.com/WordTwist

Improving and Sharing Your Writing

Whether you're an accomplished writer or an aspiring one, whether you write poetry or prose, whether you write for hire or for fun, Facebook is the place to be when you put down your pen (metaphorically or otherwise). That's because there are a lot of fantastic resources on Facebook that can help you improve your skills, share your writing with others, and learn more about the business of writing.

A great place to get started is the Writing.com Facebook Page (www.facebook.com/writingcom; see Figure 9.10), which is a very popular and very useful online community for writers of all levels.

9.10 The Writing.com Facebook page is a great resource for writers.

Other useful resources for writers on Facebook include the following:

- **The Association of Writers & Writing Programs.** This organization is dedicated to fostering literary talent and achievement, to advance the art of writing, and to serve those who create, teach, study, and read contemporary writing.

  www.facebook.com/AWPWriter

- **The Writer's Circle.** The mission of this community of writers is to connect, encourage, and highlight writers around the world.

  www.facebook.com/writerscircle

- **The Writers Studio.** Founded in 1987 on the belief that anyone can learn to write, The Writers Studio has developed a unique method that focuses on technique and emotional connection.

  www.facebook.com/pages/The-Writers-Studio/134641415337

Writers on Facebook love to talk about writing, and they love to share their own writing and have others critique it. All this back-and-forth activity goes on in various Groups, and there are lots of them. Here's a sampling:

- **A Place for Writing.** www.facebook.com/group.php?gid=2204708700
- **Aspiring Authors.** www.facebook.com/group.php?gid=2204546223
- **Children's Book Writers and Illustrators.** www.facebook.com/group.php?gid=2347317590
- **Creative Writing.** www.facebook.com/group.php?gid=2204701103
- **Fantastic Fantasy Writers on Facebook.** www.facebook.com/group.php?gid=2370080768
- **Publishing Talk.** www.facebook.com/group.php?gid=2381074915
- **Suspense/Thriller Writers.** www.facebook.com/group.php?gid=2397748813
- **Writers Cafe.** www.facebook.com/group.php?gid=2207018293

If you're a freelance writer, or would like to become one (who wouldn't, says the freelance writer), Facebook can help. Most freelancers have practically memorized *Writer's Market*, which is *the* resource book for places to sell your writing (it's not called the "freelancer's bible" for nothing). Happily, the book has its own Facebook Group (www.facebook.com/group.php?gid=18874504145; see Figure 9.11), which has a lively Wall section and lots of discussions. I also recommend the Group called Writing and Publishing (www.facebook.com/group.php?gid=6138914001), which is run by the International Association of Writers and offers lots of tips and advice for getting published. Also check out the Facebook Page for *Writing* magazine (www.facebook.com/pages/Writers-News-and-Writing-Magazine/139711209402425).

You should also stop by Freelance Writing Tips (www.facebook.com/group.php?gid=12134975530), a Group formed by the author of the book *The Greatest Freelance Writing Tips in the World*, which offers links to useful articles for freelancers. Other freelance-related resources include Freelance Writers (www.facebook.com/group.php?gid=2351373470), Freelance Writing (www.facebook.com/group.php?gid=2214024274), Writing for Dollars (www.facebook.com/group.php?gid=59188976673), and Freelance Writing Jobs (www.facebook.com/freelancewritingjobs).

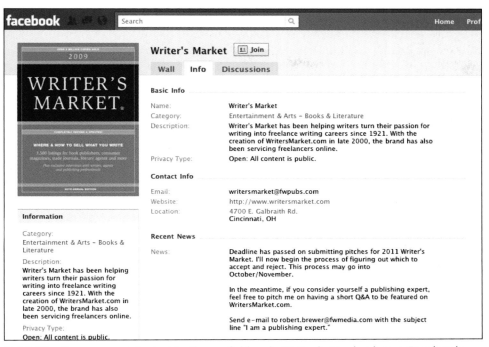

9.11 The famous and fantastically useful book *Writer's Market* has a Facebook Group.

Of course, every writer needs to watch out for scam artists and other shady operators who might try to take advantage of you. Two Facebook resources cover this sort of thing and offer lots of tips, warnings, and advice: Writer Beware (www.facebook.com/pages/Writer-Beware/374157262457) and Warnings for Writers (www.facebook.com/group.php?gid=9113492596).

Status Update as Art Form

The writing of status updates is somewhat of an art form in and of itself. Much like the structure of a haiku poem (three lines, with 17 total syllables) poses a special challenge, so, too, does the 420-character limit of status updates. And of course, the temporal nature of the status update— the essential "now-ness" of it—adds a certain literary urgency. As an aspiring writer, why not use your status update to practice (very) short prose? It's also an excellent platform for tossing out ideas.

If poetry is your thing, be sure to drop by the Poetry Society of America (www.facebook.com/poetrysociety), which has tons of useful and interesting content, as well as the similar Canadian Poetry Association (www.facebook.com/pages/Canadian-Poetry-Association/8313085490). The Poets & Writers page (www.facebook.com/poetsandwriters) is another excellent resource.

If you're looking for a place to post your poems, there are lots of Groups that let you do just that. Three to check out are 2:00 a.m.: A Poetry Group (www.facebook.com/group.php?gid=2209327057), Amateur Poets & Writers (www.facebook.com/group.php?gid=2383273753), and David Brazier's Poetry Circle & Workshop (www.facebook.com/group.php?gid=9671599291).

Finally, here are two applications that can help you with your writing and with sharing your writing with your Facebook friends:

- **Slates.** www.facebook.com/apps/application.php?id=4240867762
- **Writing is Freedom.** www.facebook.com/apps/application.php?id=5366791854

If you want to see even more writing resources on Facebook, or if you just have a *lot* of time to kill, then check out the Group called Creative Writing Sites on Facebook (www.facebook.com/group.php?gid=8539923410) — an Index that currently lists over 800 (!) Facebook Pages and Groups.

From Freelance to Facebook

The word freelance was coined in 1820 by Sir Walter Scott in the book Ivanhoe:

"I offered Richard the service of my Free Lances, and he refused them — I will lead them to Hull, seize on shipping, and embark for Flanders; thanks to the bustling times, a man of action will always find employment."

He was talking about mercenary knights of the Middle Ages who, in "bustling times" would sell their warrior skills to the highest bidder. By the end of the 19th century, the word had come to mean a self-employed journalist or writer. Nowadays it can refer to anyone who is self-employed, but it still has a special resonance for writers.

Sharing Documents with a Group

Suppose you want to share the latest draft of your novel manuscript with a group of writer friends. With Facebook, you can easily do so using a special feature called Docs. Docs works in conjunction with Facebook groups to enable you to collaborate on a simple document. For example, with Docs, you can share a passage of your manuscript (or any other content) with a Facebook group populated with your writer friends. Within the group, choose the Doc link above the Publisher to get started. Group members can then view and/or edit your document to provide feedback.

Connecting with Fellow Hikers and Campers

What's the opposite of Facebook? That might sound like an odd question, but let's think about it: Facebook is often a sedentary, indoor activity (the odd updating-my-status-while-walking-around-town mobile user notwithstanding), so its opposite would be something that's active and takes place outdoors. Many pastimes meet those qualifications, of course, but perhaps the two that best exemplify them are the quintessential outdoorsy activities of hiking and camping. But even though Facebook may be the opposite (whatever that really means) of hiking and camping, it's an excellent place to connect with other hikers and campers, share stories, discuss interesting places to go, get tips, and lots more.

Hikers are legion on Facebook, with vast numbers of members adding this activity as an interest on their profiles. This makes for a lively Community Page (www.facebook.com/pages/Hiking/105525412814559), which also features a good Wikipedia entry on hiking that includes links to different types of hiking, including backpacking, hillwalking, freehiking, day hiking, and heli hiking. Many of these alternative forms of hiking also have their own Community Pages:

- **Backpacking.** www.facebook.com/pages/Backpacking/113703391980553
- **Day Hiking.** www.facebook.com/pages/Day-Hiking/376721493897
- **Freehiking.** www.facebook.com/pages/Freehiking/103106883062897

- **Hillwalking.** www.facebook.com/pages/Hillwalking/111941145489962
- **Ultralight backpacking.** www.facebook.com/pages/Ultralight-backpacking/102141773160862

Whether you hike for fitness or just to get in a little *forest bathing* (a recently coined term that refers to time spent in a forest or similar natural setting), Facebook has tons of other resources to help you get more out of this pastime no matter what your level or interest. A good place to start your trek is the selection of hiking-related magazines on Facebook, which include *Backpacker* (www.facebook.com/backpackermag), *Adirondack Life* (www.facebook.com/pages/Adirondack-Life/108927182465247), and *Vermont Sports* (www.facebook.com/pages/Vermont-Sports/52173623149).

Another great place to hang out with hikers is the Group for the American Hiking Society (www.facebook.com/group.php?gid=2421032047), which is dedicated to promoting and protecting hiking.

If hiking in the mountains is your thing, then consider joining the very popular Group called Mountaineering | Mountain Climbing | Alpine Trekking, Backpacking & Hiking (www.facebook.com/group.php?gid=2343408030), which offers lots of lively discussions.

If you're looking for hiking news, tips, equipment reviews, books, and more, be sure to check out Hiking Trip Report (www.facebook.com/hikingtips; see Figure 9.12). And although not specifically focused on hiking, no hiker's Facebook resource list would be complete without the Pages for the National Parks Service (www.facebook.com/nationalparkservice), which offer lots of great information about the U.S. national parks, and Parks Canada (www.facebook.com/ParksCanada), which is the Canadian equivalent.

Quote, Unquote: Forest Bathing

"One study published in January included data on 280 healthy people in Japan, where visiting nature parks for therapeutic effect has become a popular practice called Shinrin-yoku, or forest bathing. ... The scientists found that being among plants produced 'lower concentrations of cortisol, lower pulse rates, and lower blood pressure' among other things." — Anahad O'Connor, "The Claim: Exposure to Plants and Parks Can Boost Immunity," *The New York Times,* July 6, 2010

9.12 Check out Hiking Trip Reports for tons of hiking tips, news, and reviews.

If you're into *thru-hiking* (hiking a long trail from one end to the other), you'll find plenty of like-minded trekkers in the Thru-Hiking Page (www.facebook. com/Thruhike), which features tips, discussions, and lots of thru-hiking photos.

Hiking is all about trails, of course, so most hiking-related resources on Facebook are devoted to trails in general, or to specific trail systems. Here's a sampling:

- **American Discovery Trail.** www.facebook.com/ AmericanDiscoveryTrail

- **American Trails.** www.facebook.com/pages/American-Trails/ 175325010812

- **Appalachian Trail Conservancy.** www.facebook.com/ATHike

- **The Buckeye Trail Association.** www.facebook.com/group. php?gid=67039793763

- **The Colorado Trail Association.** www.facebook.com/pages/ The-Colorado-Trail-Foundation/115337198486403

- **Continental Divide Trail.** www.facebook.com/group. php?gid=8047999779

- **Continental Divide Trail Alliance.** www.facebook.com/group. php?gid=5750447595

- **The Green Mountain Club.** www.facebook.com/GreenMountainClub

- **The John Muir Trail.** www.facebook.com/group. php?gid=2240988980

- **The Mountains-to-Sea Trail.** www.facebook.com/pages/ Friends-of-the-Mountains-to-Sea-Trail/144643271890

- **The North Country Trail Association.** www.facebook.com/ northcountrytrail

- **The Pacific Northwest Trail Association.** www.facebook.com/ pacificnorthwesttrail

- **The Sheltowee Trace Association.** www.facebook.com/group. php?gid=100397517759

- **Superior Hiking Trail Association.** www.facebook.com/suphike

- **Trails BC.** www.facebook.com/TrailsBC

- **Trans Canada Trail.** www.facebook.com/transcanadatrail

- **Vancouver Trails.** www.facebook.com/vancouvertrails

This list only scratches the surface, so if you're looking for a specific trail, or for trails in a specific location, searching Facebook can help. If you're searching for Groups, choose the Sports & Recreation category, and then Outdoor Sports subcategory. For example, a search on "Appalachian" returns a number of groups, including the following: The Appalachian Trail (www.facebook.com/ group.php?gid=2218013389), Appalachian Long Distance Hikers Association (www.facebook.com/group.php?gid=26249723354), and Appalachian Trail Hikers (and Hopefuls) (www.facebook.com/group.php?gid=2223185107).

Similarly, if you belong to a hiking club you should search for the club on Facebook because many now have their own Pages or Groups.

Finally, here are a few applications you can use to enhance your hikes and share them with friends:

- **HikeJournal.** You can use this application to share your hiking journal.

  www.facebook.com/apps/application.php?id=58812245830

- **Live Trails.** This application lets you find out the latest conditions for trails.

  www.facebook.com/apps/application.php?id=104990126785

- **Map My Hike.** This application helps you to map, log, and share your hikes.

  www.facebook.com/mapmyhike

- **Summit Book.** This application lets you share your hiking trip with friends and meet other hikers.

  www.facebook.com/apps/application.php?id=2780481349

- **Trimble Outdoors.** This application lets you post location updates to your Wall section using GPS data from the same company's smartphone app.

  www.facebook.com/trimbleoutdoors

TIP If there are numerous hikers or campers in your Facebook set, consider creating a group to swap stories, share photos of recent outings, and trade information about hiking and camping locales? You can also use Facebook's Events feature to organize outdoor outings.

Camping is even more popular than hiking on Facebook. The Community Page (www.facebook.com/pages/Camping/105426616157521) offers lots of camping-related Facebook posts, as well as an in-depth Wikipedia article on the subject. There are also Community Pages for different types of camping, including the following:

- **Canoe Camping.** www.facebook.com/pages/Canoe-camping/ 116342461709389

- **Motorcycle Camping.** www.facebook.com/pages/ Motorcycle-Camping/376300418811

- **Tent Camping.** www.facebook.com/pages/Tent-Camping/ 390740662280

- **Winter Camping.** www.facebook.com/pages/Winter-Camping/ 378998128937

- **Work Camping.** www.facebook.com/pages/Work-Camping/ 374275807644

There aren't many magazines solely devoted to camping, but there are a few, and most are also on Facebook, including *Camping Life* (www.facebook.com/pages/Camping-Life-Magazine/16267630738; see Figure 9.13), and *Go Camping Australia* (www.facebook.com/pages/Go-Camping-Australia-Magazine/111203612247347).

9.13 *Camping Life* magazine's Facebook home.

If you're trying to decide where your next camping trip should be, a great place to start your search is the Facebook Page for the U.S. National Forest Campground Guide (www.facebook.com/USNFCG), which offers descriptions on nearly 2,400 campgrounds.

For Canadian campers, check out Camping in Canada (www.facebook.com/ CampSource), which lists more than 4,000 campgrounds. You should also check out the Local Camping application (apps.facebook.com/localcamping), which maps local camping sites.

Of course, it's one thing to know that a campground exists, but it's quite another to know whether the site is any good. To help out, the Facebook Page called 5 Star Campgrounds (www.facebook.com/5starcampgounds) rates and reviews campgrounds through the United States and Canada.

If you want to know where campers are congregating on Facebook, look no farther than the Camping Page (www.facebook.com/pages/Camping/12795133724), which boasts more than 650,000 fans and offers lots of discussions and photos. There'sanotherCampingPage(www.facebook.com/pages/Camping/73067872879) that has even more fans (more than 750,000!), but its Wall section is marred by ads and spam, so it's less useful.

Some of the camping retailers have set up shop on Facebook, and the better ones also offer camping tips, gear reviews, and more. See, for example, Camping Survival (www.facebook.com/pages/Camping-Survival/48301221510) and, for RVers, Camping World (www.facebook.com/campingworld).

If roughing it isn't to your taste, consider *glamping*, a form of camping that includes expensive equipment, fine food, and other luxuries (the word is a blend of glamour and camping), and check out Glamping Girl — Putting the Glam in Camping (www.facebook.com/glampinggirl; see Figure 9.14).

Quote, Unquote: Glamping

"Open from May through September, this Canadian resort is a top destination for 'glamping,' or glamour camping. Guests at Clayoquot stay in one of 20 tents, but these canvas contraptions are tricked out better than most city apartments: fancy carpets, oil lamps, antique furniture, a cozy fire at the push of a button. In other words, heavy on the glamour, light on the camping." — Lori Rackl, "Nature or nurture?," *Chicago Sun Times,* September 19, 2007.

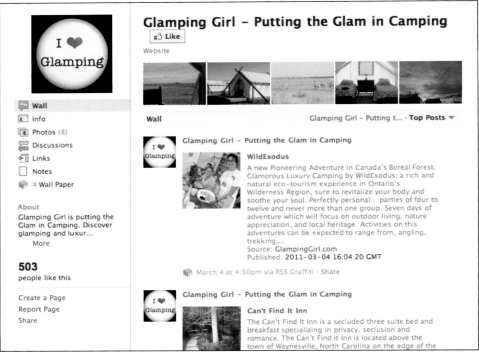

9.14 If luxury camping is more your style, Glamping Girl can help.

Facebook is also home to lots of location-specific camping Pages and Groups, so search for "camping *location*", where *location* is where you're interested in camping. Examples of location-specific Facebook camping resources include Camping and RVing BC Coalition (www.facebook.com/pages/Camping-and-RVing-BC-Coalition-CRVBCC/97939190814), California RVing and Camping (www.facebook.com/CaliforniaRVing), and Camping Ontario (www.facebook.com/group.php?gid=2225913310).

Making Sports Social

To say that sports are popular is akin to saying that night is dark: It's true, certainly, but so obviously so that it's barely useful as a starting point for discussion. We can put some flesh on those bones by talking about how popular sports are in Facebook. Millions of Facebookers list Sports as an interest on their profiles. Similarly, there are a dozen sports where at least 1 million

Facebook users have declared themselves fans of the sport. In fact, here's a list of the 20 most popular sports on Facebook (in descending order of fans), along with each sport's Community Page:

- **Association Football (soccer).** www.facebook.com/pages/Association-football/108501195841933

- **Basketball.** www.facebook.com/pages/Basketball/108614982500363

- **Fishing.** www.facebook.com/pages/Fishing/104056309631975

- **American Football.** www.facebook.com/pages/American-football/108067645881905

- **Baseball.** www.facebook.com/pages/Baseball/108379982523213

- **Tennis.** www.facebook.com/pages/Tennis/105650876136555

- **Golf.** www.facebook.com/pages/Golf/105942022769573

- **Volleyball.** www.facebook.com/pages/Volleyball/109446562415595

- **Snowboarding.** www.facebook.com/pages/Snowboarding/107496599279538

- **Hunting.** www.facebook.com/pages/Hunting/108654529159055

- **Skiing.** www.facebook.com/pages/Skiing/103780659661402

- **Bowling.** www.facebook.com/pages/Bowling/112198422125473

- **Ice Hockey.** www.facebook.com/pages/Hockey/104044816297627

- **Cricket.** www.facebook.com/pages/Cricket/103992339636529

- **Cycling.** www.facebook.com/pages/Cycling/114031331940797

- **Track and Field.** www.facebook.com/pages/Track-Field/115268138486823

- **Rugby.** www.facebook.com/pages/Rugby/114694351878815

- **Boxing.** www.facebook.com/pages/Boxing/105648929470083

- **Sailing.** www.facebook.com/pages/Sailing/107733585923064

- **Table Tennis.** www.facebook.com/pages/Table-tennis/108167272538953?

For team sports, many people are fans of specific teams within each sport, of course, and most professional sports teams have Facebook Pages these days where fans can get the latest team news, game highlights, announcements of special events, and so on. Here are the top ten professional sports team Pages on Facebook (in terms of total fans):

You can use your Facebook profile to show your team spirit before a big game. Post a team-oriented status update, start a discussion on the Wall section of a friend from the opposing team, or even add fun profile pics to show your love!

- **Galatasary.** www.facebook.com/Galatasaray
- **Fenerbahçe.** www.facebook.com/Fenerbahce/138432502881936
- **Los Angeles Lakers.** www.facebook.com/losangeleslakers
- **Manchester United.** www.facebook.com/manchesterunited
- **New York Yankees.** www.facebook.com/Yankees
- **Beşiktaş.** www.facebook.com/BesiktasTaraftarSayfasi
- **Boston Celtics.** www.facebook.com/bostonceltics
- **Arsenal.** www.facebook.com/ArsenalFC
- **Juventus.** www.facebook.com/pages/Juventus-Club/8460495804
- **Persib Bandung.** www.facebook.com/pages/PERSIB-Bandung/21164211233

Check out the Facebook-run Sports on Facebook page (www.Facebook.com/Sports) for ongoing updates on various sports around the world.

Sports leagues are also all over Facebook, and they can be great resources for getting an overview of what's happening in a sport. Some league Pages to check out are the National Basketball Association (www.facebook.com/nba), the National Football League (www.facebook.com/NFL), Major League Baseball (www.facebook.com/mlb), the Professional Golfers' Association (www.facebook.com/PGATour), and the National Hockey League (www.facebook.com/NHL).

Are you passionate about college basketball? If so, check out the NCAA Final Four bracket that CBS Sports issues on Facebook each year (www.facebook.com/apps/application.php?id=5713520924).

Facebook Fantasy Sports

If you participate in a fantasy league, you can use Facebook to communicate with other league members. The best approach is to create a group solely for league members; they can use it to share stats, make trades, and of course, talk a little trash. And of course, you can use Facebook's Events feature to plan gatherings to watch games and to organize your league's draft day. Facebook also offers various applications that enable you to participate in site-wide fantasy leagues (not to mention other sports-related applications that you can play with your friends).

For sports news, articles, profiles, and results, check out the general sports magazines on Facebook, including *Sports Illustrated* (www.facebook.com/SportsIllustrated), *Sporting News* (www.facebook.com/sportingnews), and *Inside Sport* (www.facebook.com/insidesportmagazine). All the major sports networks also have a presence on Facebook, but go the extra mile by integrating Facebook into their live sports coverage. To see how these networks will be using Facebook to cover the next big event, check out ESPN (www.facebook.com/home.php/ESPN), Fox Sports (www.facebook.com/home.php/foxsports), and Versus (www.facebook.com/VersusTV).

Clearly, spectator sports are huge on Facebook, but so are participatory sports. I talked about a few of these earlier in the book, including cycling, swimming, triathlon, and particularly running, all in Chapter 7. For other sports, you can usually find lots of Pages and Groups that offer instruction, tips, and equipment reviews, as well as discussions among fans.

For example, golf is very popular on Facebook. So, not surprisingly, all the major golf magazines have Facebook Pages, including *Golf Digest* (www.facebook.com/GolfDigestMag), *Golf* (www.facebook.com/SI.Golf), *Golf World* (www.facebook.com/GolfWorldMag), and *Golf Journal* (www.facebook.com/GOLFJOURNAL).

If you're looking for tips to help with your swing, course strategy, club selection, and more, check out the Golf Channel (www.facebook.com/GolfChannel) and The Golf Fix with Michael Breed (www.facebook.com/TheGolfFix).

Finally, there are also lots of golf equipment manufacturers on Facebook, including adidas (www.facebook.com/adidasGolfUS), Calloway (www.facebook.com/Callaway), Nike (www.facebook.com/nikegolf), PING (www.facebook.com/PINGGolfFans), and TaylorMade (www.facebook.com/TaylorMadeGolf). These pages can tell you about new equipment, promotions, reviews, and more.

| **Wall** | Info | Photos | Notes |

Facebook for Foodies

If you consider yourself a foodie — that is, a person with an above-average interest in or knowledge of food and drink — then chances are you don't dine "al desko" (you know. Al fresco? At your desk?). So it's unlikely that you eat and play around with Facebook at the same time. That's a good thing (those crumbs can play havoc with your keyboard), but it doesn't mean you can't combine food and Facebook in other ways. With Facebook, the social nature of food in general and of eating in particular are on full display, so here you find shared recipes, cooking tips, pointers to fantastic wines and beers, nutrition advice, reviews of restaurants, and much more.

Trading Recipes

Almost everyone who enjoys cooking not only likes to talk about cooking (as you learn in the next section of this chapter), but also loves to share recipes, read other people's recipes, and adapt those recipes for personal tastes and culinary needs. Recipe-sharing sites abound on the Web, so it's no surprise that thousands upon thousands of Facebook cooks also are eager to swap recipes.

The easiest way to find a particular type of recipe on Facebook is to run a search on "*style* recipes," where you replace *style* with whatever type of meal you want to serve. For example, a search for "Thai recipes" turns up Thai Recipes Today (www.facebook.com/pages/Thai-Recipes-Today/164572013576497; see Figure 10.1) and a few other Pages. Besides specific cuisines, you can also search for a region, ingredient, holiday, or cooking style.

10.1 Search for "style recipes" to locate recipes in the style you're craving.

NOTE There are many Facebook addresses in this section. All of them are case sensitive, and some of them quite long. Rather than typing the addresses by hand, see the Facebook page for this series: www.facebook.com/FBGseries. Alternatively, you can type a page's name in Facebook's Search box to locate it. Please note that Facebook does not endorse the sites listed in this book.

To give you the flavor of what's available on Facebook, here's a taste of some recipe resources that are devoted to specific cuisines, styles, or regions:

- **Assamese Cuisine and Recipes.** www.facebook.com/assameserecipes

- **Best Southern Recipes from the Deep South.** www.facebook.com/SouthernRecipes

- **Caribbean Recipes.** www.facebook.com/caribbeanrecipes

- **Chinese Cooking.** www.facebook.com/pages/Chinese-Cooking/50786852571

- **Karina's Kitchen — Recipes from a Gluten-Free Goddess.** www.facebook.com/GlutenFreeGoddess

- **Old Biloxi Recipes, by Sonya Fountain Miller.** www.facebook.com/pages/Old-Biloxi-Recipes-by-Sonya-Fountain-Miller/103019296349

- **Pakistani Recipes Exchange.** www.facebook.com/group.php?gid=99624580146

- **Persian Recipes.** www.facebook.com/persianrecipes

- **Pinoy Food Recipes.** www.facebook.com/pinoyfood

- **Sri Lankan Recipes.** www.facebook.com/pages/Sri-Lankan-Recipes/143048564070

- **Vegetarian Recipes.** www.facebook.com/vegrecipes

- **Vita-Mix Recipes.** www.facebook.com/VitaMixRecipes

There are also lots of Pages and Groups that take a more general approach and aren't focused on a particular style or cuisine. Here are some to check out the next time you're hungry:

- **365 Tupperware Recipes in 365 Days.** This Page is maintained by a woman who is cooking a different Tupperware recipe each day for one year, and more than 10,000 fans are going along for the ride. People love their Tupperware!

www.facebook.com/pages/365-Tupperware-Recipes-in-365-Days/ 112218045488047

- **All Recipes.** This Page is the Facebook home of AllRecipes.com, a busy Web site for sharing all kinds of recipes.

  www.facebook.com/allrecipes

- **Best Recipes.** The Page asks fans to post their favorite recipes.

  www.facebook.com/bestrecipes

- **Better Recipes.** This popular Page focuses on "homespun family favorites."

  www.facebook.com/betterrecipes

- **CopyKat Recipes.** This unique and fun Page is devoted to trying to come up with recipes that re-create specific restaurant meals.

  www.facebook.com/pages/Copykat-Recipes/247258983605

- **Crock Pot Recipe Exchange.** This large and lively Group is centered around recipes for the crock pot ("one of man's greatest inventions," according to the Group description).

  www.facebook.com/group.php?gid=263037202669

- **Crockpot/Simple Casserole Recipes.** This is another popular Group devoted to crock pot cooking.

  www.facebook.com/group.php?gid=176453769322

- **Epicurious.** This popular and busy Page (see Figure 10.2) is the Facebook home of the famous Epicurious Web site.

  www.facebook.com/epicurious

- **Healthy Blender Recipes.** On this Page, Tess Masters, aka The Blender Girl, shares some blender-based recipes.

  www.facebook.com/healthyblenderrecipes

- **Laura's Best Recipes.** This very popular Page is run by Laura Levy, a cooking enthusiast who scours the Web for the best recipes she can find, and then posts them.

  www.facebook.com/laurasrecipes

10.2 The Facebook page for the Epicurious recipe-sharing Web site.

- **Recipe Binder.** This popular application enables you to store and share recipes with friends.

  www.facebook.com/recipebinder

- **Recipe of the Day.** This Epicurious application sends you a new recipe every day.

  www.facebook.com/recipeoftheday

- **Recipe.com.** This Page offers lots of interesting recipes from around the world.

  www.facebook.com/recipedotcom

- **Recipes.** On this Group, more than 13,000 people share recipes from all over.

  www.facebook.com/group.php?gid=49864617122

- **Visual Recipes — Recipes with Step-by-Step Photos.** This Page offers links to recipes that include copious photos of the preparing and cooking process.

  www.facebook.com/pages/Visual-Recipes-Recipes-with-Step-by-Step-Photos/309311555558

Improving Your Cooking

We all have to eat, and someone has to cook that food, so from a purely utilitarian perspective, cooking is about as routine and everyday as human activities get. And yet there's just something about cooking that fires people's imaginations and stokes their creativity. Perhaps that's why cooking is one of the most popular pastimes on Facebook. In fact, only music, reading, and travel are more popular.

If you want to learn how to cook, improve your cooking skills, and learn new techniques and styles, you can connect with all kinds of people on Facebook who can certainly help. A fantastic place to start is the Community Page for Cooking (www.facebook.com/pages/Cooking/113970468613229), which offers tons of Facebook posts and an in-depth Wikipedia article that gets into cooking history, ingredients, methods, food safety, cooking science, and more.

There are also Community Pages for each of the main cooking methods. Here are just a few examples:

- **Baking.** www.facebook.com/pages/Baking/105992459431332
- **Barbecuing.** www.facebook.com/pages/Barbecuing/108281252539877
- **Crockpot Cooking.** www.facebook.com/pages/Cooking-With-a-Crockpot/373135692461
- **Curing.** www.facebook.com/pages/Curing/376587708849
- **Frying.** www.facebook.com/pages/Frying/103763689661821
- **Grilling.** www.facebook.com/pages/Grilling/108130762547784
- **Microwave Cooking.** www.facebook.com/pages/Cooking-With-a-Microwave/375466165869
- **Pressure-Cooking.** www.facebook.com/pages/Pressure-cooking/106023082770449

- **Roasting.** www.facebook.com/pages/Roasting/103126086393999

- **Steaming.** www.facebook.com/pages/Steaming/113673731976606

- **Stewing.** www.facebook.com/pages/Stewing/108613029169475

- **Stir Frying.** www.facebook.com/pages/Stir-frying/108213449199047

Other great sources of new cooking lore and skills are the various cooking magazines, many of which have a presence of Facebook. These magazines include the following:

- *Appetite.* www.facebook.com/pages/Appetite-Magazine/121793322353

- *Bon Appétit.* www.facebook.com/bonappetitmag; see Figure 10.3

10.3 The foodies at *Bon Appétit* have their own Facebook page.

- *Cooking Light.* www.facebook.com/CookingLight

- *Cook's Illustrated.* www.facebook.com/CooksIllustrated

- *Fine Cooking.* www.facebook.com/pages/Fine-Cooking/188608890800

- *Food and Wine.* www.facebook.com/foodandwine

- *La Cucina Italiana.* www.facebook.com/pages/La-Cucina-Italiana/ 51344486486
- *Olive.* www.facebook.com/olivemagazine
- *Yummy.* www.facebook.com/yummymagazine

Reading about cooking is one thing, but a great chunk of the population prefers to watch cooking, hence the perpetual popularity of cooking shows. Lots of those shows are on Facebook, too, and they use their Pages to post recipes, preview upcoming shows, and talk about cooking. At the network level, you'll find the Food Network (www.facebook.com/FoodNetwork) and the Cooking Channel (www.facebook.com/CookingChannel).

At the show level, most of the highest rated shows are on Facebook, including the following:

- *America's Test Kitchen TV.* www.facebook.com/ AmericasTestKitchenTV
- *Cake Boss.* www.facebook.com/CakeBoss
- *Good Eats.* www.facebook.com/GoodEatsTV
- *Hell's Kitchen.* www.facebook.com/HellsKitchen
- *Iron Chef.* www.facebook.com/pages/Iron-Chef/18541316042
- *Iron Chef America.* www.facebook.com/pages/Iron-Chef-America/ 25351617408
- *Man v. Food.* www.facebook.com/ManVFood
- *Top Chef.* www.facebook.com/TOPCHEF

There are tons of other Pages and Groups that you can check out to learn new techniques and styles of cooking. Here's a list to whet your appetite:

- **Baking**. Bakers use this popular Page to share baking tips, techniques, and recipes.

  www.facebook.com/pages/Baking/120332470773
- **Cooking.com.** This popular Page (see Figure 10.4) is the Facebook version of the Cooking.com Web site.

  www.facebook.com/Cookingcom

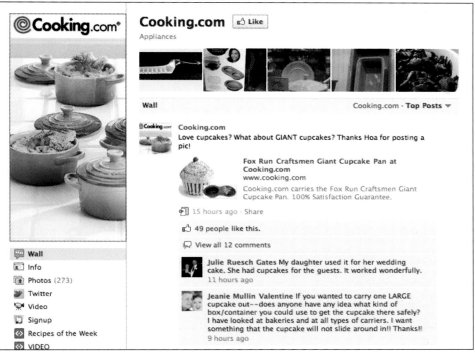

10.4 The Cooking.com Page is a busy and useful place for cooks of all abilities.

- **Cooking Club of America.** This Facebook Page is based on the popular Web site (cookingclub.com) that's devoted to people who love cooking and food.

  www.facebook.com/CookingClub

- **Cooking for Busy Moms.** This Page is based on a popular blog where busy moms swap tips and information for feeding their families.

  www.facebook.com/cookingforbusymums

- **Cooking with All Things Trader Joe's.** Cooking notes and posts courtesy of the Trader Joe's brand.

  www.facebook.com/CookingWithTraderJoes

- **George Foreman Cooking.** If you're joined at the hip with your George Foreman Grill, this Page lets you commune with 35,000 like-minded chefs.

  www.facebook.com/GeorgeForemanHealthyCooking

- **Grilling Out.** If you're looking to improve (or boast about) your grilling skills, this popular and lively Page is the place to go.

  www.facebook.com/pages/Grilling-Out/72717210769

- **Kosher Gourmet Cooking.** This Group offers lots of posts and discussions about kosher cooking.

  www.facebook.com/group.php?gid=118207589553

- **Texas Cooking.** This Page offers recipes and techniques for cooking it Texas style.

  www.facebook.com/texascooking

- **What I'm Cooking.** With this application from the folks at Epicurious, you can share with friends what you're cooking or what you're craving.

  www.facebook.com/apps/application.php?id=4225774935

Restaurants and Chefs on Facebook

As long as you still have taste buds, then chances are you like to eat out (or take out) every once in a while as your budget permits. That might explain the astonishing popularity of some restaurants on Facebook, particularly the larger fast-food chains such as McDonald's (www.facebook.com/McDonalds), Taco Bell (www.facebook.com/tacobell), and Kentucky Fried Chicken (www.facebook.com/KFC).

Quote, Unquote: Facebook and Restaurants

"Facebook has given us the chance for more interaction, response, and suggestions direct from customers. We're able to let everyone know where we're going to be, what specials we will be featuring, including pictures, as well as updates on when we're running out of anything." — Akash Kapoor, owner of Curry Up Now (www.facebook.com/curryupnow), quoted on The Facebook Blog, July 1, 2010

Why become a fan of a large restaurant chain? For many people, it's just a way of underlining their enjoyment of that chain's food, but it also gets them information on promotions, new products, and special deals.

However, it's not just the big chains that are taking advantage of Facebook: Many smaller restaurants also use social networking to connect with their customers and promote their brand. For example, an Irish local pub in Toronto called The Céilí Cottage uses its Facebook Page (www.facebook.com/TheCeiliCottage; see Figure 10.5) to tell fans what's on the menu each night, to announce upcoming events (such as oyster-shucking competitions), and more.

Some restaurants go even farther for their fans. A great example is the famous Gramercy Tavern in New York. Its Page (www.facebook.com/pages/Gramercy-Tavern/113135062061277) includes menu updates, food photos, upcoming events, Notes related to the restaurant and its food, and even a Reservations tab (see Figure 10.6) that lets people reserve a table without leaving Facebook.

10.5 Smaller restaurants such as The Céilí Cottage use Facebook to let fans know what's on the menu and what events are coming up.

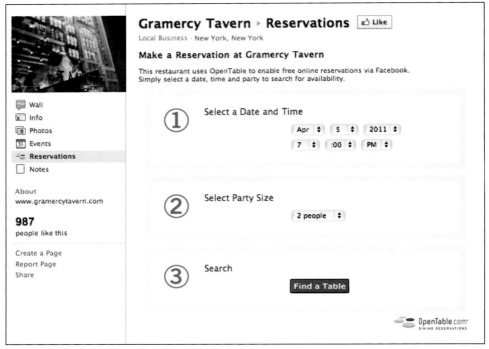

10.6 At the Gramercy Tavern Facebook Page, you can reserve a table without leaving the site.

There are also lots of Pages devoted to restaurant reviews. Probably the most famous and the most popular is Zagat (www.facebook.com/Zagat), which offers reviews of restaurants around the world. Most restaurant review pages are more limited, typically serving a single city, multiple cities, or a region. If you have a review service you use regularly in your area, search for it on Facebook. Here are some examples:

- **B.R. Guest.** This database serves New York, Las Vegas, and St. Pete Beach, Florida.

  www.facebook.com/BRGuestHospitality

- **Dining Out In the NorthWest.** This is a promotional Page for restaurants in the U.S. Northwest.

  www.facebook.com/pages/Dining-Out-In-The-NorthWest/106194646415

- **Dining out in Central Mass.** This Page covers restaurants in central Massachusetts.

  www.facebook.com/pages/Dining-out-in-Central-Mass/274718986142

- **Dine Here.** You can use this service to find reviews in Vancouver, Victoria, and Whistler, British Columbia.

  www.facebook.com/dinehere

- **Martiniboys.com.** This Page covers New York, Miami, Toronto, Montreal, Vancouver, and Calgary.

  www.facebook.com/group.php?gid=52080325298

If you find a particularly good restaurant, you should share the joy with your friends. (Conversely, if you suffer through a particularly bad restaurant, you should share the pain with your friends, to help them avoid the same fate.) Here are three applications that can help you do just that:

- **Living Social: Restaurants.** www.facebook.com/LivingSocial

- **Local Picks.** www.facebook.com/LocalPicks

- **My Restaurants.** www.facebook.com/apps/application. php?id=4206848155

If you want to find new restaurants to try, you can visit City Search (www.city search.com) and Yelp (www.yelp.com). Both sites have integrated with Facebook to enable users to see reviews posted by Facebook friends.

TIP If several of your Facebook friends are known to regularly dine out, consider creating a group for those friends and urging them to post reviews of their favorite local spots. You could also use Facebook's Events feature to schedule regular eatings—er, outings—to local eateries.

If you have a favorite chef, particularly someone you follow on television, chances are he or she has a Facebook Page that you can "like" to keep up with the chef's latest creations and happenings. To save you some legwork, here's a list of some top chefs that have Facebook Pages:

- **Barefoot Contessa (Ina Garten).** www.facebook.com/pages/ Barefoot-Contessa/49929963034

- **Mario Batali.** www.facebook.com/MarioBatali

- **Anthony Bourdain: No Reservations.** www.facebook.com/ AnthonyBourdainNoReservations

- **Alton Brown.** www.facebook.com/pages/Alton-Brown/ 37908558111

- **Paula Deen.** www.facebook.com/PaulaDeen

- **Giada De Laurentiis.** www.facebook.com/giada
- **Thomas Keller.** www.facebook.com/ChefThomasKeller
- **Emeril Lagasse.** www.facebook.com/Emeril
- **Jamie Oliver.** www.facebook.com/jamieoliver
- **Wolfgang Puck.** www.facebook.com/wolfgangpuck
- **Rachael Ray.** www.facebook.com/TheRachaelRayShow
- **Alice Waters.** www.facebook.com/pages/Alice-Waters/74837008344

Learning about Wine and Beer

A meal isn't complete unless it has a tasty beverage to go along with it, and that often means a nice wine or a complimentary beer. Facebook is home to a large population of wine and beer aficionados, so it's a great place to learn more about these beverages, get recommended pairings, and more.

TIP

The next time you stumble upon a great vintage or brew, why not post a status update that sings its praises it or upload a photo of the label? No doubt, your fellow Facebook quaffers will appreciate the tip!

Wine

Hundreds of thousands of Facebook users include wine as an interest on their Facebook profiles, so there's no shortage of wine knowledge and wisdom just waiting to be uncorked. The Community page (www.facebook.com/pages/Wine/109455512414846) is a real gem, with lots of Facebook posts and an astonishingly comprehensive Wikipedia article that covers wine history, varieties, classifications, tasting, and much more. There are also lots of Community Pages devoted to wine types. Here's a taste:

- **Beaujolais.** www.facebook.com/pages/Beaujolais/109380539081589
- **Bordeaux.** www.facebook.com/pages/Bordeaux-wine/104035846300781
- **Cabernet Sauvignon.** www.facebook.com/pages/Cabernet-Sauvignon/108219445873643
- **Chardonnay.** www.facebook.com/pages/Chardonnay/108503985840231

- **Chianti.** www.facebook.com/pages/Chianti/105560616145420
- **Gewürztraminer.** www.facebook.com/pages/Gewurztraminer/ 106143526083460
- **Malbec.** www.facebook.com/pages/Malbec/107335025962992
- **Merlot.** www.facebook.com/pages/Merlot/112644778751146
- **Muscat.** www.facebook.com/pages/Muscat/111806508836134
- **Pinot Grigio.** www.facebook.com/pages/Pinot-Grigio/ 110288878994189
- **Pinot Noir.** www.facebook.com/pages/Pinot-noir/112381532112532
- **Riesling.** www.facebook.com/pages/Riesling/103143556391896
- **Sauvignon Blanc.** www.facebook.com/pages/Sauvignon-blanc/ 109406339077928
- **Syrah (Shiraz).** www.facebook.com/pages/Syrah/109251949100851
- **Zinfandel.** www.facebook.com/pages/Zinfandel/107925102569228

The world is awash in wine magazines, and many of them have tasted the Facebook nectar and decided to settle in for the long haul. The most notable of them are the following:

- *Champagne.* www.facebook.com/pages/Champagne-Magazine/ 37644459276
- *Food and Wine.* www.facebook.com/foodandwine
- *Quarterly Review of Wines.* www.facebook.com/pages/ Quarterly-Review-of-Wines-Magazine/320416641980
- *Sommelier Journal.* www.facebook.com/pages/Sommelier-Journal/ 85876392412
- *Touring and Tasting.* www.facebook.com/touringandtastingfans
- *Wine Enthusiast.* www.facebook.com/WineEnthusiast
- *Wine Spectator.* www.facebook.com/WineSpectator; see Figure 10.7

If there are wine critics whom you follow, they just might be on Facebook. Notable wine critics on Facebook include Jancis Robinson (www.facebook.com/ pages/Jancis-Robinson/118866221457959) and James Suckling (www.facebook. com/jamessuckling).

NOTE If you're wondering why I didn't mention Robert M. Parker, probably the world's most famous wine critic, it's because Mr. Parker's Facebook page (www.facebook.com/pages/Robert-M-Parker/62313773016) is currently not well-maintained. But there is a Community Page about him, where you can find information posted by others.

If you're looking for wine reviews and tasting notes, I highly recommend Wine Searcher (www.facebook.com/winesearcher), which offers wine-related stories, discussions, notes, as well as a Tasting Club where people post their own wine reviews.

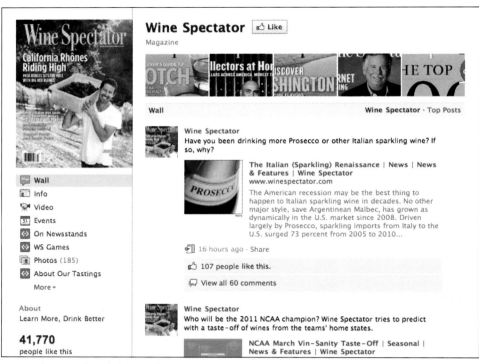

10.7 The Facebook home for the famous *Wine Spectator* magazine.

Other useful Pages for furthering your wine education are Wine Library TV (www.facebook.com/winelibrarytv), Wine.com (www.facebook.com/winecom), Wine Harlots (www.facebook.com/pages/Wine-Harlots/123462161494), Snooth (www.facebook.com/snooth), Wine of the Month Club (www.facebook.com/Wineofthe MonthClub), and Wine Encyclopedia (www.facebook.com/WineEncyclopedia).

Facebook is also home to thousands of vineyards and vintners, from large, industrial operations to mom-and-pop wineries. Some examples include Bollinger (www.facebook.com/Bollinger.Champagne), Kim Crawford Wines (www.facebook.com/kimcrawfordwines), J. Lohr Vineyards & Wines (www.facebook.com/pages/J-Lohr-Vineyards-and-Wines/108123525882236), Robert Mondavi (www.facebook.com/robertmondavi), and Rodney Strong (www.facebook.com/Rodney.Strong.Vineyards). Search Facebook for your own favorites.

Ever wanted to own your own vineyard? Various Facebook applications can give you a taste of what that's like. My Vineyard (www.facebook.com/MyVineyard) and Vineyard Country (www.facebook.com/VineyardCountry) are game applications that enable you to create your own virtual vineyard, where you harvest grapes, make delicious wine, and share it with your friends.

To round out your look at Facebook's wine-related resources, here are a few popular places to check out:

- **100% Cork.** This Page is dedicated to preserving cork as the material of choice for wine closures (instead of plastic stoppers or metal screw caps).

   www.facebook.com/100PercentCork

- **The California Wine Club.** This popular Page is the place to be if you enjoy California wines.

   www.facebook.com/cawineclub

- **ChampagneGuide.net.** If a bottle of the bubbly is more to your taste, there is plenty to like on this Page.

   www.facebook.com/champagneguide

- **Community Wine Tastings on Twitter.** Yes, it's a Twitter thing, but this Facebook Page has lots of info on tastings and other wine goodness.

   www.facebook.com/TasteAndTweet

- **I Love Wine.** This Page's motto is *Nunc est bibendum*, Latin for "Now is the time for drink," which pretty much tells you what this lively Page is all about.

   www.facebook.com/pages/I-Love-Wine/63818445465

- **Moms Who Need Wine.** A gathering place for mothers (or, really, anyone) who enjoy a glass of vino at the end of the day (see Figure 10.8).

   www.facebook.com/MomsWhoNeedWine

- **Naked Wine Show.** Just what it says: It's a wine show where your host Susan Sterling delivers video wine reviews in the buff (tastefully, of course).

  www.facebook.com/pages/Naked-Wine-Show/21739852869

10.8 The Facebook Page for Moms Who Need Wine.

- **VINTUBA.** This Page's description says that it's "Where the Everyman's Wine Snob meets the Wine Snob's Everyman." I don't know what that means, either, but the Page has all kinds of useful info and links.

  www.facebook.com/vintuba

- **Wine Beagles.** This application lets you review and share your wines with your friends.

  www.facebook.com/apps/application.php?id=2426439300

- **Wine Industry Network.** Ostensibly aimed at people in the wine trade, this Page still offers lots of interesting content for the rest of us.

  www.facebook.com/WineIndustryNetwork

- **Women & Wine.** This Page is a gathering place for women who like wine, although men are also welcome.

  www.facebook.com/womenwine

- **World Wide Wine Network.** This is another Page aimed at wine insiders, but there's plenty here for wine outsiders, too.

  www.facebook.com/WorldWineWineNetwork

Beer

Thousands upon thousands of Facebookers have added beer as an interest on their Facebook profiles, so there's lots of beer expertise and experience out there just waiting to be tapped. The Beer Community Page (www.facebook.com/pages/Beer/112570395422274) is a frothy mixture of Facebook posts and a very nice Wikipedia entry that talks about beer history, brewing methods, beer varieties, and more. There are also many Community Pages devoted to beer varieties, including the following:

- **Ale.** www.facebook.com/pages/Ale/107957452560801
- **Lager.** www.facebook.com/pages/Lager/112599732084698
- **Berliner Weisse.** www.facebook.com/pages/Berliner-Weisse/ 108087099213581
- **Bock.** www.facebook.com/pages/Bock/112257498785189
- **Brown Ale.** www.facebook.com/pages/Brown-ale/104047522964483
- **Dunkel.** www.facebook.com/pages/Dunkel/105519902815983
- **India Pale Ale.** www.facebook.com/pages/India-Pale-Ale/ 107813739242034
- **Kellerbier.** www.facebook.com/pages/Kellerbier/108163415872379
- **Lambic.** www.facebook.com/pages/Lambic/109672099059459
- **Pale Ale.** www.facebook.com/pages/Pale-ale/108121599216105
- **Pilsner.** www.facebook.com/pages/Pilsner/114514665227284
- **Porter.** www.facebook.com/pages/Porter/107854065902883
- **Stout.** www.facebook.com/pages/Stout/107489519280239
- **Weissbier.** www.facebook.com/pages/Weissbier/109758809050281
- **Wheat Beer.** www.facebook.com/pages/Wheat-beer/112613652083477

You can learn more about beer and get reviews of tasty ales and lagers by checking out the beer magazines that have set up shop on Facebook, including *All About Beer* (www.facebook.com/pages/All-About-Beer-Magazine/148352285181483), *Beer Connoisseur* (www.facebook.com/BeerConnoisseur), and *DRAFT* (www.facebook.com/draftmagazine).

There's something satisfying (albeit thirst inducing) about a good beer review (or a review of a good beer), and there are plenty of resources on Facebook that can supply you with not only beer reviews but also beer news, beer views, and photos of just-poured beers. Some of the better places to pull up a stool are RateBeer (www.facebook.com/pages/RateBeer/153277718016808), RealBeer.com (www.facebook.com/pages/RealBeercom/114676775825), and Beer Universe (www.facebook.com/beeruniverse). For beer reviews from a female perspective, check out Lipstick on the Rim (www.facebook.com/LipstickontheRim).

Craft brewing — that is, brewing beer in small batches using traditional methods and aiming for a distinct and flavorful taste — has become very popular over the past 10 or 15 years, and that popularity is reflected on Facebook, which offers lots of craft brewing resources.

A few that are worth checking out are CraftBeer.com (www.facebook.com/CraftBeers), American Craft Beer Week (www.facebook.com/AmericanCraftBeerWeek), the Great American Beer Festival (www.facebook.com/pages/Great-American-Beer-Festival/77791416708), and SAVOR: An American Craft Beer & Food Experience (www.facebook.com/SAVORcraftbeer). There are also lots of craft brewers on Facebook, including Dogfish Head Beer (www.facebook.com/dogfishheadbeer), Great Lakes Brewing Company (www.facebook.com/greatlakesbrewingco), and Rogue Ales (www.facebook.com/rogueales; see Figure 10.9).

If you're into crafting your *own* beer, you'll find plenty of fellow brewers on Facebook. Start with the useful Community Page (www.facebook.com/pages/Homebrewing/112140972130434), and then progress to the American Homebrewers Association (www.facebook.com/pages/American-Homebrewers-Association/19834173309), *Brew Your Own* magazine (www.facebook.com/BrewYourOwn), Homebrewing (www.facebook.com/pages/Homebrewing/87091467550), Fine Beer and Homebrew (www.facebook.com/group.php?gid=2240993730), and Beer and Home Brewing (www.facebook.com/group.php?gid=2465905843).

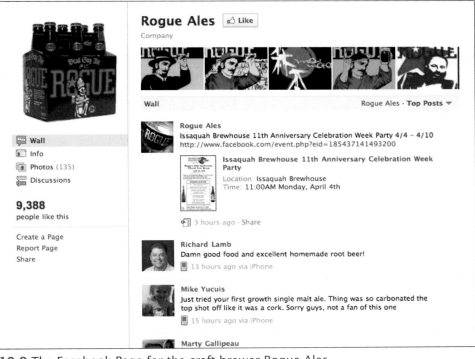

10.9 The Facebook Page for the craft brewer Rogue Ales.

Increasing Your Nutrition Know-How

After all this talk about mouth-watering recipes, fabulous restaurants, heavenly wines, and tasty beers, perhaps it's best to balance things out by concluding this food chapter with a few pointers to some useful nutritional information. Sure, great recipes and restaurant meals don't necessarily have to be decadent, and a list of studies as long as your arm has shown that moderate drinking is good for you (better for you than abstaining, in fact). However, one of the keys to a long and healthy life is to make most of your meals (although not necessarily all of them) healthy, balanced, fresh, and nutritious. If you're not sure how to go about doing that, or if you'd like to try to do better, Facebook can help by connecting with people and resources that offer lots of good information on nutrition and healthy eating.

You can start with the Nutrition Community Page (www.facebook.com/pages/Nutrition/104072772962473), which boasts lots of posts and a lengthy Wikipedia article that covers all aspects of nutrition. From there, check out the Healthy Diet Community Page (www.facebook.com/pages/Healthy-diet/110635775623183), which offers plenty of common-sense info on dietary recommendations.

Facebook also has Community Pages on various aspects of nutrition:

- **Antioxidants.** www.facebook.com/pages/Antioxidants/105811936126038
- **Carbohydrates.** www.facebook.com/pages/Carbohydrates/110568088971937
- **Fat.** www.facebook.com/pages/Dietary-fat/114859388527905
- **Fiber.** www.facebook.com/pages/Dietary-fibre/108216189212991
- **Minerals.** www.facebook.com/pages/Dietary-mineral/108648392501305
- **Nutrient.** www.facebook.com/pages/Nutrient/107914272565202
- **Protein.** www.facebook.com/pages/Protein/106942099345041
- **Vitamins.** www.facebook.com/pages/Vitamins/110314108998156
- **Whole Protein.** www.facebook.com/pages/Whole-protein/129730057068752

To continue your nutrition education, head over to the American Heart Association Nutrition Center (www.facebook.com/heartofhealth; see Figure 10.10), which offers regular posts on nutrition advice, healthy dieting, nutritious recipes, and more.

I also highly recommend the American Dietetic Association (www.facebook.com/AmericanDieteticAssociation), as well as the Facebook page for *Eating Well* magazine (www.facebook.com/EatingWell).

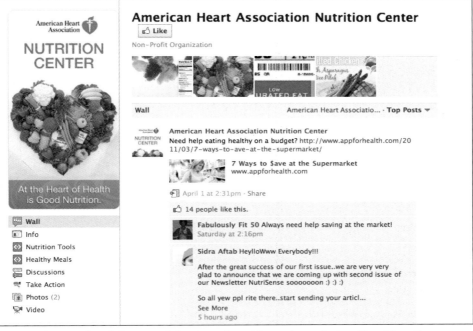

10.10 The Facebook home of the American Heart Association Nutrition Center.

Here are a few other Facebook resources related to nutrition and healthy eating:

- **Calorie Count.** This Page offers sensible advice on dieting.

  www.facebook.com/caloriecount

- **Diet & Calorie Counter.** This application lets you search a large food database for nutrition and calories data.

  www.facebook.com/apps/application.php?id=2355854671

- **Food Insight.** This Page is run by a nonprofit that promotes a science-driven food policy, but it also posts lots of information on food safety and healthy eating.

  www.facebook.com/pages/Food-Insight/143670749291

- **Food Science and Nutrition.** This Page is maintained by the medical publisher Elsevier, and it features links to nutritional studies, sample chapters, and more.

  www.facebook.com/elsevierfoodscience

- **National Association of Nutrition and Aging Services Programs.** This organization is devoted to providing older adults healthy food using community-based services.

  www.facebook.com/pages/National-Association-of-Nutrition-and-Aging-Services-ProgramsNANASP/297513753613

- **Nutrition Diva.** I'll let this Page's host, Monica Reinagel, describe her creation: "What do you get when an underemployed opera singer goes back to school and ends up with an awesome second career as a nutrition guru? The Nutrition Diva, of course."

  www.facebook.com/NutritionDiva

- **Nutrition Evolution.** This Page is run by a certified nutrition educator, and it offers lots of great advice on healthy eating.

  www.facebook.com/NutritionEvolution

- **NutritionData.** This Page offers detailed nutrition data on over 10,000 foods, as well as nutrition tips and advice.

  www.facebook.com/nutritiondata

- **Today's Diet & Nutrition Digital Magazine.** This is the Facebook home of *Today's Diet & Nutrition*, a digital magazine that focuses on healthy eating and nutrition information.

  www.facebook.com/pages/Todays-Diet-Nutrition-Digital-Magazine/125446324160776

- **U.S. Department of Agriculture.** This government Page has some nutrition information. The USDA also runs a Group related to the Food Guide Pyramid (www.facebook.com/group.php?gid=483697245547).

  www.facebook.com/USDA

- **The Vegetarian Resource Group.** This Page is dedicated to educating people about vegetarianism.

  www.facebook.com/thevegetarianresourcegroup

- **We Can - Ways to Enhance Children's Activity & Nutrition.** This Page is maintained by the National Institutes of Health, and offers tips and advice on nutrition for children.

  www.facebook.com/nihwecan

| **Wall** | Info | Photos | Notes |

Tips for Travelers

When it comes to popular pastimes on Facebook, few are as popular as traveling. If you count the number of users who've added either "traveling" or "travel" to their Facebook profiles, you come up millions of people who have various forms of wanderlust, making it one of the most popular Facebook activities. When you have that many people with a travelling Jones in one place, travel-related resources can't be far behind, and so it is on Facebook. There are Pages and applications to help you plan your trip, airlines and hotels with Facebook Pages to help when you're ready to set up your trip, and applications that help you share your adventures with your friends.

Getting Inspired

In the pre-digital world, people shared their travels by inviting all their friends over for the obligatory post-journey slide show—which, for those viewing the show, inevitably seemed to last longer than the voyage it depicted. Thanks to Facebook, slide projectors are no longer required. Travelers can share their vacation photos with Facebook friends all over the globe with a simple click of a mouse, and those friends can peruse those images at their leisure. If you're looking for travel ideas, you may not need to look any farther than your Facebook News Feed!

You can also scratch your travel itch by perusing any of the travel magazines that have set up operations on Facebook. Some of the best are *National Geographic Traveler* (www.facebook.com/NatGeoTraveler; see Figure 11.1), *NationalGeographicAdventure*(www.facebook.com/pages/National-Geographic-ADVENTURE-magazine/30049274825), *Travel + Leisure* (www.facebook.com/travelandleisure), *Condé Nast Traveler* (www.facebook.com/CondeNastTraveler Magazine), and *Caribbean Travel + Life* (www.facebook.com/pages/Caribbean-Travel-Life/67005253365).

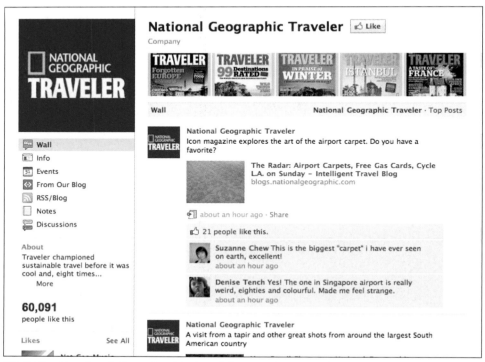

11.1 The Facebook Page for *National Geographic Traveler* magazine.

NOTE There are many Facebook addresses in this section. All of them are case sensitive, and some of them quite long. Rather than typing the addresses by hand, see the Facebook page for this series: www.facebook.com/FBGseries. Alternatively, you can type a page's name in Facebook's Search box to locate it. Please note that Facebook does not endorse the sites listed in this book.

Also, lots of travel guides have Facebook homes, and they're often great places to learn about interesting and exciting destinations. One of the best is Frommer's (www.facebook.com/Frommers; see Figure 11.2), which regularly adds destination-themed blog posts, videos, and photo slide shows, as well as travel news and deals. You should also check out the Page for the Travel Channel network (www.facebook.com/TravelChannel), which offers links to travel-related stories, show snippets, and more.

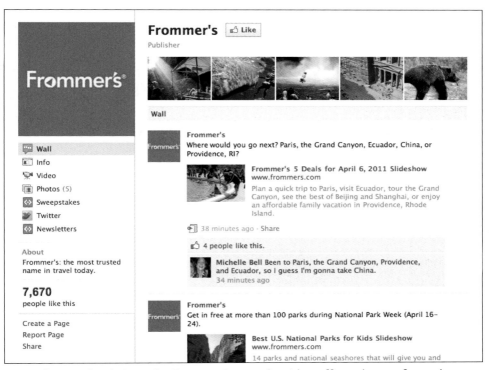

11.2 The Facebook Page for Frommer's travel guides offers plenty of travel inspiration in the form of photo slide shows and destination videos.

If you're still looking for that perfect getaway spot, here are a few more Facebook resources that can help:

- **BBC Travel.** First-rate travel journalism from the BBC.

  www.facebook.com/BBCTravel

- **BootsnAll.** This popular and lively Page is aimed at the "independent traveler," and it features lots of articles about traveling to the sound of a different drum.

  www.facebook.com/BootsnAllTravel

 TIP BootsnAll also features an application called Traveler Connect that enables you to connect with people who are going to the same place. Either click the Travel Connect tab on the BootsnAll Page, or head directly to the application: www.facebook.com/apps/application.php?id=214724428860.

- **Brave New Traveler.** This is the Facebook home of "the largest indie travel publication on the Web," and it features copious links to interesting and inspiring travel articles.

  www.facebook.com/bravenewtraveler

- **Gadling.** This Page offers links to travel ideas and suggestions on its popular blog.

  www.facebook.com/gadling

- **IgoUgo.** This Page encourages people to share their latest trips and vacations, so it's a great way to learn about new and interesting destinations.

  www.facebook.com/igougo

- **Jaunted.** This fun Page bills itself as the Pop Culture Travel Guide, and it's loaded with travel stories from all over the world.

  www.facebook.com/Jaunted

- **Lonely Planet.** This very popular Page is loaded with travel ideas and tips and even offers free travel itineraries.

  www.facebook.com/lonelyplanet

- **Lonely Planet Images.** The Page is brought to you by the Lonely Planet people, and it features lots of terrific and inspiring travel photography.

  www.facebook.com/pages/Lonely-Planet-Images/343012405305

Quote, Unquote: Facebook and Travel

"I saw an interesting ad on Facebook regarding a ski and snowboard festival called Snow Explosion. I liked the idea, so I clicked the ad. I exchanged a few e-mails with the guys from Snow Explosion and in 10 days I moved from Oradea to Bucharest. So: a Facebook ad + a few e-mails + 10 days = My life changed :)." — D. N., Bucharest, Romania

- **Matador Travel.** The popular Page is the Facebook home of an online travel magazine, and it offers tons of travel tales from every corner of the world.

  www.facebook.com/matadornetwork

- **Rand McNally.** This Page is hosted by the famous map and atlas company, and it features lots of interesting and unique idea for trips and adventures.

  www.facebook.com/randmcnally

- **Travel Talk.** This Page comes from the same folks who do Gadling, and it consists of links to podcasts about travel destinations, tips, and news.

  www.facebook.com/gadlingtv

- **Traveling.** More than 32,000 people are fans of this Page, so there are tons of travel stories and photos to inspire your next trip.

  www.facebook.com/pages/Traveling/36942391532

Planning Your Trip

Once you have a destination in mind, you'll want to get some advice on the best time to go, how to get there, where to stay, how to get around, places to visit, and so on. Facebook can help here, too. First and foremost, you should pump your Facebook friends for information about the locale. After all, what better way is there to prepare your itinerary than to ask members of your own trusted circle for some insight? If you know a friend has visited your destination before, send him or her a message to ask for advice. Alternatively, use your status update to ask your friends to share their thoughts on the trip you're planning.

TIP Are you planning a vacation with friends? If so, consider creating a Facebook group for you and your travel companions. That way, as each of you researches your destination and makes travel plans, you can quickly share information.

In addition to seeking advice from your Facebook friends, you can use any number of the trip-planning resources found on Facebook. For starters, all the major trip-planning sites have their own Facebook Pages. The most popular is TripAdvisor (www.facebook.com/TripAdvisor) which boasts a busy Wall section and Discussions tab, so there's no shortage of advice. In addition, TripAdvisor's main Web site (www.tripadvisor.com) has partnered with Facebook to enable you to see reviews posted by your Facebook friends.

Nearly as popular is the Travelocity Page (www.facebook.com/Travelocity), which offers lots of news on destinations and deals. In fact, Travelocity offers the Deals on a Map application (apps.facebook.com/deals-on-a-map/; see Figure 11.3), which, given a departure location, can show you a map of flight (or flight plus hotel) deals for different destinations.

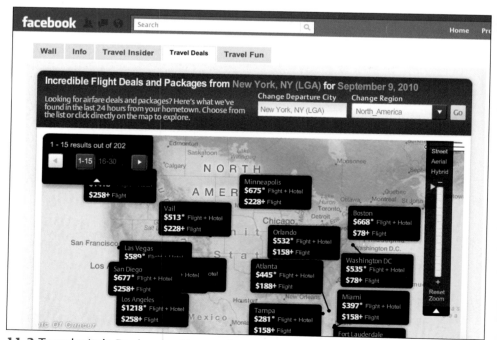

11.3 Travelocity's Deals on a Map application displays a map of flight deals to multiple destinations.

Here's a list of the other major trip-planning sites that are on Facebook:

- **Expedia.** www.facebook.com/expedia
- **Flight Centre.** www.facebook.com/pages/Flight-Centre/ 54103434078
- **Orbitz Travel.** www.facebook.com/Orbitz

Here are a few other Facebook resources that might also help you plan your trip:

- **AOL Travel.** This popular Page offers travel news, advice, and useful tidbits.

  www.facebook.com/AOLtravel

- **Everett Potter's Travel Report.** Check out this Page for travel news and deals.

  www.facebook.com/pages/Everett-Potters-Travel-Report/ 179601199911

- **Family Travel Logue.** This is the Facebook home of the BootsnAll Family Travel Logue, a blog written by Sheila Scarborough that features tips and advice for traveling with family.

  www.facebook.com/FamilyTravelLogue

- **Family Vacation Critic.** This Page offers advice geared toward family vacations.

  www.facebook.com/FamilyVacationCritic

- **SmarterTravel.** This popular Page offers travel news, tips, and deals.

  www.facebook.com/smartertravel

- **Top Trips.** This very popular Page offers trip tips, advice, and deals.

  www.facebook.com/toptrips

- **Travel Gear Blog.** This useful Page offers links to posts about travel equipment, gear, and gadgets.

  www.facebook.com/travelgear

- **Travel Rants.** This edgy Page is maintained by Darren Cronian, who regularly rants about travel annoyances and problems, but also offers lots of useful tips and advice for avoiding holiday disasters.

  www.facebook.com/travelrants

Quote, Unquote: Facebook and Travel

"I have been a Facebook user for about a year now. It helped me and my mom have the most FANTASTIC trip to France in June 2010! Via Facebook, I was introduced to a reporter who lives in Amboise, France, with his lovely wife and two cute boys, and through our Facebook communications, he invited us to actually come and stay for two nights in his home! So we did, and it was the most fun we had during our 10 days there!" — C. N., Manchester, New Hampshire

TIP One of the great things about Facebook is it enables you to keep in touch with friends all over the world. As you plan your travels, why not use Facebook to connect with friends near your destination and see if they can join you?

Booking Your Flight

Many of the trip-planning sites that I talk about in the previous section (Travelocity, Expedia, Flight Centre, and Orbitz) are also happy to book your flight for you. This is often the best way to get a good deal because these services have access to insider deals and can negotiate lower prices. However, airlines often offer special deals to customers who book directly with them (and they're often a lot quicker to help you if something goes awry with your flights), so it pays to check with the airlines to make sure you're getting the best deal.

All of the major airlines are on Facebook, but the features and services you see vary widely. As I write this, probably the most innovative carrier on Facebook is Delta Air Lines (www.facebook.com/delta). In addition to offering travel news and deals on its Wall section and interacting with customers, it also offers the Delta Ticket Window, a Facebook application that lets you locate and book flights (and share the good news with your friends), all without leaving the comfy confines of Facebook (see Figure 11.4).

Other airlines are garnering significant audiences on Facebook by offering special deals. By far the most successful so far has been Southwest Airlines (www.facebook.com/Southwest), which as I write this is approaching 1.5 million fans, at least in part because it offers deals like the one shown in Figure 11.5.

11.4 The Delta Ticket Window lets you find, book, and share flights right in Facebook.

There are probably hundreds of airlines with their own Facebook Pages, so I won't list them all (or even a small percentage of them). Instead, here's a list of some of the more popular airlines on Facebook:

- **Air France.** www.facebook.com/airfrance
- **American Airlines.** www.facebook.com/aa
- **Cathay Pacific.** www.facebook.com/cathaypacific
- **Continental Airlines.** www.facebook.com/continentalairlines
- **EasyJet.** www.facebook.com/easyJet
- **Emirates.** www.facebook.com/pages/EMIRATES/6339308479
- **JetBlue Airways.** www.facebook.com/JetBlue
- **KLM.** www.facebook.com/KLM
- **Lufthansa.** www.facebook.com/lufthansa
- **Qantas.** www.facebook.com/Qantas

- **Singapore Airlines.** www.facebook.com/pages/Singapore-Airlines/ 6352578678
- **United Airlines.** www.facebook.com/unitedairlines

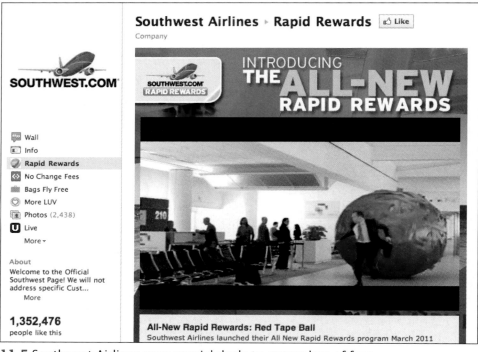

11.5 Southwest Airlines uses special deals to garner lots of fans.

Also, here are three Pages that can help you find the right seat on the right flight for the right price:

- **Airfarewatchdog.** This Page tells you about airline sales and flight deals, and even lets you sign up for e-mail alerts when there are low fares departing from your location.

  www.facebook.com/Airfarewatchdog

- **Priceline Negotiator.** This famous discount airfare purveyor uses its Facebook Page to let you know about flight deals.

  www.facebook.com/priceline.negotiator

- **SeatGuru.** This is the Facebook home of SeatGuru, a Web site that offers maps of the seating in each flight and can advise you on the best seats to choose. (*Time* magazine named SeatGuru one of its 50 Best Websites for 2010.)

  www.facebook.com/SeatGuru

Reserving Your Hotel Room

When you're ready to book your hotel room, first check to see whether your travel agent or trip-planning service offers combined flight and hotel deals, which can save you some money. However, you can also sometimes eke out a good deal by dealing with the hotel directly. Most of the larger chains have Facebook sites, and you can use those Pages to get updates on special deals and upcoming events.

Some chains strive hard to engage their customers by offering extra goodies on the Facebook pages. For example, the Embassy Suites hotel chain (www.facebook.com/EmbassySuitesHotels) has amassed thousands of fans by engaging with customers on the Wall section, running contests, enabling you to check room availability (although the results are displayed in a separate Web page), and the Atrium, a tab that lets people send virtual drinks, get complimentary meals, and more (see Figure 11.6).

Here's a list of some other major hotel chains that operate Facebook Pages:

- **Best Western.** www.facebook.com/BestWestern
- **Courtyard by Marriot.** www.facebook.com/courtyard
- **Days Inn.** www.facebook.com/pages/Days-Inn/56456219978
- **Delta.** www.facebook.com/deltahotels
- **Fairmont.** www.facebook.com/fairmonthotels

- **Four Seasons.** www.facebook.com/FourSeasons
- **Hilton.** www.facebook.com/Hilton
- **Holiday Inn.** www.facebook.com/HolidayInnHotels
- **Mandarin Oriental.** www.facebook.com/MandarinOriental
- **Motel 6.** www.facebook.com/motel6

11.6 Embassy Suites engages with its customers and offers freebies in the Atrium.

- **Omni Hotels.** www.facebook.com/omnihotels
- **Ramada.** www.facebook.com/ramada
- **Relais & Châteaux.** www.facebook.com/RelaisAndChateaux
- **Ritz-Carlton.** www.facebook.com/ritzcarlton
- **Sheraton.** www.facebook.com/SheratonHotelsandResorts
- **Starwood.** www.facebook.com/starwood
- **Super 8.** www.facebook.com/Super8

Quote, Unquote: Facebook and Travel

"Since 2008, I have been on a constant move — traveling in three continents and four countries. Whenever I was in trouble and the phone did not work, I was able to connect via Facebook to friends and family, as well as make new friends in my ever-changing location." — A. K., Boston, Massachusetts

- **Swissôtel.** www.facebook.com/swissotelhotelsresorts
- **Wyndham.** www.facebook.com/WyndhamWorldwide

Note, too, that thousands of individual hotels large and small have Facebook Pages, so if there's a particular hotel you're interested in, see if you can find it by searching for it on Facebook. If you know your destination, a Page search on "hotels *location*", where *location* is the city or place you want to stay, should turn up a few hits.

To help you find a hotel and book your stay, several resources on Facebook offer reviews and stories:

- **Accessible.travel.** This Page focuses on finding and booking hotels for people with disabilities.

  www.facebook.com/pages/accessibletravel/50291531091

- **Hotel Chatter.** This fun Page offers stories and articles about hotels around the world.

  www.facebook.com/pages/HotelChatter/24662241754

- **Oyster Hotel Reviews.** This useful Page features lots of hotel reviews and photos.

  www.facebook.com/oysterhotels

- **Tablet Hotels.** This very popular Page offers reviews of boutique and luxury hotels around the world.

  www.facebook.com/pages/Tablet-Hotels/38896221569

- **Travel Intelligence.** If you're looking for a boutique or luxury hotel, this Page offers reviews of hotels, hotel news, and more.

  www.facebook.com/pages/Travel-Intelligence/109084550766

Also, the people who run LastMinute.com (see www.facebook.com/lastminute.com) also operate several Pages that offer hotel reviews and deals:

- **England Hotel Experts.** www.facebook.com/englandhotelexperts
- **Europe Hotel Experts.** www.facebook.com/southafricahotelexperts
- **Ireland Hotel Experts.** www.facebook.com/englandhotelexperts
- **London Hotel Experts.** www.facebook.com/theLondonHotelExpert
- **Paris Hotel Experts.** www.facebook.com/parishotelexperts
- **Scotland Hotel Experts.** www.facebook.com/scotlandhotelexperts
- **South Africa Hotel Experts.** www.facebook.com/southafricahotelexperts

Booking Your Cruise

If cruising is your style, Facebook offers lots of useful resources for researching, locating, and booking your trip. All the major cruise lines have Facebook Pages, although there are significant differences between them in terms of interaction with customers, promotions, and other goodies.

Carnival Cruise (www.facebook.com/Carnival) has garnered over 650,000 fans by running one of the best Facebook pages, with lots of custom interaction, special deals for fans, a Meet the Crew feature, profiles of ports, and ship photos

Here are some other big-time cruise lines on Facebook:

- **Celebrity Cruises.** www.facebook.com/celebritycruises
- **Costa Cruises.** www.facebook.com/costacruises.na
- **Cunard.** www.facebook.com/cunard
- **Disney Cruises.** www.facebook.com/DisneyCruiseLine
- **Holland America Line.** www.facebook.com/HALCruises
- **MSC Cruises.** www.facebook.com/MSCCruiseLine
- **Norwegian Cruise Line.** www.facebook.com/Norwegiancruiseline
- **Princess Cruises.** www.facebook.com/PrincessCruises
- **Royal Caribbean.** www.facebook.com/royalcaribbean
- **Star Cruises.** www.facebook.com/starcruises

Quote, Unquote: Facebook and Travel

"My wife and I are moving from the east coast all the way to California. During this time, I have used Facebook to connect with friends along the way and come up with accommodations. Meanwhile, I have been uploading photos of our adventures of moving cross-country to a Facebook album, and using an event to let people know about our move as well."
— M. W., Billings, Montana

Facebook boasts a large and passionate community of cruisers, so there are lots of resources you can turn to for researching and booking your cruise. Here's a sampling:

- **All Things Cruise.** Check in with this Page for all the latest cruise news and reviews.

  www.facebook.com/AllThingsCruise

- **Cruise Addicts.** This Page is a gathering place for people who love to cruise.

  www.facebook.com/CruiseAddicts

- **Cruise Compete.** With this service you select a cruise and then receive competing offers from discounter travel agents.

  www.facebook.com/wholesalecruises

TIP
A similar Page is ResortCompete (www.facebook.com/AllInclusiveResorts), which lets you field competitive offers for resorts.

- **Cruise Critic.** This very popular Page offers reviews, news, and other information about cruise vacations.

  www.facebook.com/CruiseCritic

- **Cruise News Weekly.** This is the Facebook home of a Web site (www.cruisenewsweekly.com/) that offers cruise news and information.

  www.facebook.com/cruisenews

- **CruiseCrazies.** This is a social network for cruisers, so you'll find lots of cruise reviews and information.

  www.facebook.com/CruiseCrazies

- **Cruises Only.** This is a cruise agency, but it's a popular Page (nearly 40,000 fans), so the Wall section contains lots of good information on cruises and ships.

  www.facebook.com/CruisesOnly

- **uCruiser.com.** This Page encourages people to share recent cruise experiences, plus the Page proprietors post lots of cruise news and articles, so it's a useful place to research cruises.

  www.facebook.com/ucruiser

Sharing Your Travels

Trips and vacations are wonderful adventures, and the next best thing to getting away is returning home and telling all your family and friends what a great time you had. Of course, Facebook makes this easy by letting you post a trip-related status update, photo album, video, Note, or whatever. If Facebook Places is available in your home country, you can use it to "check in" to restaurants, hotels, museums, and other sites while you're away. However, there are also lots of Facebook applications you can use to make it even easier to share your travels with your friends.

Quote, Unquote: Cybercasing

"Data stored in digital photographs can help criminals locate individuals and plot real-world crimes, a practice two researchers called cybercasing in a recently published paper. The site Pleaserobme.com was one of the first to expose the problem by displaying tweets tagged with location information, although it has since stopped the practice." — Niraj Chokshi, "How Tech-Savvy Thieves Could 'Cybercase' Your House," The Atlantic, July 22, 2010

CAUTION You may want to update your location throughout your trip, either by changing your current location in your profile, by posting pictures, or by using Facebook Places, if it's available where you're traveling. However, there are thieves who look for this kind of information to perform *cybercasing*: using online location data and services to determine when a home is unoccupied with a view to robbing it. By all means, you should share your travels on Facebook, but make sure you know who you are sharing with or maybe wait until *after* you get home to post.

By far the most popular of these applications is TripAdvisor — Cities I've Visited (www.facebook.com/CitiesIveVisited). This application enables you to add to your profile a map that shows all the cities you've visited (or would like to visit), as shown in Figure 11.7.

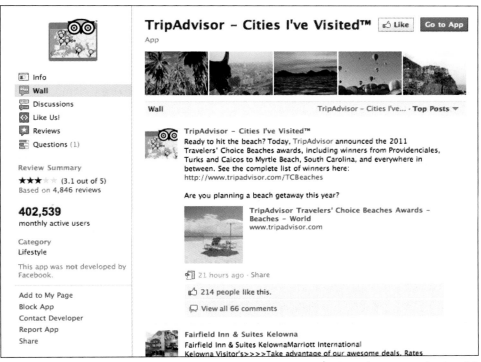

11.7 TripAdvisor offers the very popular Cities I've Visited application, which adds a tab to your profile with a map that shows the cities you've visited.

Here are some other applications you can use to share your travels with your Facebook friends:

- **Travel Buddies.** You can use this application to share a travel calendar, plot your trip on a map, send postcards to your friends, and more.

  www.facebook.com/travelbuddies

- **Travel Map.** This application enables you to plot your trip on a map.

  www.facebook.com/TravellerspointTravelMap

- **TripAdvisor TripWow.** From the same folks who created Cities I've Visited, this application lets you create a beautiful slide show of your trip photos.

  www.facebook.com/apps/application.php?id=111769535518503

- **Where I've Been.** This popular application (currently with more than 1 million monthly users), lets you show where you've been, write reviews, and more.

  www.facebook.com/apps/application.php?id=2603626322

application A program that runs within the Facebook site and usually enables you to connect with and share experiences with your friends. Most applications are built by third-party developers, not by Facebook.

comment A message that a person adds to a story posted by a friend.

defriend To remove a person from your Facebook friends list.

Event A Facebook item associated with an offline Event, such as a wedding, celebration, rally, or simple get-together, which enables you to invite people to the Event and to communicate with the attendees.

friend (noun) A person on Facebook with whom you've agreed to share information.

friend (verb) To connect with another Facebook user by becoming that person's friend.

friend list A subset of your friends.

friend request A notification that a person receives when another Facebook user wants to become that person's friend.

friends list The collection of Facebook users that a person has friended.

Group A collection of people who share a common interest, such as a hobby, a passion, a cause, a protest, or just something fun or silly. There are two types of Groups on Facebook: small groups that you create to include your friends, and larger groups that span the Facebook community.

like (verb) To indicate that you have a positive response toward a Facebook item or an item on a third-party website.

Like button An icon that appears along with a Facebook item, such as a story or Page, or an item on a third-party website that, when clicked, enables you to tell your Facebook friends that you liked that item.

link A story that includes a link to a third-party website.

memorialized profile A profile of a Facebook user who has died, which retains its Wall section so that people can write remembrances, but hides some profile information and ensures the person does not come up in a search or in friend suggestions.

message Text — possibly augmented with a link, photo, or video — that gets sent directly to a friend.

Most Recent The view of your News Feed that shows you all of your friends' recent activity, sorted chronologically, with the most recent at the top.

News Feed The automated collection of stories generated by the activities of your friends, the Pages you like, the Groups you've joined, and the Events you're attending.

note A message that can be as long as you need and that can include formatting.

notification A message that Facebook sends to you whenever someone else does something on Facebook that relates to you, such as requesting to be your friend, accepting your friend request, commenting on a story, or sending you a message.

page A special, nonpersonal Facebook profile designed to help businesses communicate with customers, organizations to communicate with users, and public figures or entities to communicate with fans.

photo album A collection of related photos.

profile The collection of information about yourself that you've shared on Facebook, including your location, relationship status, interests, activities, education, work history, and contact info.

share To add a friend's story to your Wall section or to share a link to another site on your profile.

social capital The value generated by a person's social relationships.

social networking Using a website to connect with people you know or who share similar personal or professional interests.

social plugin A website feature that enables you to interact with that website via your Facebook account, and view items shared or liked by your friends. Examples include the Like button and a Facebook login.

status update A simple message that you use to share what you're doing, where you're going, how you're feeling, or whatever happens to be on your mind.

story Any item that appears on your News Feed, including status updates, shared links, photos, and videos, changed profile settings, likes, and application updates.

tag To identify a person in a photo, video, or place as one of your Facebook friends.

target To direct a Facebook ad only at people who might be interested in your product or service.

Top News The view of your News Feed that shows only those friend activities that Facebook has calculated are relevant to you.

Wall section A section of your Facebook profile that shows the stories you've posted, and where your friends can add stories. Many Pages, Groups, and Events also come with their own Wall sections.

Wall-to-Wall A Facebook conversation where messages are exchanged by writing on each other's Wall section.

index

Index

Index